D1482732

Southern Literary Studies
LOUIS D. RUBIN, JR., EDITOR

Allen Tate
and the Augustinian
Imagination

Allen Tate
and the Augustinian Imagination

A Study of the Poetry

ROBERT S. DUPREE

Louisiana State University Press
Baton Rouge and London

Manufactured in the United States of America

Designer: Barbara Werden
Typeface: Linotron Janson
Typesetter: G&S Typesetters, Inc.

LIBRARY OF CONGRESS CATALOGING IN PUBLICATION DATA

Dupree, Robert S., 1940–
Allen Tate and the Augustinian imagination.

(Southern literary studies)
Includes index.
1. Tate, Allen. 1899– —Criticism and interpretation. 2. Augustine, Saint, Bishop of Hippo—Influence.
I. Title. II. Series.
PS3539.A74Z65 1983 811′.52 83-7990
ISBN 0-8071-1100-7

Publication of this book has been assisted by a grant from the Andrew W. Mellon Foundation.

TO LOUISE COWAN

Saber non ay ni sen per lieys lauzar,
Tant a d'onor que pus non y cabria,
E tant de ben que res no.l creysseria.
Doncx ma lauzors de que la pot honrar?
Ieu prenc l'onor, quar no.n puesc dir mas ver.

—GUIRAUT RIQUIER

Contents

Abbreviations

The following short titles are used in the notes. Unless otherwise noted, all citations from the poetry and prose of Allen Tate are taken from these editions.

Collected Poems	*Collected Poems, 1919–1976* (New York: Farrar, Straus and Giroux, 1977)
The Fathers	*The Fathers and Other Fiction*, rev. ed. (Baton Rouge: Louisiana State University Press, 1977)
Memoirs	*Memoirs and Opinions, 1926–1974* (Chicago: Swallow Press, 1975)
Essays	*Essays of Four Decades* (Chicago: Swallow Press, 1968)
Letters	*The Republic of Letters in America: The Correspondence of John Peale Bishop and Allen Tate*, ed. Thomas Daniel Young and John J. Hindle (Lexington: University Press of Kentucky, 1981)
Correspondence	*The Literary Correspondence of Donald Davidson and Allen Tate*, ed. John Tyree Fain and Thomas Daniel Young (Athens: University of Georgia Press, 1974)

Preface

The poetry of Allen Tate constitutes a body of work formidable not so much for its size, although ample enough, as for its demands on the intellectual tenacity of readers. These demands have been partially met by a small body of essays of considerable merit, informative and rewarding to the patient searcher for a full comprehension of Tate. The task of explication is never complete, of course, and the finest of commentaries will always display lacunae. Thus certain poems, crucial for an interpretation of Tate's achievement but almost totally neglected, have never received adequate elucidation. These unexplored texts, seemingly intransigent for the critic, constitute a serious barrier to the complete understanding of his poetry. Nevertheless, the principal gap in our knowledge of Tate lies elsewhere. The unity of his work, his poetry and prose together, has escaped the critical net. Despite some laudable attempts to demonstrate the integrity of Tate's career, its basis has remained obscure for most readers. As a result, few have grasped the magnitude of his achievement.

Tate himself insisted that his work be approached in its entirety. In the preface to *Poems: 1928–1931*, he declared, "The books of a poet are finally one book; this author is writing to that end." A year later, he wrote to John Peale Bishop that "every phrase and line, in every poem of an author, implies every other phrase and line, and takes its place with reference to the whole body of his work."[1] Tate returned to this principle in his brilliant analysis of the mind of Edgar Allan Poe. Summing up T. S. Eliot's earlier comments, he notes that "continental critics habitually view an author's work as a whole; whereas English and American critics view each work separately and, in the case of Poe, have been stopped by its defects."[2] Ironically, Tate's poetry has also been the victim of such piecemeal scrutiny. Indeed, a tendency among critics to be "stopped by its defects" has flawed even the most ambitious attempts to account for Tate's work as a whole.

1. Allen Tate to John Peale Bishop, December 23, 1933, in *Letters*, 94.
2. Allen Tate, "The Angelic Imagination: Poe as God," in *Essays*, 402.

It is for this reason that I have adopted something of a "continental" approach to Tate's poetry, setting aside the legitimate but distracting judgment of individual poems and passages for the sake of a more philosophical perspective. Much criticism of Tate has focused on biographical, regional, and historical themes. Tate's skill as a craftsman of verse, his unusual style, his astonishing imagery, and his energetic syntax have been frequently noted and delineated. However, for all the dramatic intimacy and personal vigor that characterize it, Tate's is primarily a poetry of ideas. What keeps it from lapsing simply into an intellectual exercise in verse is his insistence that ideas are effective in poetry only when embodied in human actions and feelings. In Tate's work, then, personal intensity is inseparable from a commitment to intellectual integrity. His rejection of what he calls "romanticism" is a refusal to segregate the truth of the heart from that of the mind.

Thus Tate's work should be given the kind of consideration accorded other twentieth-century poets—such as Yeats, Eliot, or Pound—who combine an intimate focus on personal experience with an extensive grasp of the Western intellectual tradition. Though the play of ideas in Tate's writings is often limited to a small core of closely related themes, the range of his awareness is broad indeed. He can speak of Carneades, Proclus, or Iamblichus in one breath and of Mistral, Madame de La Fayette, or St-John Perse in the next. He brings a well-informed mind to his criticism of Civil War histories and to his judgment of philosophies of history. He is a truly cosmopolitan author whose principal concern is European rather than American culture, even when the American South plays a central role in his meditations. Yet it is precisely this focus on the European tradition that has eluded many of Tate's critics. Despite some incisive studies of Tate's use of Virgil and Dante, this European orientation has not received the attention it deserves. My aim, in the pages that follow, is not only to take a continental view of Tate's poetry but to demonstrate its essentially European perspective. In searching for an appropriate vehicle for exploring this dimension of Tate, I have been almost inevitably drawn to the one historical figure, Augustine of Hippo, who seems close to him in character and convictions. Moreover, the intellectual and poetic unity of Tate's work emerges with admirable clarity when viewed as analogous to the achievement of a man whom some would call "the father of the West."

This reexamination of Tate's work through the figure of Augustine has resulted in some unusual readings of several well-known poems. They are intended to be fresh, not definitive, interpretations, put forward in an effort to supplement the fifty-year-old accumulation of criticism devoted to the poetry. I regret that lack of space has prevented me from referring to or citing from Tate's major critics. However, having read nearly everything published on Tate, I would feel neglectful if I did not at least acknowledge my obvious debt to the pioneering commentaries of Cleanth Brooks, Louis D. Rubin, R. K. Meiners, and Radcliffe Squires. I hope that other critics who have written fewer but not necessarily less important pages on Tate will accept this general expression of gratitude for the illumination they have provided.

I should like to thank Mrs. Alice Puro for helping me track down many obscure items in periodicals difficult of access and Donald A. Cowan for his encouragement and support over a long period of time. My greatest debt is owed to the person who inspired and fostered this book. Not knowing how to thank her, I have dedicated it to her. I hope that she will find in Guiraut Riquier's verse, if not in my prose, a fitting expression of my gratitude and admiration.

Allen Tate
and the Augustinian
Imagination

Introduction

George Hemphill has remarked that Allen Tate's "way of writing history is the same as Gibbon's, the same as Milton's in the last two books of *Paradise Lost*, and the same as St. Augustine's in *The City of God*. Civilizations rise and fall as they hold fast to or lose an active faith."[1] This theme of active faith is central to Tate's work, arising from his prolonged contemplation of the decline of Western civilization as exemplified in the demise of the American South. The southerner, Tate maintains, has lacked an adequate faith. He has been unable to "fall back upon his religion simply because it was never articulated and organized for him." His alternative is to invent a faith through political means: "He must use an instrument, which is political, and so unrealistic and pretentious that he cannot believe in it, to re-establish a private, self-contained, and essentially spiritual life."[2] The southerner can be comfortable as neither believer nor unbeliever. He is forced into a trap, the only escape from which is the invention of a past that never existed.

This dilemma is at the heart of one of the most difficult poems Tate ever wrote. Published in 1935, "To the Romantic Traditionists" has been avoided by most of Tate's critics. Its difficulty stems from an ambiguity so radical as to render its plain sense virtually inaccessible. Nevertheless, it is an extremely important poem for an understanding of Tate's intellectual struggles, for it was written at a crucial moment in his career, midway between his secular and religious stages of development.

An initial interpretive question about the poem arises from its title: what or who are the "romantic traditionists"? Both the adjective and the noun recur frequently in Tate's works. He has published poems such as "To a Romantic Novelist" (1925) and "To a Romantic" (1925) in which he speaks of the progressive modern who rejects the past altogether and denies that it has meaning. "To a Romantic" ends, for example, with an image of the dead as ghosts who "arise/ Westward and

1. George Hemphill, *Allen Tate* (Minneapolis, 1964), 16.
2. Allen Tate, "Religion and the Old South," in *Essays*, 575–76.

fabulous." This variety of romantic turns his eyes toward a future that he sees as stretching infinitely "into the vagrant West"—like Tennyson's Ulysses. But the West is also the place where the dead reside, according to folklore, and the young romantic with the "iron mood" of Ozymandias (an ironic allusion to Shelley) has cast his idealistic eyes not upon unending horizons but upon the "doors to a narrow house." "To a Romantic" and "To the Romantic Traditionists" share a similar irony and at least one common image (that of the dead bored with the living), but the earlier poem does not give many clues to what Tate is doing in its successor ten years later. It does not explain how a romantic can be a traditionist.

Indeed, the linking of "romantic" and "traditionist" in the title of the poem is virtually oxymoronic, if one bears in mind Tate's definition of traditionists, in his essay "Liberalism and Tradition," as "those who believe in the value of tradition."[3] Yet the two terms can be reconciled, for Tate apparently means by "romantic traditionist" something on the order of "idealizer and idolizer of the past" and may be referring specifically, though not at all exclusively, to the modern southern idealist, the sentimental traditionist of the twentieth century who romanticizes history.

The poem is not immediately clarified, however, by an explication of its title. The verses that follow are a bewildering tangle of "I," "We," "You," and "They," and the literal sense of the poem hinges critically on a proper interpretation of each pronoun.

> I have looked at them long,
> My eyes blur; sourceless light
> Keeps them forever young
> Before our ageing sight.
>
> You see them too—strict forms
> Of will, the secret dignity
> Of our dissolute storms;
> They grow too bright to be.

The poem is addressed to the romantic traditionists of the title, who are referred to as "you" in the poem itself. The poet and his like-minded

3. Allen Tate, "Liberalism and Tradition," in *Reason in Madness* (New York, 1941), 196–216.

contemporaries (avant-garde in language and style but believing in the value of tradition) are referred to consistently as "we" and "us." The remaining third-person pronouns must refer, then, to those men from the past who are idealized by the addressees of the poem. Both the poet and his romantic-traditionist contemporaries see the same figures, but they regard them in utterly different fashions. The poet asks for a description of them:

> What were they like? What mark
> Can signify their charm?
> They never saw the dark;
> Rigid, they never knew alarm.

The romantic sees the figures as larger than life, as fearless, immaculate, and possessed of a changeless perfection. They are veritable gods, Olympian in their separation from the decadent present. Objects of worship, they have turned into bloodless abstractions:

> Immaculate race! to yield
> Us final knowledge set
> In a cold frieze, a field
> Of war but no blood let.

But they are not the actual men and women who have lived before us; they are vague projections of our own desires, "strict forms/ Of will." In an ironic query, the poet wonders what might be the response of these distant figures to a request for their portrait:

> Are they quite willing,
> Do they ask to pose,
> Naked and simple, chilling
> The very wind's nose?

Have these great men of the past given their consent to this glorification of their persons, or have they been transformed into such aloof images by idolatrous successors?

In an essay of 1934, "Three Types of Poetry," Tate speaks of the "romantic will" in terms that clarify the first six stanzas of the poem. He paraphrases Hart Crane's verses to Pocahontas:

> The poet confesses that he has no access to a means of satisfying his will, or to a kind of vision where the terms are not set by the

> demands of the practical will. He returns to a fictitious past. There he is able to maintain, for a moment, the illusion that he might realize the assertion of his will in a primitive world where scientific truth is not a fatal obstacle.

Tate then points to "a special property of the romantic imagination" that "has no insight into the total meaning of actual moral situations; it is concerned with fictitious alternatives to them, because they invariably mean frustration of the will. This special property of escape is the Golden Age, used in a special fashion. The romantic poet attributes to it an historical reality."[4] The more one gazes on these historical fictions, the more they become pure abstractions of the will, divorced from time and "forever young/ Before our ageing sight." The "sourceless light" of their self-contained perfection makes them dazzle our eyes until they lose all relation to contingent existence and "grow too bright to be." We may ask, "What were they like?" but they have become so archaically brilliant through the romantic imagination that we are incapable of knowing them for what they truly were.

The only escape from the cycle of solipsistic projection that the romantic will creates is a refusal to participate:

> Do not the scene rehearse!
> The perfect eyes enjoin
> A contemptuous verse.
> We speak the crabbed line.

If modern poets speak constantly in fragmented and satirical lines of man's failures, it is because they cannot accept the romantic image of the past as true to reality. In "Three Types of Poetry," Tate argues against his friend Edmund Wilson that the refusal of certain contemporary poets to take either romantic or scientific points of view is not escapism but commitment. If the "cold frieze" of these Golden Age figures, this "immaculate race," is not a scene that the poet cares to rehearse, he must ask if the men of the past are "willing . . . to pose" in all their naked essences and submit to his scrutiny. He will greet them in the "contemptuous verse" that their "perfect eyes" seem to provoke.

In order for the Golden Age figures to take on the plausibility that a real tradition requires, they must be made to enter into the bloodstream

4. Allen Tate, "Three Types of Poetry," in *Essays*, 184–85.

of our present existence rather than stand aloof from it. The poet imagines them as asking him the great romantic question "How to live?" One is immediately reminded of Stein, in Conrad's *Lord Jim*, who answered that one must submit "to the destructive element." This, too, is the poet's response:

> They ask us how to live!
> We answer: Again try
> Being the drops we sieve.
> What death it is to die!

Tate would agree with Stein that one must submit to the realities of the present. The past lives only in us. Its continuation into the present is a matter of selection by the living, and so men of the past must be constantly absorbed into a new identity, must die again and enter into the life of the present.

One way of understanding these strange lines is to see in them a reference to tradition as a sacrificial experience. Martin Heidegger has spoken of a "listening to the tradition that does not give itself up to the past but thinks of the present." The need for this attention is emphasized by other modern writers. In Ezra Pound's "Canto I," the past is presented as an evocation of ghosts from the underworld through the sacrificial offering of blood. Pound's Odysseus beats back all but Tiresias, who alone can tell him what he needs to know about himself. Even Antikleia, Odysseus' mother, must be kept back from her son until Tiresias has spoken. Odysseus must hold the dead in check and not be overwhelmed by them if he is to learn how to live the remainder of his life.

Likewise, German critic Walter Benjamin has spoken of the constant need to make new what remains from the past: "The genuine picture may be old, but the genuine thought is new. It is of the present. This present may be meager, granted. But no matter what it is like, one must firmly take it by the horns to be able to consult the past. It is the bull whose blood must fill the pit if the shades of the departed are to appear at its edge."[5] While doubtless agreeing with such conceptions of

5. Walter Benjamin, *Schriften*, II, 314, as cited by Hannah Arendt in her "Introduction" to Benjamin, *Illuminations*, trans. Harry Zohn (New York, 1968), 44. The citation from Martin Heidegger, *Kants These über das Sein* (Frankfurt, 1962), 8, is given by Hannah Arendt in her "Introduction," p. 46.

tradition, Tate would go a step further, for he sees that the present is not merely meager but dead. It has been sucked dry by an illusion that has drunk all its blood, like the empty men of the later poem "Jubilo." In "To the Romantic Traditionists," the sacrifice is ineffective:

Therefore because they nod,
Being too full of us,
I look at the turned sod
Where it is perilous

And yawning all the same
As if we knew them not
And history had no name—
No need to name the spot!

The Golden Age figures are depicted as vampires who have fed to satiety on the present; they are like the "sleepy dead" of "To a Romantic." But if the men of the past would be bored with us, Tate implies ironically, their nods could be answered in kind by the "yawning" grave. Therefore, the poet chooses to concentrate his attention on the "turned sod" of the grave. By refusing to take these romanticized figures as real, he kills a past that has its immortality in the present will alone. The grave is the most effective refutation of the romantic will. If such a perfection has never existed in the past, then it can never exist in the present.

Tate opposes memory, which, as he was to say later, "has its own life and purposes" and "gives what *it* wills" to the personal will. Once memory is destroyed, there is no point in imposing identities upon places: "No need to name the spot!" In such a condition, "All places are equally the wrong places," as Tate once wrote to Donald Davidson.[6] What the poem shows is that there is a force which the will cannot control. The romantic traditionist attempts to overcome this obstacle by projecting his desire upon an epoch beyond anyone's experience. This divorce of past from present in the narrow vision of scientific method and liberalism or the worship of primitivism by the romantic is a form of death. History must feed the present, not feed on it. Since the romantic dream has no place for the present, the present has no place for

6. Allen Tate, "A Lost Traveller's Dream," in *Memoirs*, 12, and Allen Tate to Donald Davidson, February 18, 1929, in *Correspondence*, 223.

the dream. It will die completely, and these vain figures of the personal will show "What death it is to die!" These brilliant but empty figures will vanish without a trace, as though "history had no name."

The worship of the past creates golden ages that never existed; the worship of the future creates utopias that will never come into existence. Both attitudes are built upon a lie that emerges from a diseased imagination. When grasped analogically, these images of the past or future can contribute to an understanding of human history and destiny. Viewed as true pictures of the human order, complete in every detail, they are worse than misleading; for their shadowy darkness, like the images of Plato's cave, is perversely taken to be light. The truth about man must include the literal, if unpleasant, fact of his limitedness in time, space, and vision. The false imagination—Tate later calls it "angelic" or "unliteral"—promises liberation but succeeds only in producing enslavement.

Thus, while other twentieth-century writers have spoken of "the necessary angel" or "the right to dream," Tate has written both of "the limits of poetry" and of "literature as knowledge." He refuses to make claims for the imagination that it cannot sustain, but he insists on defending the uniquely vital kind of understanding that only poetry can provide. He is, in fact, one of this century's great defenders of the poetic way of knowing, yet he never severs the imagination from its roots in culture, history, and the human condition. Unlike those supposedly wise in the ways of the heart but innocent of the world, Tate has immersed himself in a study of the social and economic relations that set the stage for human actions. Nevertheless, he has not forgotten the inescapable origin of all human action in myth, ritual, and belief. Without them, men must perish as surely as did the American South.

In Tate's view, then, the true traditionist is a radical, even a destroyer, for he responds to his dilemma in the present by "cutting away the overgrowth and getting back to the roots."[7] A sacrificial violence may be the only means for saving a moribund culture. One year after he wrote "To the Romantic Traditionists," Tate cast the insights of his poem into another form as a prose defense of poetry. The concluding paragraph of the "Preface" to *Reactionary Essays on Poetry and Ideas* identifies this kind of romantic as a bad reader of literature:

7. Tate, "Religion and the Old South," 576.

> There are all kinds of poetry readers. The innocent reader and the reader till lately called the moralist, who is now the social reader, are different from the critical reader, and they are both incurably intellectual. Their heads buzz with generalizations that they expect the poet to confirm—so that they will not have to notice the poetry. It is a service that the modern poet, no less amiable than his forebears, is not ready to perform: there is no large scheme of imaginative reference in which he has confidence. . . .
>
> The innocent reader lives in the past; he likes to see in poetry, if not the conscious ideas, then the sensibility of a previous age. Our future sensibility the social reader, wise as he is, has no way of predicting, because he ignores the one source of that kind of prophecy—the present—grasped in terms, not of abstractions, but of experience. . . . The poet—and it is he who is the critical reader—is aware of the present, any present, now or past or future. For by experiencing the past along with the present he makes present the past, and masters it; and he is at the center of the experience out of which the future must come. . . . The greater poets give us knowledge, not of the new programs, but of ourselves.[8]

The romantic traditionist, like the "innocent reader," lives in the past and hopes to recover "the sensibility of a previous age." His opposite is the modern liberal whom Tate depicts in "Eclogue of the Liberal and the Poet." In his rejection of the past, the liberal corresponds to the "social reader." Like the Syracusan of "Epistle: To a Syracusan Much Too Late at Rome," he pursues a "busy quest" that is an attempt to replace myth with technology, augury with statistics. The "Eclogue," however, presents the liberal as a kind of sentimentalist who has replaced "place" (Europe) with "face" (emotions), "hope" with "soap." In a parody of John Denham's "Cooper's Hill," Tate suggests that these rhymes are "not tired" but "expired," like the tradition of rational clarity they represent. Liberal optimism, shaken by the violence of twentieth-century wars, has turned place into "the big weeping face/ And the other abstract lace of the race." The liberal and the romantic traditionist are both worshipers of an abstraction that they have taken

8. Allen Tate, "Preface to *Reactionary Essays on Poetry and Ideas*," in *Essays*, 613–14.

for reality. In their loss of a sense of analogy, they have been forced to base their metaphysics on mere feelings. The definiteness of place has been replaced by the vagueness of sentiment. Paradoxically, it is the poet, the "critical reader," who refuses to base his art on feelings alone and seeks to remain "at the center of experience" from which come both past and future.

It is this center of experience to which Tate returns repeatedly as the norm for the imagination. Its mode of presentation is symbolic; and its reach, as Tate says, "is perhaps no longer than the ladder of analogy, at the top of which we may see all, if we still wish to *see* anything, that we have brought up with us from the bottom, where lies the sensible world."[9] The principal means of attaining this vision is a device that Tate, paraphrasing Erich Auerbach, calls *figura*, "the symbolic dimension rooted firmly in a literal image or statement that does not need the symbolic significance in order to be immediately understood."[10] Auerbach gives an extensive description of the "figural interpretation" of reality. It establishes, he points out, "a connection between two events or persons, the first of which signifies not only itself but also the second, while the second encompasses or fulfills the first. The two poles of the figure are separate in time, but both, being real events or figures, are within time, within the stream of historical life."[11] It is the symbolic imagination, source of the figural interpretation of reality, that informs the intelligence of the critical reader. *Figura* remains always in the concrete realm of person and action. It eschews abstract categories or reduction to a lowest common denominator. Experience is given meaning not by the imposition of an intellectual program but in terms of another experience. A historical person draws his significance not from his place in a grand scheme but through his relationship, in time, to another person. The virtue of the figural method of interpretation is that its terms are composed of human realities, even when its goal resides beyond them. This, then, is the center of experience to which Tate returns repeatedly as the normative way of the imagination. He does not simply extol the imagination as the highest human faculty. He is careful to discriminate among its verities and identify those that lead to that

9. Allen Tate, "The Angelic Imagination," in *Essays*, 422.

10. Allen Tate, "The Unliteral Imagination; Or, I, too, Dislike It," in *Essays*, 453.

11. Erich Auerbach, "Figura," in *Scenes from the Drama of European Literature*, trans. Ralph Manheim (New York, 1959), 53.

personal wholeness he refers to as "salvation." The symbolic imagination offers the richest and most complete way of understanding, uniting high and low in a single experienced complex.

Opposed to the symbolic imagination are what Tate calls the "unliteral or roundabout imagination," on the one hand, and the "angelic imagination," on the other. The three kinds of imagination bear an obvious relation to Tate's earlier description of the three varieties of reader and the trio of romantic traditionist, liberal, and poet. The unliteral imagination is the way of a naïvely applied scientific method. Tate discerns its operation in much modern literary scholarship, of which a notable, if eccentric, example is John Livingston Lowes's famous "roundabout" study of Coleridge. The unliteral imagination never encounters the true object of its attention; it mistakes something else for the reality supposedly under its scrutiny. The angelic imagination, in contrast, lies at the opposite pole from the unliteral. It goes straight to the heart of the matter—to pure essence without recourse to the bodily senses, as an angel is presumed to know things through his special, unmediated intuition of reality. But the angelic imagination suffers from "an incapacity to represent the human condition in the central tradition of natural feeling" and entails "the loss of the entire order of experience."[12]

Although Tate clearly preferred the way of the symbolic imagination, he saw his own modern cast of mind as uncomfortably prone to the unliteral and angelic temptations of the romantic. One of Tate's most startling *tours de force* is his essay "Our Cousin, Mr. Poe," in which he applies a figural interpretation to himself and explores the origins of his own spiritual dilemma in the romantic imagination he has inherited from the nineteenth century. Tate describes Poe as a writer whose "relationship, almost of the blood . . . we must in honor acknowledge: what destroyed him is potentially destructive of us." What distinguishes Poe from authors like Hawthorne or Melville, whose "large, articulate scheme of experience . . . we may partly sever from personal association, both in the writer and in ourselves," is the "wilderness of mirrors" with which this "cousin" surrounds us. In him "we see a subliminal self endlessly repeated, or, turning, a new posture of the same figure."[13]

12. Tate, "The Angelic Imagination," 403.
13. Allen Tate, "Our Cousin, Mr. Poe," in *Essays*, 387.

Such a figure appears often in Tate's poetry; the best example is the form that the poet glimpses in the mirror of "The Maimed Man," a "forlorn demon" that is not exorcised until the last lines of "The Buried Lake."

The importance of "Our Cousin, Mr. Poe" resides in its method. An indirect confession of its author's own inadequacies, the essay is, at the same time, a perfect—though negative—example of figural interpretation. Tate insists, before embarking on his investigation of Poe, that "in discussing any writer, or in coming to terms with him, we must avoid the trap of mere abstract evaluation, and try to reproduce the actual conditions of our relation to him."[14] This warning is equally relevant to the student of Tate. What this essay provides is an invaluable model of a kind of criticism not much practiced in our time and never applied to Tate himself. Tate modestly suggests that his main literary forebear is Edgar Allan Poe. I would claim for him a more appropriate *figura* in St. Augustine.

In the following study, I hope to show that Tate shares with Augustine more than a common tradition. Tate's poetry, taken as a whole, depicts the same action of conversion that Augustine describes in *The Confessions*. The major Augustinian themes of history, memory, confession, and the two cities are all prominent in Tate's mature work and are present even in his earliest writings. Like Augustine, he knew that he was born into a declining world. The temptation for a sensitive person, faced with this knowledge, is to turn inward. Thus the most popular stance among poets of the last few decades is the so-called confessional posture. But the Augustinian perspective represents a turning inward in an entirely different sense. Tate has written, concerning the modern practice of confession, that "it is always a question whether one's egoism can be made to look unique, or anything but conventional and boring."[15] He speaks of being incapable of letting himself "indulge in the terrible fluidity of self-revelation" for fear of having "to tell what was wrong with me."[16] Certainly, he never proclaims, as he accuses André Gide of doing, his "intellectual virtue." Nevertheless, he does reveal his own faults and limitations, if only indirectly and dramatically. This

14. *Ibid.*

15. Allen Tate, "Preface to *The Man of Letters in the Modern World*," in *Essays*, 623.

16. Allen Tate, "Preface" to *Memoirs*, ix.

kind of self-revelation has its roots in Augustine, who, according to Robert J. O'Connell, "looks on the stuff of his own life as food for probing reflection, and finds it not untypical of what the mass of mankind has known. So, he prods our minds to ponder a series of his own life experiences, of the sort, he is confident, that we will recognize as our own, or so very like our own as to spark in us the recognition he hopes will dawn."[17] Tate's poetry reveals not his personal life but a kind of *figura*—Mr. Tate, our cousin, our double, our brother.

Poe and Augustine, then, are opposed *figurae* of Tate. Poe is associated with the narcissism of the mirror, Augustine with the outward gaze of the window. The "hypertrophy of the three classical faculties: feeling, will, and intellect" in Poe[18] is countered by Augustine's trinity of memory, understanding, and will in the unified soul. Poe's unhistorical imagination, finally, is confronted by Augustine's vision of the two cities and his analogical theory of reality. Though little is said of Poe in this study, I hope that these contrary figures will be understood as main contenders for the soul of the modern poet. Poe longed for cosmic annihilation. The author of *The City of God* moved away from the fragmentation and brutality of his civilization without forsaking the present. He sought a society built on the heart, a stable community of men directed toward a common, transcendent goal. Tate found in Augustine's example a means of carrying out the mandate that is the subject of all his writings—the task of preserving from the ravages of a civilization in collapse those elements of permanent value.

The nine chapters of this book are an account of this quest for order, presented in terms of its main themes and in an approximation of chronological order. The first five chapters describe Tate's encounter with and consideration of the claims of science, tradition, heredity, sexuality, and history on his loyalties. Without rejecting any of these models of order outright, Tate recognizes their radical insufficiency as a basis for a modern faith, even when all of them are embraced at once. The last four chapters are about the transformation these models undergo as Tate begins to recover that unique but decisive shift in Western intellectual sensibility toward a new order I call the "Augustinian per-

17. Robert J. O'Connell, *Art and the Christian Intelligence in St. Augustine* (Cambridge, Mass., 1978), 189.

18. Tate, "The Angelic Imagination," 403.

criterion, and probability is the only acceptable one. Man can never grasp the truth; he can only approximate it mathematically. The twin infinities of the reading experience are linked with the girl's despair over the abstract, asymptotically distant reality that man can never know. Since she has experienced the immediacy and truth of love, the girl destroys herself rather than allow the riddling mind to dominate her emotional grasp of human realities.

Her action of dashing her brain is reminiscent of another early poem, "Homily," which is a witty extension of the biblical injunction to pluck out the eye if it offend. It is the "linear sight" of the eye, the "straight line of pessimism," that is countered by the body's seeming impenetrability. The abstracting vision of the head leads to the imposition of a static spatiality on a world of flux, but this mathematical refinement of the world of experience destroys the stuff of life. The reader who encounters the death of the duchess is caught in the same dilemma. Like the Greek girl, he is trapped in a world that offers only "mouthings of probability," but unlike her, he refuses to take action. The girl and the duchess die for something that Tate calls "the myth." The form of their lives is supported by a myth that gives meaning to love, and both lose their lives for love. The modern, on the other hand, is content to live in a world of mechanical movement and illusion, incapable of committing himself to any action that bears an ultimate meaning. The tragic catharsis of the play leads to his discomfort and boredom. What the "Horatian Epode" shows is the terrible inability of man to love if his world has no meaning. Tate sees this condition of rationality-dominated inaction—what he later calls in "Ode to the Confederate Dead" the "cold pool left by the mounting flood,/ Of muted Zeno and Parmenides"—as the characteristic modern disease. In this realm of mechanical order and abstraction, twentieth-century man finds the means of avoiding any contemplation of death.

A return to the poem "Homily," mentioned briefly above, will show this escape for what it is. If the consciousness of death offend thee, Tate says wittily, then tear it out of your mind. But if this advice is taken literally, as the poem suggests, the result is self-destruction. The head's "linear sight" cannot exist without the palpable body that sustains it, just as the "form requires the myth" in the story of the Greek girl. The head is "unutterable"—that is, the intellect is unspeakably bold but altogether inarticulate in its abstract rage. The poem renders a feeling of impotent anger at the inability of man to escape his fate. Speech is creative, the bringer of life; failure of speech is death. The "unutterable head" is balanced by its nemesis, the "loquacious bed," where life begins. Through love one can fall "down and [bruise] the stars/ With the glitter of superior light," as Tate puts it in an earlier version of the poem.[4] Because modern man cannot bring himself to contemplate or speak of death, he must hunt out and destroy the impulse that leads to thinking about it. In this silence is the rejection of the complexities of human existence, the intricate "wars" between love and death "That wove their interior smoke its way" through the mind. The inarticulateness of modern man, coupled with his native pessimism and fear of death, is a constant theme in Tate's later poetry. Here it receives a macabre, if witty, expression.

The attempt to escape death through an absorption into mechanical order (the streetcars of "Horatian Epode") or an annihilation of thought (the ironic conclusion of "Homily") is the subject of another poem of this early period, the much-anthologized and discussed "Death of Little Boys." Among numerous readings of the poem, Donald Davidson's interpretation, contained in a letter to Tate, stands out for its clarity and accuracy. He compares the poem to a scene in Tate's later novel: "Abstraction threatens, is indeed imminent, but does not quite prevail at the funeral of Lacy's mother, in The Fathers. In Death of Little Boys, it has prevailed; the result is raw fear rather than grief; the 'guests' turn down their palms to repress indecorous (unmodern) manifestations of grief; people, place, objects lack identification and connection; in the end there is 'calm' but not consolation."[5]

The poem is an intricate study of spatial relationships manifested by psychological reactions to the natural world. It is about a communal response to the death of a young person known and loved, but the impact of the death on the person addressed in the poem is overwhelming. His feelings are projected by images of things, such as the drenched aster, that seem to threaten from without. The battered flower peers in, as it were, on the scene inside. It possesses a nightmarish quality of natural fury against life—a psychological echo of the tousled head of the dying boy whose hair has been "torn in two" by death. The event

4. Allen Tate, "Homily," *Fugitive*, IV, ii.
5. Donald Davidson to Allen Tate, January 15, 1963, in *Correspondence*, 391.

has a cosmic terror about it that "will rage terrific as the sea." The "little town" that should offer communal solace "reels like a sailor drunk in his rotten skiff." The impact of death on the community is described as a kind of vertigo, triggered by the cold, crashing sea of the north, inhospitable and sterile, that threatens below the imaginary "cliff/ Of Norway where you ponder"—another psychological image of remoteness and separation. The waving flower outside the window, the dizzying perspective from the cliff, and the shipwreck all give a sense of helplessness in the face of death. The awesome energy of nature that is deployed in the death-event, even in this quiet room, is met by fear and near-paralysis. The onlookers can find relief only in motion through space without any definable goal—the "chill precision of moving feet" that takes them away from the fearful scene. Whatever may be true of Tate's other writings, this poem works through a logic of suggestion rather than through definite literary allusions.

A more unusual aspect of "Death of Little Boys" is its treatment of light. Throughout Tate's poetry, light is ambivalent; it has negative as well as positive connotations—or rather, to speak more precisely, it may reveal death as readily as symbolize life. The results are often interestingly complex, for light is usually associated with space, while time is associated with death. Thus the sudden explosion of light that fills the "crumbling room" is a disruption of spatial calm. Death transforms the meaning of light. Space is turned into time. It is in this "chipped music" at the end of the poem that the abstraction is given curiously concrete qualities; a temporal art is treated sculpturally. Furthermore, the scene outside the window has taken on a sense of discontinuity, of gold "deftly intricate with gray" among the fields of wheat, as an echo of the event within. Space has been destroyed by time and no longer offers a refuge from the fate of all humanity. The dead boy's hair is "torn in two," but the phrase is ambiguous enough to refer also to the person who touches the boy's head. Everything has been divided by mortality—youth and age, nature within and without, the psyche and the body. The impact of this harsh reality, where the form is no longer supported by the myth, is felt on every level.

In "A Pauper," formerly entitled "Poem for My Father," Tate shows that the family itself has been divided by paralysis and the inability to speak. A Latin epigraph, omitted from later printings of the poem, sums up the situation: father and son are joined in space but not in time

("*Coniuncti pater filiusque sed non tempore*").[6] The division between husband and wife, who live in the same house but are estranged from each other, is described in meteorological terms: "cold rain," "winter," "ice," and "stiff wind." The son is a pauper in both words and feelings. He cannot speak; he has neither attitude nor mood to express. Communication between husband and wife has been reduced to the written word. The stony silence and darkness are like a "cairn," a heap of rocks left as a landmark. The son cannot remove this obstruction from the past, "heave these mighty stones" that clutter the memory "futurewards." To speak would be to prostitute language, to have "words/ As strumpets only." The final image in the poem is a burning letter, as the father remains "Deaf to the commensurate pathos up the stair" of his wife, halted by the "stiff wind" of their separation.

This shattered world that is the subject of Tate's early poetry offers no foundation for a young man to build on. Without a myth, there can be no action. What is necessary, as Tate was to recognize a few years later, is a larger perspective than immediate experience can offer. In an early review, he recognizes the importance of imaginative order in the establishing of some stable perspective.

> To represent as action, and as a whole, any human experience, one must make a fable, and when the fable is typical of one kind of action it becomes a myth, which conveys its meaning dramatically. . . . Our great myths make their appeal to those people, at last remarkably few, who have a sense of destiny, of poise above life, and who look at the vast distraction of the world, its shift and disintegration, with a controlling detachment.[7]

To enter the level of myth is to establish oneself above the slender range of daily life that always distorts one's view of the whole of reality. Nevertheless, a larger perspective offers no help if it provides detachment but not self-control. The poet cannot change or affect events, but he can affect the understanding of them. The poet has a major responsibility to his society; for he can make his own self-understanding available, through his writings, to the understandings of others.

By 1925 Tate had already begun to reach a "sense of destiny" and a

6. Allen Tate, "A Pauper," In *Mr. Pope and Other Poems* (New York, 1928), 20–21. The original title, "Poem for My Father," appears in *Voices*, III, 47.

7. Allen Tate, "A Note on Milton," *New Republic*, LXVIII, 267.

"poise above life" that provided him with some detachment from his earliest work. In a letter to Donald Davidson, he looks back on the poetry he had written as a member of the Fugitive group:

> Mine was a little more ragged and violent, being produced by a young man, than the other work; but it was in the same drift toward defeatism. I am not writing any poetry now; and the reason is obvious: I have no idiom for a Vita Nuova, for it will take a long time for me even to understand it. For poetry is the triumph of life, not a commentary on its impossibility.[8]

In this dual allusion to Dante and Shelley, Tate stakes out the limits of his dilemma. He cannot assert the Romantic optimism of Shelley or the medieval optimism of Dante because he lacks the language to make either perspective convincing. But a few months later, he had already begun to develop his more serious reflections on the meaning of history and myth. His fascination with these subjects was no doubt boosted by the appearance of two books, both of which he read at this time. One was Alfred North Whitehead's *Science in the Modern World*; the other was Oswald Spengler's *Decline of the West*, Volume I, which he reviewed for *The Nation*. Tate seems to have studied them carefully, but even so their influence should not be misconstrued. They simply reinforced a line of thought he had already been following for some years and they constitute only a small part of his voluminous reading during this period, when he contributed several reviews a month to various publications. They also gave him some new points of reference, and themes from both books—particularly from Spengler's—are especially evident in Tate's first serious collection, *Mr. Pope and Other Poems*, persisting in a subtle fashion throughout his career. What makes these two books stand out, among so many others he read during the twenties, is their fresh cultural perspective.

Whitehead and Spengler have in common a critical point of view that organizes the data they examine. While their interpretations of that data coincide only occasionally, both writers possess the kind of controlling detachment that allows them to maintain an awareness of their own limitations. As Carl Becker was to write a few years later, "We necessarily look at our world from the point of view of history and from

8. Allen Tate to Donald Davidson, November 26, 1925, in *Correspondence*, 148.

the point of view of science."[9] It was precisely the impact of these two points of view on each other that was the focus of Tate's study in 1926. Since both science and history had taken on a new progressivist character by the middle of the nineteenth century, they had come to stand for the very vanguard of modern secular positivism. What Tate found valuable in Whitehead is suggested by two sentences from the opening pages of *Science and the Modern World*: "Men can be provincial in time, as well as in space. We may ask ourselves whether the scientific mentality of the modern world in the immediate past is not a successful example of such provincial limitation."[10] This notion of provincialism in time was to inspire some fruitful discussion later in Tate's career; but in the twenties it lent authority to anti-positivist skepticism, pessimism about human progress, and rejection of the universal claims of the scientific method. It had a useful negative impact on Tate, confirming what he had already begun to suspect: that the scientific mentality is not an immutable way of thinking about reality but a historically relative cultural perspective.

It is interesting to pursue the later development of Whitehead's idea in essays by both Tate and T. S. Eliot. In "What Is a Classic?" Eliot reflects:

> In our age, when men seem more than ever prone to confuse wisdom with knowledge, and knowledge with information, and to try to solve problems of life in terms of engineering, there is coming into existence a new kind of provincialism which perhaps deserves a new name. It is a provincialism, not of space, but of time; one for which history is merely the chronicle of human devices which have served their turn and been scrapped, one for which the world is the property solely of the living, a property in which the dead hold no shares. The menace of this kind of provincialism is, that we can all, all the peoples on the globe, be provincials together; and those who are not content to be provincials, can only become hermits.[11]

9. Carl Becker, *The Heavenly City of the Eighteenth-century Philosophers* (New Haven, 1932), 27.

10. Alfred North Whitehead, *Science and the Modern World* (New York, 1925), ix.

11. T. S. Eliot, "What Is a Classic?" in *On Poetry and Poets* (New York, 1961), 72.

At the same time Eliot's essay appeared, Tate published "The New Provincialism," where a similar distinction is made. It is not clear what, if any, relationship existed between the two essays, apart from their common inspiration in Whitehead's book; but the difference between them is enlightening. Unlike Eliot, Tate sees an alternative way of life to that of the hermit. He calls it "regionalism."

> Regionalism is . . . limited in space but not in time.
>
> The provincial attitude is limited in time but not in space. When the regional man, in his ignorance, often an intensive and creative ignorance, of the world, extends his own immediate necessities into the world, and assumes that the present moment is unique, he becomes the provincial man. He cuts himself off from the past, and without benefit of the fund of traditional wisdom approaches the simplest problems of life as if nobody had ever heard of them before.[12]

Almost two decades later, then, Tate was drawing on the insights he had gained from his reading of Whitehead and coming to conclusions consonant with but not identical to those of his old friend Eliot. Tate's commitment to place, less grandiose than Eliot's attempt to preserve what remained of classical Europe, rings truer than his older contemporary's adopted citizenship abroad.

In his correspondence with Davidson during the twenties, Tate was already beginning to appreciate the advantages of belonging to a definite place; and this growing awareness is an important clue to the shift in intellectual perspective he was undergoing. The first mention of Whitehead occurs in a letter outlining a proposed essay on "fundamentalism." The essay was never published, but its ideas were worked into other pieces; and it is from them that a clear picture of Tate's evolving views on history, science, religion, and myth begins to emerge.

In a letter to Davidson dated March 3, 1926, Tate shows clear evidence of his interest in *Science in the Modern World*.

> For over a month I have been collecting notes for an essay. The essay, I fear, will contain a discussion of Fundamentalism; not

12. Allen Tate, "The New Provincialism," in *Essays*, 539.

> what the Methodist Bishops think it is, but what it really is. My purpose is to define the rights of both parties, science and religion. . . . The principle is, Science as we inherit it as Mechanism from the 17th century has nothing to say about reality: if the Church or a fishmonger asserts that reality is fundamentally cheese or gold dust or Bishop Berkeley's tar water, Science has no right to deny it. On the other hand, the Church has no right to forestall *all* criticism by simply saying Science is wrong. . . . More abstractly, Science is, according to tradition, classification; religion, or more properly philosophy, is organization. As A. N. Whitehead puts it, philosophy is nature viewed as organism; science as mechanism.[13]

Tate's conviction that "those who attack science should attack science from principle, philosophically" was to receive an unusual confirmation from an unexpected quarter. Two months later Tate published a review of *Decline of the West* under the title "Fundamentalism."

Spengler's book is an even more radical criticism of science than the one Tate had entertained, for it demolishes the pretensions of science to universal knowledge not through philosophic but through historical principles. According to *Decline of the West*, man is trapped in his own time and culture. No progression or development takes place in history apart from periods within the organic cycles that make up the repeated growth and demise of cultures. Up until and including our time, history has consisted of a limited number of cultures, each completely autonomous and dominated by a "prime symbol," which Tate calls "the basic assumption of Spengler's philosophy." This "destiny," as Spengler likes to call it, is what is specific to each culture. Study of it is undertaken through "the symbolism of history and its analogies." Everything a culture is or does, from religion to science, is simply an aspect of its "destiny."

The purpose of Spengler's book is to provide an exhaustive definition of these particular entities that are called cultures. Spengler claims that his aim is to "be clear as to what culture *is*, what its relations are to visible history, to life, to soul, to nature, to intellect, what the forms of its manifestations are and how far these forms—peoples, tongues, and epochs, battles and ideas, states and gods, arts and craft-works, sci-

13. Allen Tate to Donald Davidson, March 3, 1926, in *Correspondence*, 158.

ences, laws, economic types and world-ideas, great men and great events—may be accepted and pointed to as symbols."[14] Spengler illustrates this "fundamentalism" of perspective with a vast repertory of concepts, images, and symbols organized according to a primary set of opposing pairs. He begins with a spatial mode of organization, which he calls "polarity," and a temporal one, which he calls "periodicity." Corresponding to them are further distinctions: mathematical law identifies "dead forms" and analogy gives an understanding of living ones. The essential components of history, form and movement, can be seen as corresponding to them. In the perspective of the natural sciences, reality appears to be "the world-as-nature." Spengler counters this version with his own: "the world-as-history." He elaborates his essentially temporal view of reality with a long series of distinctions: mechanical world-impression is distinguished from the organic; law is distinguished from image; formula and system from picture and symbol; constantly possible from instantly actual; experience dissecting according to scheme from imagination ordering according to plan; and mathematical from chronological number. There is a "logic of space" and a "logic of time." Spatial logic is necessarily part of human understanding, but it tends dangerously in our time to dominate all else; for the logic of time "suffuses the whole of mythological religions and artistic thought and constitutes the essence and kernel of all history." Therefore, according to Spengler, the historiographic goals of the school of Leopold von Ranke are mistaken, for the philosopher does not attempt to give an "ensemble picture inclusive of everything known" but "a picture of *life*," presented as "things-becoming," not as "things-become."

Decline of the West offers an extensive critique of the point of view Tate was beginning to attack. It provided him with a better organized set of terms than he had mustered for himself. In his review of Volume I, Tate gives a summary of Spengler's system along with brief critical comments on it. In one paragraph he anticipates some points made in later essays.

> Physiognomic and Systematic, organic and mechanical are . . . distinguished as the Becoming and the Become—Time and Space: Time is the form of the organic, Space the form of the

14. Oswald Spengler, *The Decline of the West*, trans. Charles Francis Atkinson (New York, 1939), I, 3.

> mechanical-mathematical. Spengler points out that the living sense of direction (time) is in science reduced to another mathematical dimension which includes it in the law of reversible action; this law, strictly spatial, denies time as direction and destiny; it denies organism in the reduction of organism to causality. Again, Space is Time not felt but perceived—Time actualized. And Spengler revises Kant: Time is the form of perceiving, Space the form of the perceived. Now every culture (men in life-unity) must perceive; every culture, then, must have its idea of Time and its own way of actualizing the idea. Therefore the way in which a culture actualizes its idea of Time is the way in which it envisages Space; the conception of Space is thus the index to the spirituality of a particular culture, the key to its "prime symbol."[15]

Though Tate found much to object to in Spengler—particularly in his identification of biological and cultural entities—many of the German scholar's specific insights were of value. In any case, according to Tate, Spengler "makes no pretension to empirical foundations; the conception is deductive and visionary." Spengler acknowledges his point of view and makes no attempt to conceal it or disguise its implications. He exempts nothing, not even his own system, from universal relativism. Spengler thus offers some powerful arguments, along with those of Whitehead, against exclusivist claims for scientific method. Almost eight years after his review, Tate cited a remark concerning religion and science from the second volume of Spengler's work: "Always science has grown up on religion . . . and always it signifies nothing more or less than an abstract melioration of these doctrines, considered as false because less abstract."[16]

Tate uses Spengler in "Three Types of Poetry" (1934) to illustrate his contention that the allegorist and the scientist are of "one origin and purpose." Religion, magic, poetry, and science are all creations of the imagination, but the popular notion of the scientist's activity adds a new component—the will. The kind of detachment that the imagination gains through myth is lost in the development of a scientific per-

15. Allen Tate, "Fundamentalism," *Nation*, CXXII, 532–33.

16. Allen Tate, "Three Types of Poetry," in *Essays*, 182, n. 1. The citation is from Spengler, II, 13.

spective, where the ability to change the world and not simply to contemplate it becomes paramount. Tate links the personal will, which attempts to impose an order on reality, with the scientific and allegorical methods, which are early and late versions of what he calls "romanticism." Allegory is religion made abstract by the will, just as science is allegory made even more abstract. It is the false dream of progress, which Spengler shows to be an imaginative structure rather than a physical law, that gives a spurious moral basis for these abstract meliorations.

Nevertheless, Spengler's revelation that all intellectual phenomena are products of the symbol-producing imagination fails to resolve the issue with which Tate was grappling. In 1935 he reviewed *The Hour of Decision*, using the occasion for a final assessment of its author's significance: "The deepest question of all he leaves, as every one must leave, unanswered. Since Spengler's philosophy of history is also a philosophy of historical values enjoining us to see all 'late' forms of society as a decadence from the rooted life of property and land, how far are we entitled to will and to restore those values? How shall we set about it?"[17] Thus Spengler appears at the opposite pole from the scientist. He denies that the human will has any significance whatsoever. Yet even Spengler seems uncomfortable with this stance; and in *The Hour of Decision* he attempts to argue, not quite coherently, that man is free to choose and decide some aspects of his destiny. Although Spengler offered Tate some cogent arguments against the crude assertions of uncritical spokesmen for scientific method, he could not offer a satisfactory solution to the fundamentalist dilemma.

In a letter to Davidson on March 24, 1926, Tate mentions another part of his fundamentalist project; he has been invited by T. S. Eliot to "contribute an essay . . . on Paul Elmer More."[18] The essay did not appear until three years later, as "The Fallacy of Humanism," but it seems to have absorbed many of the ideas from the projected article that was never published. It is in this essay that Tate begins to develop his more serious reflections on the meaning of history, and some of Spengler's vocabulary is occasionally in evidence as he probes the works not only of More but also of co-humanists Norman Foerster and Irving Babbitt. While admitting that these three men have attempted nobly to

17. Allen Tate, "Spengler's Tract Against Liberalism," *American Review*, III, 47.
18. Allen Tate to Donald Davidson, March 24, 1926, in *Correspondence*, 160.

offer an alternative to the cultural decline of the present and the increasingly "naturalistic" tendency of modern thought, Tate accuses Foerster of transforming "the idea of an increasingly distant temporal past into the idea of a logical series which is quite timeless." Such a notion of time depends upon the "scientific interpretation of history, through a method which would impose an abstract mathematical pattern upon the past." The ironic result of Foerster's efforts to save the times will be to dehumanize the past: "The 'historical method' has always been the antihistorical method. Its aim is to contemporize the past. Its real effect is to de-temporize it. The past becomes a causal series, and timeless; and as a quantitative abstraction . . . valueless."[19]

In extending his analysis Tate continues to use ideas concerning spatial and temporal themes that he had encountered in Spengler and Whitehead:

> Now the logical series is quantitative, the abstraction of space. The temporal series is, on the other hand, space concrete. Concrete, temporal experience implies the existence of a temporal past, and it is the foundation of the religious imagination; that is to say, the only way to think of the past independently of Mr. Foerster's naturalism is to think religiously; and conversely, the only way to think religiously is to think in time. Naturalistic science is timeless. A doctrine based upon it, whether explicitly or not, can have no past, no idea of tradition, no fixed center of life.[20]

Tate's reflections on the opposition between religion and science, brought into sharper focus by his struggle to define their proper roles, has begun to develop into a powerful argument that will continue throughout his career.

19. Allen Tate, "Humanism and Naturalism," in *Memoirs*, 180–82. (Originally published as "The Fallacy of Humanism.")

20. *Ibid.*

Two

The Buried City

In his essay "Homer and the Scholars," George Steiner has noted the central importance of the city in the first works of Western literature:

> At the core of the Homeric poems lies the remembrance of one of the greatest disasters that can befall man: the destruction of a city. A city is the outward sum of man's nobility; in it, his condition is most thoroughly humanized. When a city is destroyed, man is compelled to wander the earth or dwell in the open fields in partial return to the manner of a beast. That is the central realization of the *Iliad*. Resounding through the epic, now in stifled allusion, now in strident lament, is the dread fact that an ancient and splendid city has perished by the edge of the sea.[1]

This theme of a fallen world lies at the heart of Tate's work. In a letter to John Peale Bishop (June, 1931) he speaks of the way that "Southerners are apt to identify the great political and social failure with their characters, or if they are poets and concerned with themselves, with their own failure." He continues by speaking of the imaginative unity that obliges a poet to act out the meaning of destruction in his own life:

> The older I get the more I realize that I set out about ten years ago to live a life of failure, to imitate, in my own life, the history of my people. For it was only in this fashion, considering the circumstances, that I could completely identify myself with them. We all have an instinct—if we are artists particularly—to live at the center of some way of life and to be borne up by its innermost significance. The significance of the Southern way of life, in my time, is failure. . . . What else is there for me but a com-

1. George Steiner, "Homer and the Scholars," *Atlantic Monthly*, CCVIII, 78.

plete acceptance of the idea of failure? There is no other "culture" I can enter into, even if I had the desire.[2]

These remarks should not be interpreted as those of a defeatist. In a later letter to Bishop, Tate implies that their friend Edmund Wilson is the real defeatist: "He seems to think that the modern breakdown . . . is necessarily permanent . . . but another historical argument would hold that such breakdowns are strictly temporary, and that the normal sequence is not logical but rather up and down." Far from being simply negative about the present, Tate recognizes the existence of another community remembered by the poet, a society existing not in the past but in the timeless realms of imagination. Its presence is sustained, even in failure, as Tate observes when he points out to Bishop that "the old Southerners did not reach perfection in the style that they developed, or the style that they lived up to." A culture exists both as a lived "style" and as a shared, if seldom realized, paradigm.

Tate's chief concern as an essayist is the nature and historical meaning of Western culture in relation to its paradigm. But as poet, he is intent on articulating the way in which culture is essential to the life of the individual. In his poems he writes, as he explains to Bishop, "from the point of view of an Ideal Self" that provides the possibility of a "greater sensuous range" and a perspective beyond his "personal observation." The common man is unconscious of any relationship between his private life and the greater network of historical and cultural elements that sustains it. A sense of one's culture in relation to himself requires an ability to meditate and interpret. The poet provides the occasion for men to develop this awareness through direct participation. He must, of course, experience the world before attempting to know it in relation to himself; but the poet begins by assuming that relationship as a given experience. He offers not theories or analyses that lead to a reading of the world but analogical experiences that require meditation and interpretation in themselves.

In "Emily Dickinson" (1928), Tate describes his subject as a type of the contemporary poet, "balanced upon the moment when . . . a world is about to fall." She "was born into the equilibrium of an old and a new order," and her principal advantage as a poet was that she did not "reason about the world she saw; she merely saw it. The 'ideas' implicit in

2. Allen Tate to John Peale Bishop, early June, 1931, in *Letters*, 34.

the world within her rose up, concentrated in her immediate perception." Tate continues by speaking of the relationship between the poet and this implicit "world" he bears within :

> That kind of world at present has for us something of the fascination of a buried city. There is none like it. When such worlds exist, when such cultures flourish, they support not only the poet but all members of society. For, from these, the poet differs only in his gift for exhibiting the structure, the internal lineaments, of his culture by threatening to tear them apart: a process that concentrates the symbolic emotions of society while it seems to attack them. The poet may hate his age; he may be an outcast like Villon; but this world is always there as the background to what he has to say. It is the lens through which he brings nature to focus and control—the clarifying medium that concentrates his personal feeling.[3]

In discussing Yeats's poetry, which he believes "is nearer the center of our main traditions of sensibility and thought than the poetry of Eliot or Pound," Tate defends the Irish poet's "system" as a necessary metaphorical structure: "Any statement about 'life' must have philosophical implications, just as any genuine philosophical statement must have, because of the nature of language, mythical implications. Yeats's doctrine of the conflict of opposites says nothing about the fundamental nature of reality; it is rather a dramatic framework through which is made visible the perpetual oscillation of man between extreme introspection and extreme loss of the self in the world of action."[4] Yeats's dramatic framework, then, is one that allows him to reconcile the solipsistic extreme of the isolated person and the totally impersonal extreme of a faceless public involvement "in a concrete relation to life undiluted by calculation and abstraction." The fallen city is given meaning by being referred to some paradigm; or, as Tate puts it, Yeats's "symbols are 'made good' in the poem; they are drawn into a wider convention (Mr. Blackmur calls it the 'heaven of man's mind') than they would imply if taken separately."[5]

3. Allen Tate, "Emily Dickinson," in *Essays*, 295–96.
4. Allen Tate, "Yeats's Romanticism," in *Essays*, 307–308.
5. *Ibid.*, 309.

This "heaven of man's mind" is what Tate calls, quoting Shelley, "a fixed point of reference"[6] for the sensibility that prevents the personal will from creating eccentric utopias out of private feelings. Tate sees this city in the imagination, towards which the fragments of the past are always directed for assembly, as "an imperative of reference": "The perfect traditional society has never existed, can never exist and is a delusion. But the perfect traditional society as an imperative of reference—not as an absolute lump to be measured and weighed—has always existed and will continue to haunt the moral imagination of man."[7] Thus even if the "perfect traditional society" is thought of as existing only in the "heaven of man's mind," it is still vital as the means of transcending the fragile historical basis of man's existence. Tate sees man as engaged in a constant task of interpreting the world. The poet plays an especially prominent role in this process. By acknowledging his stance in a culture, he can give positive significance even to a fallen city or a failed civilization. In a realm that has become almost placeless, the poet refuses to allow culture to become uniform and dimensionless. His necessary self-awareness does not lead to solipsism; it must, on the contrary, reveal the values of the eternal community. But the poet cannot evoke a fallen and buried city without invoking his own personal share in its past. Where he differs from other men is in an ability to give his private experiences a paradigmatic meaning.

In *Mr. Pope and Other Poems* (1928), Tate had already sketched the broad contours of these important dimensions. The book is divided into three sections: "Space," "Time," and "History," reflecting his early concern with the categories of science and the imaginative modes of myth and history. In poems like "The Subway" he gives a concise portrait of the mechanical secular world that destroys human freedom. But the opening title poem, "Mr. Pope," acts as a balancing assertion of the role of the poet. Pope, strolling through London, seeing, evaluating, interpreting, is in sharp contrast to the "idiot" in his "cold revery" after the subway ride. Tate's placement of these two poems in prominent positions, at the beginning and end of the first part of his book ("Space"), shows that he is concerned in "Mr. Pope" with more than a world of art, removed from both space and time in its ideal existence. He is con-

6. Tate, "Emily Dickinson," 294.

7. Allen Tate, "Liberalism and Tradition," in *Reason and Madness* (New York, 1941), 214–15.

cerned about the health of the human community. The poem is about the quest of the artist to overcome the paralysis of the imagination in a world given over to radically dissociated notions of space, time, and history.

As a paradigm for the entire volume, Pope represents the alienated but respected poet who could still pull together enough of his cultural experience to make a coherent statement about the whole of things. Other poets are alluded to in the remaining poems of this first collection—Sappho, Catullus, Propertius, Dante, Webster, Donne, Baudelaire, and Rimbaud. The epigraph from Blake's "London," on the title page of the volume, reminds the reader that Pope was quite different from all of them, for his London is not yet the unreal city of Blake and Baudelaire. His poetry is poised between two epochs. In Pope's eighteenth-century city, a traditional society is still part of the imagination. It is not in need of being reinvented, as it was already by the time of Blake. Yet like the modern southerner, Pope was a man aware of what it meant to be a foreigner in his own country. A recusant Catholic, he was barred from politics and other means of direct participation in society. A hunchback, he was physically repulsive even in Hogarth's London. A satirist and a great poet, he was both admired and feared by his contemporaries; for he showed them how great the power of poetry can be, overcoming through it all the limitations of his handicaps.

In Tate's poem, Pope is both part of the city in which he strolls and apart from it. He walks in it, while the ladies who lean out "more out of fear than pity" are riding in carriages. His "goat's" back contrasts with the "glint of pearl and gold sedans." He is not integrated into the normal life of the city; he is an outsider inspiring the fear that all invaders provoke, a strange animal wandering the streets. He strikes the ladies as a strange person, but his peculiar intensity cannot be dismissed; indeed, it causes them to strain from their habitual places of comfort. What they see in him is more than a pitifully deformed hunchback. They see a dangerous masculine force, like the one feared by Belinda in *The Rape of the Lock*. The "strict" glint of their sedans is matched by his "tight" back.

The two middle stanzas of the poem continue this opposition of the feminine and masculine, the contained and the uncontainable. The urn, we are told, "should have more bones," according to the conventional way of thinking about both art and funerals (the urn stands for both). It should contain more evidence of the man. But the "jar is empty; you may break/ It only to find that Mr. Pope is gone." The urn has become more than the "funeral shell" of the preceding stanza. It is now a vase, like the jar that Wallace Stevens set in Tennessee or the Chinese jar of Eliot's *Four Quartets*. In the oriental world, the jar stands for oneness and the still movement of art and intelligence which triumphs over birth and death. But the jar itself will be destroyed if we try to discover more of Mr. Pope inside it than nature will allow to remain.

The reason that the urn seems to be so fragile is that it has about it an air of feminine receptivity incapable of containing the masculine energy of Mr. Pope's strange person. Opposed to the feminine image of the jar—comparable to Keats's "unravished bride of quietness"—is the masculine image of the serpent. They are opposed in other ways as well—one represents space and death, the other time and fertility. Pope is said to have "dribbled couplets like a snake/ Coiled to a lithe precision in the sun." Apollonian wit and satire, combined with the extreme fecundity of his art, constitute a fertile marriage of the linear with the cyclical, life with death, good with evil, space with time. Perhaps the formal urn could never have contained all the freely emanating dribble, but the couplet manages to keep form and energy together, whatever has become of the poet; for Pope as craftsman was more than a maker of vases. His serpentine creations are a different kind of symbol of the triumph of art over birth and rebirth. In its eternal stillness, the urn remains a spatial art form. Poetry is a time art. The serpent, an old symbol of immortality, renews itself through time.

The brilliant linking of images in the last stanza of the poem draws all these oppositions together into a final statement. What was Pope's rage? It was not sexual (though the ladies fear him) nor moralistic (we still enjoy the poetry, though we no longer care for the moral). The snakelike bite of the satiric tongue, the "wit and rage between his teeth," can still interest us, whatever originally prompted it. Mr. Pope the historical personage is no more, and all his personal quarrels with other men are forgotten. As W. H. Auden said of Yeats, he has become his poems. But what has triumphed in them is the masculine energy of the snake, not the feminine receptivity of the jar. In the last two lines of the poem—"around a crooked tree/ A moral climbs whose name should be a wreath"—the snake is unified with another large symbol, the "crooked tree" that stands both for Pope's physical body and for something greater that supports his poetry. Together, snake and tree represent the triumph of the imagination over the limitations of time, space, and history in the wreath that crowns Pope's efforts. The snake is not merely coiled around the tree—it climbs. The symbolic entanglement of the snakelike moral with the earth-bound tree of life is a reminder of the caduceus, the healing wand of the ancient world. Yet it is also a reminder of moral dualism and ambivalence. The tree is the ancient symbol of the life of the cosmos, and Pope's poetry—if not the man—remains to move up this axis of immortality. Nevertheless, the spiraling serpent figure, symbol of triumph, also recalls the temptation of the knowledge of good and evil that led man to his fall from innocence. Pope is vital to modern man because he not only speaks of what we should do but, more necessary in our times, reminds us of our human limitations, our own physical and moral imperfections, our own crookedness. Pope overcame his imperfections through his imagination of a realm of order; he deserves his laurel wreath because, like the classical hero, he helped to restore a city.

Pope stands in Tate's volume for something irrecoverable; his bones can never be retrieved from the urn. He was a poet in a time of crisis who was still very much a part of his society, however difficult his position in it. He was the last poet, Tate suggests, who could draw on a whole tradition for his vision. A generation later, poets resided in a changing world that affected all too directly their ability to enjoy this communion. In 1926, speaking of Eliot, Tate wrote, "It is evident that he for some reason—like Gray who also lived in a critical transition period—cannot 'speak out.'"[8] A few years later, Tate wrote of "the intensive literary cultivation of a few men who by the very act of taking up the profession of letters exile themselves from society."[9] The poet in the early eighteenth century was still capable of speaking out because he existed in a genuine, if decaying, community. Echoing historian Carl Becker, Tate later claims in "The Man of Letters in the Modern World"

8. Allen Tate, Review of T. S. Eliot's *Poems: 1909–1925*, in *New Republic*, XLVII, 173.

9. Allen Tate, Review of T. S. Eliot (ed.), *London: A Poem*, in *New Republic*, LXVIII, 23.

that the "Heavenly City was still visible, to Americans, in the political economy of Thomas Jefferson."[10] Thus America was able to hold on to the notion of a traditional society a bit longer than could Europe. Pope and Jefferson stand for the last major figures to whom the unity of Western culture was still available. In a series of epigrams entitled "Historical Epitaphs" (1930), Tate provides a brief résumé of nineteenth-century American history, from Thomas Jefferson to John Brown, in which he traces the movement from an appreciation of tradition to an embracing of abstract moralism. Among poets, the movement is from Pope to Blake, whose "poetry of the Prophetic Books fleshes out the homemade system,"[11] and to Keats, who "lacks an ordered symbolism through which he may *know* the common and the ideal reality in a single imaginative act."[12]

As sympathetic with and admiring of these poets as he was, Tate recognized that there was something spiritually unhealthy about the world into which they were thrust and with which they were forced to contend as poets. In his introduction to Hart Crane's *White Buildings*, Tate speaks of his friend's "repudiation of the commonly available themes of poetry" in favor of a "ready-made theme" that narrows or attenuates the poet's vision.[13] It is a condition that poets have faced and reacted against since the time of Baudelaire and Rimbaud, who had to "reinvent" the concept of the city and the meaning of love in order to survive as men of letters. Hence, "the important contemporary poet has the rapidly diminishing privilege of reorganizing the subjects of the past. He must construct and assimilate his own subjects. Dante had only to assimilate his." In Baudelaire, for instance, there still lingers an ability to see the presence of the eternal in the squalor of the contemporary metropolis; but despite the "Ideal" that he opposes to the "Spleen" of his reaction to the "fourmillante Cité," Baudelaire's unity of the high and the low inheres in a private system of his own invention, derived from an eccentric thinker like Swedenborg rather than from a community to which he belongs. However, Baudelaire could show, according to Tate, that "the sordid and the sublime could be grasped in a single complex of experience" through the one fragment of tradition that still

10. Allen Tate, "The Man of Letters in the Modern World," in *Essays*, 6.
11. Tate, "Yeats's Romanticism," 308.
12. Allen Tate, "A Reading of Keats," in *Essays*, 271.
13. Allen Tate, "Introduction to *White Buildings* by Hart Crane," in *Memoirs*, 111–12.

remained within his grasp—formal versification. He could still speak out because he had inherited the rigorous style of seventeenth-century French classicism. After Baudelaire, perhaps only Yeats, among the major poets of the modern era, managed to remain in touch with the central modes of the Western tradition. For Yeats, too, has his two cities—the "darkness and abstraction, quantitative relations without imagination" of "Babylonian mathematical starlight" opposed to the "monuments of unaging intellect" of Byzantium. Yeats's Byzantium is not, Tate asserts, a utopian but a pastoral image of the city, "where men enjoy full unity of being." It is, very simply, the "picture of a perfect culture." Indeed, Tate goes so far as to compare Yeats with Dante, noting that "both poets strove for a visible structure of action which is indeed necessary to what they said, but which does not explain what they said." Neither Dante's exile nor Yeats's "lower mythology" kept them from the world. What both poets received from their experiences was "not a mythology at all, but rather an extended metaphor."[14]

Although Tate recognizes in his criticism that it is possible for the contemporary poet to overcome the handicaps of exile and inability to speak or act, he is honest enough to admit as poet that he has not yet achieved that triumph. He wrote to Bishop in 1932, "For some reason I never doubt that I know what the truth is; I doubt my capacity to state it."[15] On the whole *Mr. Pope and Other Poems* has a powerful negative character, for Tate had not yet developed his concept of regionalism as an alternative to provincialism in time. It was this emphasis that led Donald Davidson to accuse Tate of wielding "your own favorite word—*failure* . . . on every possible occasion."[16] He had not yet come around to Davidson's positive assessment of southern culture; in an essay published in 1925, "Last Days of the Charming Lady," Tate still sees the southerner as limited by the same provincialism as others in the modern world.[17]

A portrait of the provincial as southerner is given in Tate's difficult poem "Idiot":

> The idiot greens the meadow with his eyes,
> The meadow creeps implacable and still;

14. Tate, "Yeats's Romanticism," 302–304, 307.
15. Allen Tate to John Peale Bishop, October 26, 1932, in *Letters*, 67.
16. Donald Davidson to Allen Tate, February 15, 1927, in *Correspondence*, 187.
17. Allen Tate, "Last Days of the Charming Lady," *Nation*, CXXI, 485–86.

A dog barks, the hammock swings, he lies.
One two three the cows bulge on the hill.

In his "creative ignorance," a kind of pseudo-poetic irrationality, the idiot through whose eyes the scene is described tries to impose some kind of order on the things he sees. He attempts to project "becoming," the temporal sense of life, on a meadow scene that is "implacable and still." He "greens," that is sees life and movement where there are none (the meadow "creeps" in his imagination). In the second stanza he has spatialized everything. "Motion, which is not time," is the key to his picture of a controlled reality, like the cows who emerge in a mathematical series on the hill. He is suspended, out of contact with the scene he views—one supposes—from the front porch of his house, as he counts the cows, themselves barely separate from the landscape. Even the sunset is "long" and retarded. It is not time but some abstracting force that reduces people ("niggers") to a quantitative, repeated pattern ("a multiple of backs"). The barking dog—an image that recurs frequently in Tate's poetry and usually suggests a Cerberus-like warning of death—and the flies, grown cold, are harbingers of mortality accompanying the setting sun. Magnolias cover the ground with a suggestion of the defeat at Appomattox, yet the verb "drench" implies moisture and life.

In the long sunset where impatient sound
Strips niggers to a multiple of backs
Flies yield their heat, magnolias drench the ground
With Appomattox! The shadows lie in stacks.

The limp blossoms are at best a sentimental symbol of southern gentility and surrender. Even the shadows, another suggestion of mortality, appear to be neatly arranged. The idiot is close to death, yet he shields himself with his sister's fan, which also serves the purpose of allowing him to manipulate the visual appearance of mountains and seas.

Although everything the idiot tries to shape is expressed in or assimilated to an abstract, visual sense of space, the other senses ultimately impinge upon the control of his commanding eye. The inescapable doom that twilight and dark announce, when sight is obscured and space has vanished, is expressed in terms of the other senses: hearing, smell, touch. The "niggers" who were reduced to an abstraction are assembled into an individual, "Ashy Jim," whose grey appearance "puts murmurs" or intimations of mortality "in the day." Though he is a visual entity, Jim's effect is aural. The "julep glass" he proffers distorts the visual appearance of the black servant, but it "weaves echoes" as though the grotesque lens of the glass is countered by something inescapable that is ready to descend. The idiot's futile attempts are interrupted by the smell of "dead asters," flowers that fade and shrivel only in very late fall or early winter (like the "peeled" aster in "Death of Little Boys"). The dying season is opposed by the idiot's imaginative imposition of a spring landscape, but his assimilation of all senses to the visual—the key to his attempt at control—begins to fail in the fifth stanza:

> All evening the marsh is a slick pool
> Where dream wild hares, witch hazel, pretty girls.
> "Up from the important picnic of a fool
> Those rotted asters!" Eddy on eddy swirls
>
> The innocent mansion of a panther's heart!
> It crumbles, tick-tick time drags it in
> Till now his arteries lag and now they start
> Reverence with the frigid gusts of sin.

The meadow becomes a marsh, dominated by fantastic and perhaps decadent sexual images in a grotesque idyl. Despite his effort to assert himself ("Up from the important picnic of a fool"), the idiot is pulled down into the whirlpool of a reality he can neither transform nor escape. Time begins to assault him, and it "crumbles" the "innocent mansion of a panther's heart." His dream world is overcome by the stench of the rotting seasons. The beastlike energy of his world will yield to the forces of time, just as the buried dead of the "potter's field" will be transformed by springtime into anonymous grass. The subsequent things the idiot senses bring his defeat to a climax as the past history of man's defeat by time and death—the universal Appomattox—catches up with him. The "precise whistle" of a train "is escheat/ To the dark." The twilight takes over the decaying "mansion" of the idiot's heart as an overlord might take over forfeited land. At the end of the poem, time and the pressures of mortality overwhelm the idiot's attempt to rule the world through sight: "and then the towering weak and pale/ Covers his eyes with memory like a sheet."

Though it is clear that the idiot stands in some fashion for the solipsistic vision of modern man, one wonders if this "captain of new wars" also points to something more precise. The "memory" that blots out his vision is in part the history of defeat that man has encountered in all his efforts to impose order. Does Tate intend to say that the idiot is a symbol of the sentimental South of magnolias and mint juleps that he renounced early in his career? Is he, in short, what Tate was later to call a "romantic traditionist"? Perhaps so. Yet if the poem is about a futile attempt to hold reality to a "motion that is not time," it cannot be confined simply to a particular section of the country. The "new wars" that were ushered in by the Civil War affect all men. The southern malaise is symptomatic of the greater modern illness, and "Idiot" is certainly intended to include more in its harsh indictment than the modern southerner; it is a poem about modern provincialism in time.

"Idiot" and "The Subway" were both written at about the time Tate began to read Spengler, and their imagery may owe something to him, though they certainly continue the coherent development of themes characterizing his earliest work. In any case, the latter poem has a moral vehemence that goes beyond *Decline of the West*. It is most appropriately described as a visit to hell. Tate once defined the epic as "a judgment of human action, an implied evaluation of a civilization, a way of life." He considered Hart Crane's attempt at epic in *The Bridge* to be a failure because "to the vision of the abyss in 'The Tunnel,' a vision that Dante passed through midway of this mortal life, Crane had no alternative."[18]

Though "The Subway" is a parody of the epic hero's descent into the abyss—perhaps even an intentional allusion to Dante—it is in the form of a sonnet. The usual associations of the sonnet with the theme of love work ironically in this context to suggest a perverse relationship between man and his own creations. Crane's apostrophe to the airplane, in "Cape Hatteras," is perhaps parodied by Tate's sardonic address to

18. Allen Tate, "Hart Crane," in *Essays*, 319.

underground transportation. The poem consists of one long, complex clause:

> Dark accurate plunger down the successive knell
> Of arch on arch, where ogives burst a red
> Reverberance of hail upon the dead
> Thunder, like an exploding crucible!
> Harshly articulate, musical steel shell
> Of angry worship, hurled religiously
> Upon your business of humility
> Into the iron forestries of hell:
>
> Till broken in the shift of quieter
> Dense altitudes tangential of your steel,
> I am become geometries, and glut
> Expansions like a blind astronomer
> Dazed, while the worldless heavens bulge and reel
> In the cold revery of an idiot.

Dante's wanderings came to an impasse in a "dark forest." Here the darkness of the forest is an unnatural one; the trees are iron standards where higher and lower have come together to form a total picture of hell that is directionless. The subway takes its passengers along a path that cannot be described as going either up or down. The linear accuracy of the train is expressive of no freedom; its tracks are organized and rigid, conducting the pilgrim through echoing arches in a mock-religious ceremony of initiation into fire and thunder. The transformation of the subway traveler is the mechanical equivalent to the humiliating and dehumanizing experiences of the damned in Dante's underworld. The modern passenger is metamorphosed into a mathematical abstraction by the alchemical crucible of the train, which explodes in sparks and unholy music.

In this parody of religious conversion, the passenger emerges not to see the sublime stars that mark the end of each of Dante's stages of emergence but to stand "Dazed, while the worldless heavens bulge and reel." The subway, intended to save time, affects the human relationship with space by abstracting men from the earthly scale. In such an event, the subway causes the traveler to lose the world as a concrete experience of temporal travel through space. Time is compressed and altered in the subway because speed of movement is no longer related to the feet and body. Moreover, the subway does not even allow one to see where he is going, except as a point on an abstract map.

If Spengler's impact is present at all in the poem, it may be in the poet's ironic echo of St. Paul and Tennyson. "I am become geometries" recalls both St. Paul's "I am become as sounding brass" and Tennyson's "I am become a name" ("Ulysses"). It suggests that the speaker has succumbed to the lust for abstraction that Spengler called "Faustian geometry," a new conception of space introduced by Descartes and his contemporaries: "In place of the sensuous element of concrete lines and planes—the specific character of the Classical feeling of bounds—there emerged the abstract, spatial, un-Classical element of the *point* which from then on was regarded as a group of co-ordered pure numbers. The idea of magnitude and of perceivable dimension . . . was destroyed and replaced by that of variable relation-values between positions in space."[19] The "geometries" of the modern world, based on algebraic relations rather than on optically perceptible figures, are an apt analogy for the disorientation of the subway traveler. Spengler's Faustian geometry is an interesting parallel to Tate's poetic presentation of modern existence. In the subway a journey that should be a fresh contact with the reality of the world is altered, by incessant daily repetition, into a glut of changing places without the spiritual experience of the spaces that lie between them. By removing him from a world in which he has a sense-oriented scale of judgment, the subway destroys the basis of man's moral sense. He is not simply disoriented—he is made insane, incapable of further judgment and therefore of salvation.

"The Subway" is a metropolitan companion piece to the rural "Idiot." Both are densely effective statements of the relationship between spatiality and temporality, science and religion in the modern world. But the poem that shows most profoundly the impact of Tate's meditation on these problems is his famous "Ode to the Confederate Dead." It is filled with imagery that recalls Spenglerian ideas. To dispel any doubt about that relationship, one need only turn to Tate's own explication of the poem in "Narcissus as Narcissus," where he explains:

19. Oswald Spengler, *Decline of the West*, trans. Charles Francis Atkinson (New York, 1939), I, 74.

> The closing image, that of the serpent, is the ancient symbol of time. . . . But time is also death. If that is so, then space, or the Becoming, is life; and I believe that there is not a single spatial symbol in the poem. "Sea-space" is allowed the "blind crab"; but the sea, as appears plainly in the passage beginning, "Now that the salt of their blood . . ." is life only insofar as it is the source of the lowest forms of life, the source perhaps of all life, but life undifferentiated, halfway between life and death.[20]

In fact, Tate has altered Spengler's concepts somewhat, for in *Decline of the West* space is associated with the "Become" and time with the "Becoming." Nevertheless, the principal motif is clear; and the poem, begun only a year after Tate's first encounter with Spengler's work, is haunted by the problem of knowledge through analogy.

Knowledge is impossible without the power of analogy, for the tangle of perceptions man experiences can be given some discernible structure or ontological validity only if the mind in its activity can find correlatives among things. At some point perceptions must lead to a knowledge that everything taken together constitutes a whole; but that whole can exist only as a closed system in which every object, however remote from other things, is somehow related to every other. This sense of a whole is deeply satisfying, but it can also lead to a kind of terror, for nothing in the universe can, on these terms, be understood simply in and by itself. Each thing has meaning only insofar as it can be related to something else. Knowledge of one isolated object is impossible; at least two things must be known in order for one thing to be understood. Spengler's world is built on a biological analogy and therefore should, by definition, be vitalistic. Yet his refusal to allow sufficient play in a deterministic universe for the individual will means that the only real constant in the world is death. Tate was aware of this tendency; in a review published in 1931, he notes that "the conception of life as the medium in which the organism must wear itself out toward its goal in death is as old as Western culture."[21] Nevertheless, there is an opposing view that would see the self as the most important term in all analogies.

20. Allen Tate, "Narcissus as Narcissus," in *Essays*, 600–601.

21. Allen Tate, Review of Houston Peterson's *The Melody of Chaos*, in *New Republic*, LXVII, 266.

To emphasize the self above all else is to mitigate somewhat the terrors of analogy, but the result of such a focus is to lose the specificity and weight of the world. In 1927 Tate noted a peculiar quality in the characters of Phelps Putnam; they live in a "modern neo-realist world where every position implies every other, and thus ceases to be position—where space abdicates to the event, which is not *in*, but *is* time. Putnam's heroes are symbols of time: they are nowhere, doing everything."[22] A world without positions is one that has lost its sense of analogy and must forge links between things by means of "the event." The self holds the world together by constant activity.

These two polarities—death and the self—are the tensional basis for the kind of conflict between deterministic pessimism and radical solipsism Tate depicts in "Ode to the Confederate Dead." The first stanza shows a natural order that is dominated by the closed system of "the seasonal eternity of death." The whole passage is a picture of a world with a kind of Spenglerian destiny that ignores the presence of man. There are suggestions of a system of rewards and punishments, such as might make up some mythical order of justice, but nature offers only the salvation that comes with total effacement. What is lacking is any sense of individual continuity that might break out of the terrible cycle. The stone memorials placed over the graves "yield their names" with "strict impunity." Their loss of memory will go unpunished and uncorrected. The wind shows no signs of "recollection"—the poet puns on the scattering effect of wind on the leaves in the "riven troughs" as well as the mindless energy of its whirr. The leaves themselves are "splayed," never again to be made whole; they are part of nature's "casual sacrament," an accidental rather than an intentional communion. (The word "casual" suggests the "fall" of the leaves by association with Latin *casus*.) The falling leaves have long been images of human mortality, from Homer, Virgil, and Dante to Shelley; but these leaves also take on the imagined quality of damned beings. Part of the whole of things, they lose all individuality as they are "driven . . . to their election in the vast breath." Like "The Subway," "Ode to the Confederate Dead" is a grim parody of traditional religious ideas of salvation tinged with overtones of predestinarian determinism.

If death dominates the first stanza, the self is prominent in the sec-

22. Allen Tate, Review of Phelps Putnam's *Trinc*, in *New Republic*, LIII, 76.

poet, this man at the gate, but the skeptical historian who meditates on the past of Western civilization as though he were looking at a graveyard. The gate and the wall separate the living from the dead, but the two important "sounds" in the poem—the screech-owl's call and the rioting "tongue" of the "gentle serpent"—are appeals to some kind of life. That life is not the simple organic cycle of nature but something beyond it. As the figure of the serpent makes plain, it is the life of myth, of speech through the imagination that is neither mutely paralyzed like the mummy nor rendered as a meaningless noise in the buffeting of the leaves. By yielding to time and participating in the past through memory, man can at least survive through the makeshift devices of his secular imagination, even in a declining civilization. Nevertheless, "Ode to the Confederate Dead" does not offer, as Tate explains in his essay, a "practical solution . . . for the edification of moralists," but it does imply that such a solution is possible. As Tate goes on to say, "To those who may identify the man at the gate with the author of the poem I would say: He differs from the author in not accepting a 'practical solution,' for the author's personal dilemma is perhaps not quite so exclusive as that of the meditating man."[23] It is the exclusive character of the dilemma that makes it difficult to resolve, for the alternative of science or religion at least offers the promise of a practical solution to the problem of acting in an alien universe. Unless the man at the gate can learn to see the choice between a nature dominated by mortality and a self locked in solipsism as a false presentation of alternatives, he cannot act in any decisive way.

In "Retroduction to American History"—in its original form and placement in Tate's first collection an obvious companion piece to "Ode to the Confederate Dead"—he dramatizes the figure of a person who is unable to speak out about what he understands. Perhaps influenced by the style of Eliot's "Gerontion," it is the first of Tate's truly "confessional" poems. It is also his version of Babylon, the modern city in its late Spenglerian phase of engineered abstraction and cultural decadence.

A "retroduction" is a leading back; and in this satirical version of the medieval dream vision, the poet gathers together many of the motifs of his literary criticism: language, heritage, heredity, myth, and the meaning of art in the world. The speaker reviews the character of modern

23. Allen Tate, "Narcissus as Narcissus," in *Essays*, 600.

American life from the post of observation of his own bedroom, when the metropolis is asleep. Wordsworth, viewing London from Westminster Bridge, was still able to see the modern city as a thing of beauty when its "mighty heart" was lying still. But for Tate, the "stiff unhappy silence" that comes at midnight does not encourage contemplation. Night now "flouts illumination with meagre impudence," denying man his needed rest and celebrating nature's defeat. The city has become the ultimate product of man's narcissism rather than his proudest monument. In the earlier stages of Western civilization, "Antiquity breached mortality with myths." Now mortality is attacked frontally, and myth is given spurious expression in bad architecture or speech whose "Vocabulary is confusion." Scholars, traditionally the guardians of culture, have become panders, concerned more with the "passionate underwear" of Catullus than with what he had to say about his civilization or human nature. The modern scholar is like Webster's Flamineo in *The White Devil*, for whom "simplicity is obscene" and who holds that "morality disciplines the other/ Person." Contemporary man lives in a world that has been hygienically purged of impurities that would "distract him from nonentity," and so he does not recognize that his soul is empty. He cannot hear or speak, for "his metaphors are dead" and have been detached from the natural world that gave them birth. His intellect operates exclusively by deduction, "Connives with heredity, creates fate as Euclid geometry/ By definition." Human destiny has become mathematized.

In this state of decline, the West has arrived at the extreme conditions of its audacious experiment to live out its dream of mechanized perfection. The end of this dream without image or metaphor is a nightmare in which the skeleton beneath the flesh will be disclosed in all its inescapable horror. Yet the greatest terror of all is the prospect of an inarticulate future that stretches on indefinitely towards a life without communication. This dilemma is dramatized in the earlier version of "Ode to the Confederate Dead," which is closely related in theme to the "Retroduction":

> We have not sung, we shall not ever sing
> In the improbable mist of nightfall
> Which flies on multiple wing;
> It has only a beginning and an end;

And in between the ends of distraction
Lurks mute speculation.

The "Retroduction to American History" originally bore the title "Causerie," an accurate description of its casual, rambling conversational style. A year later, Tate wrote a sequel, calling it "Causerie II." It commences, as does its predecessor, with questions and references to insomnia:

What are the springs of sleep? What is the motion
Of dust in the lane that has an end in falling?

"Springs" is ambiguous; it can mean "sources" or "seasons." In either instance it connotes motion and fresh beginnings. Yet sleep is the desired repose, the long-awaited end of motion. A road leads somewhere, but dust, stirred up by travelers and vehicles, always settles back in the same place. The dust and the lane are images of man's mortality and his passion for movement and discovery. Western man has unknowingly invested his passions in a quest "with sloops and telescopes," not in order to continue forever in motion but to find a stopping place. It is remarkable that the entire history of progress in the Western world should eventuate in this desire for repose. Nevertheless, the repose man will find is not the same as the one he seeks. In an allusion to Bosola's speech in *The Duchess of Malfi*, the poet notes that a different end awaits him, "A packet of worm-seed, a garden of spent tissues." Man will be gathered into a "rumor of light" rather than into the light of permanence.

The speaker in this poem utters a kind of impersonal confession. He has neither committed crimes nor been overly conscientious in seeking to exonerate himself. He knows that he need not worry over his "petty crimes of silence." What emerges is not the confession of an individual but of a whole civilization expressing itself through the voice of the poet:

This innermost disturbance is a babble,
It is a sign moved to my face as well
Where every tide of heart surges to speech
Until in that loquacity of visage
One speaks a countenance fitter for death than hell.

In the lines that follow, the opening images are gathered into a culminating confrontation of speech, blood, home, and dust, for they lead to a realization that man's perspective is foolish and naïve. Modern conveniences cannot hide the horrors of human failure—the hygiene of the "porcelain tub" cannot overcome the sinful ways that Webster reveals as endemic in our fathers. The only "purity" possible in the present is a provincial ignorance of what man has been in the past.

Tate names several friends—John Crowe Ransom, Robert Penn Warren, and Edmund Wilson—who wait, as he himself waits, for some revelation. Because they have no beliefs, no "doctrine," their hopes are incomplete or intellectually perverse. The poet knows that the "incredible image" of rebirth that could join life and death in a meaningful pattern is a thing of the past, not of the future: "Now/ I am sure that Purusha sits no more in our eyes." At twilight in the world-order, man loses both the blood embodying his past in a living stream of movement and the light of self-understanding. If he rejects this romanticism, he has to find other ways of escaping the mysterious puzzles of guilty desire. Through psychoanalysis he may probe his private past for "innocent acquittal," but his "essential wreckage" is not merely personal. It is a shared guilt of which his whole society would be free.

The conflict between desire for movement and desire for rest is given form in the memory. There alone resides a language that cannot be suppressed, for the "causerie" of the poem's title is a conversation carried on by every generation forced to confront its past:

> What is this conversation, now secular,
> A speech not mine yet speaking for me in
> The heaving jelly of my tribal air?
> It rises in the throat, it climbs the tongue,
> It perches there for secret tutelage
> And gets it, of inscrutable instruction.

The poet himself is not responsible for this dialogue; it comes from some unconscious impulse that he cannot quite identify. At one time it would have belonged to the communal language of myth. Now secularized, it has risen like spars from a shipwreck to haunt the surface of the contemporary mind. But the loss of myth and the degradation of language have placed the poet's enterprise in doubt. The loss of standards has not only affected public life—the Capitol with its "progeny of thieves"—but also the cultural memory of a people, whose government has reduced the great images of man in art to mere ornament:

Where now the antique courtesy of your myths
Goes in to sleep under a still shadow.

The speaker has not found repose, but his civilization has done so. The rest that modern man so eagerly seeks is the death-sleep of his own past. The poet alone is aware of the residue; and though he may not be able to find the right language for communicating to the world what is happening, he can speak out imperfectly and only half coherently, if he must, in a causerie. For in times when the Capitol of Rome is imitated architecturally but not morally and politically in the New World and the Roman orgy is lamely imitated in New York (as the epigraph from the New York *Times* recounts), the poet must yield to the pressure of this "tribal air" that rises within him.

Tate's two "causerie" poems lead naturally enough to a third, "Fragment of a Meditation," begun in 1928 but published several years later. This deliberately incomplete poem, cut short in almost comic fashion by a footnote, is a review of American public history through "the great Administrations"; yet like his other satiric poems, it has a strong personal focus. It begins with a meditation on the "thirtieth year," the turning point of life for Christ and François Villon, which the speaker will soon reach. In thinking over the imminent year that will make "of forward back," he thinks of another turning point in history, "back seventy years/ And more," when the United States had known six administrations,

and all the public men
Whom doctrine and an evil nature made
Were only errand boys beaten by the sun
While Henry Adams fuddled in the shade.

Tate offers as an alternative to the supercilious yet ineffectual Adams the "bristled intellect" of John C. Calhoun; but he knows that no political theorist could have saved the South. In an essay published in 1935, Tate wrote that the great southern "ideas were strangled in the cradle, either by the South herself . . . or by the Union armies."[24] More typical of what was to follow is the "poet against the world," the "crazy Poe," whom Tate claims in his poem his "grandfather knew well," but "who was not of our kind." Poe, like his twentieth-century successors,

24. Allen Tate, "The Profession of Letters in the South," in *Essays*, 522.

was cut off from the community for which he should have been the spokesman. Tate's allusion to this condition suggests a kinship with a poet whose vision, as well as his personal life, was obsessed by failure.

The poem ends with the poet's expectation of some prodigious event, replete with a new lamb of God, new prophetic signs, and the coming of a new trio of wise men. But there is no delegation adequate to the terrifying demands that confront the poet in his thirtieth year. He stands on the brink of his maturity knowing that he must face "the venom of the night" without any assistance from a social or religious structure of meaning. He is not sure what action to take in this era of "the irresponsible Verb" conniving "with chaos," and his verses, like Villon's, are a sort of ironic last will and testament "*en l'an trentiesme de son âge*."

Tate's satiric series forms a continuous group of poems concerned with his failure to bring the public and private realms into some kind of orderly relationship. The poet's personal destiny is so intimately a part of the cultural dilemma that his verse is marked more by anguish than by the detachment that characterizes the most successful satire.

Tate's early poetry depicts a kind of moral paralysis that is the result of this inability to act or speak. His own commitment to poetry and the imagination was a clear indication that he intended to accept the responsibility for doing both, even if he was uncertain about what course to take. The long struggle to perfect "Ode to the Confederate Dead" was perhaps the poet's attempt to reveal the next step in the journey towards a solution. Yet a practical solution is not necessarily an easy one, as the antiromantic poem "Ignis Fatuus," placed as epilogue to *Mr. Pope and Other Poems*, serves to show. The "fool's fire" of the title is the light that the modern mistakes for truth and progress, an emanation from what Tate has called "imaginative constructions of the future." This false glimmer of an abstract ideal attracts modern man to his own destruction in "the green tissue of the subterranean worm." He becomes like a pigeon that has losts its feathers and can no longer fly away or an exile trapped in a past that he is doomed to repeat as he "utters the creed of memory." Must man renounce all ideals and hope of light, or can he find in his sense of history a means of escaping from the "ignis fatuus" of disillusionment?

One's own petty failings, presented literally, are not very engrossing. To have meaning, failure must point beyond its immediate occasion. Myth and poetry are the means of detachment that allows one's own experiences to become the actualization of the present condition of the world. As Tate has said of two other poets:

> Personal revelation of the kind that Donne and Miss Dickinson strove for, in the effort to understand their relation to the world, is a feature of all great poetry; it is probably the hidden motive for writing. It is the effort of the individual to live apart from a cultural tradition that no longer sustains him.[25]

In the image of the "buried city," Tate discovered a means of objectifying failure and yet pointing beyond it to some hope that can eventually sustain the individual more surely in his search for the light of permanence.

25. Tate, "Emily Dickinson," 292.

Three

The Vain Chivalry of the Personal Will

SHORTLY AFTER 1933 Tate began a novel, later abandoned, that he intended to call *Ancestors of Exile*. In a letter to John Peale Bishop, Tate explains that it will depict his "own ancestry, beginning with Robert Reade in Va. about 1638, and bringing it down to my brothers and myself, who are fairly good types of modern America, absolutely different but motivated by the same blood traits." The narrative is based on "two chief figures to a generation, who will be dealt with simultaneously for contrast . . . between the Va. tidewater idea—stability, land, the establishment—and the pioneer, who frequently of course took on the Va. idea, even in Tenn., but who usually had some energy left over, which has made modern America."[1] In this project the "buried city" has been reconceived in terms of buried ancestors. "Provincialism in time" was to have been prefigured in the pioneer, regionalism in the "Virginia idea."

Tate gave up the book because he could not find adequate vehicles for the opposition he was attempting to express. Fortunately, he did discover the appropriate symbols in his poetry. A group of poems dating from about this period—including "Message from Abroad," "Emblems," "The Oath," "The Ancestors," "Sonnets of the Blood," and "To the Lacedemonians"—articulates this conflict almost perfectly, despite Tate's failure to find a resolution for himself. The clash between place and energy, expressed through the complementary images of blood and fire, demonstrates that the personal will has severe limitations as a means of restoring order. The poems are informed by a vision that emanates from the world of Greek tragedy rather than from a Virgilian *pax augusta*. For some reason the sacred ancestral bonds are an

1. Allen Tate to John Peale Bishop, February 11, 1932, in *Letters*, 52.

inadequate stay against the violence of man and nature. Recovery of the past through the memory is not enough; there must be some concrete evidence of its continuity into the present. Yet attempts at resuscitation succeed in evoking absences rather than presences. The imaginative act is flawed by a tragic lack arising from the loss of resolve. The figures in these poems have seen the dark and issue their warnings to those who, lacking guidance from the past, would seek salvation in the warm feral blood of kinship or in the preservation of privileges and public myths without the "law of form."

Nevertheless, the energy or "fire" of these poems is not a simple equivalent for the personal will depicted in "To the Romantic Traditionists." Without some such spark of life, the whole past will remain dead. In a note to the revised version of *The Fathers*, where these themes are given their definitive presentation, Tate says of his hero Lacy that he "has the instinct of survival, regardless of principle; yet at the same time 'principle' is back of his decision to return to the army." In the new world into which Lacy will survive after the Civil War, "not all the old traditions, which [he] partly represents, are dead."[2] It is when the fire becomes aimless in its drive that the modern dilemma arises. In the closing lines of "To the Lacedemonians," one sees a transformation of this energy into the flames of damnation, a fire that is as empty as the "bodiless flesh" Tate speaks of in "Last Days of Alice." Fire and blood are meant to balance and restrain one another. Their equilibrium is upset when the past is rejected for the sake of some desired or imagined future. The tension between settler and pioneer is ultimately a conflict of will and imagination that produces the exiled modern sensibility.

This opposition is the basis of "Message from Abroad." The epigraph to the poem, cited from a "traveller to America" in 1799, depicts the pioneers as ruddy even amidst the malarial climates of the New World; in it the contrast between self-willed assertion and the destructive energies of nature is made explicit. But unlike "Ode to the Confederate Dead," where this same contrast is presented, "Message from Abroad," more vehement in its denunciation, explores this loss of form from an international perspective. The poem consists of the reflections of an American after crossing the ocean to reside in Europe. There he discovers that he cannot find a formal role in which to cast his behavior.

2. Allen Tate, "Note," in *The Fathers*, 314.

In his encounter with the past that Europe represents, he loses all sense of identity as an American; yet he has no sense of destiny as a European. In a letter contemporary with the poem, Tate writes to Davidson, concerning Englishmen he has met: "They feel a certain remoteness from their own past almost as great as the breach that we feel as transplanted Europeans."[3] One cannot return to the past because there is no longer a place where it is to be found. The pioneering drive of the Yankee intent on escaping the past at all costs blinded him to the values of the civilization he was rejecting; now that those values have become inoperative, he has no possibility of turning back from his destructive push forward.

The poem is concerned with discovering how one can know and use the past. Mere history in the abstract is not enough:

> What years of the other times, what centuries
> Broken, divided up and claimed? A few
> Here and there to the taste, in vigilance
> Ceaseless, but now a little stale, to keep us
> Fearless, not worried as the hare scurrying
> Without memory. . . .

Memory is man's only means of countering his fears. What he remembers is not simply the past, but "the intensest expression, or communication, the past has reached," as Tate puts it in a letter. The past speaks no more readily in Europe than in America. Where Aeneas sought unknown shores, modern man sifts through past civilizations that he knows are safely dead; he makes little attempt to discover the remnants of his own tradition:

> Provence,
> The Renascence, the age of Pericles, each
> A broad, rich-carpeted stair to pride
> With manhood now the cost—they're easy to follow
> For the ways taken are all notorious,
> Lettered, sculptured, and rhymed.

These periods of achievement stand out in the historical imagination because something still remains of them in the present, but the suffer-

3. Allen Tate to Donald Davidson, October 24, 1928, in *Correspondence*, 217.

ing that made their achievement possible has been forgotten. Simply to imitate the achievements of the past without undergoing the conditions that made them possible is easy, but such performances do not place one in touch with a tradition. The other ages, "incuriously complete, lost," that are "Not by poetry and statues timed," may have as much integrity and as much to teach as the outstanding ones. An artist may be better off if he is still informed by such ignored traditions than if he is dominated by the artificial demands of formal imitation. Indeed, despite the antihistorical tendencies of American culture, the South possessed just this kind of advantage for men of Tate's generation. Yet the nineteenth-century South produced no great art; and without such aesthetic records, a tradition can easily fall into oblivion.

The northern Yankee rejected tradition, and the southerner failed to give his culture some kind of permanent form. Thus the southerner is just as lost in the chaotic wash of modern rootlessness as his northern countryman; both live in a culture that is marked by "emblems of twilight." The "red-faced and tall" man who is the central figure in "Message from Abroad" is the pioneering American of indomitable but ignorant will forging his way across the continent in an effort to tame and subdue it. He rejects both the past and the natural world that sustains him in his progress. He seems to depend on nothing at all:

> In the day of his strength
> Not as a pine, but the stiff form
> Against the west pillar,
> Hearing the ox-cart in the street—
> His shadow gliding, a long nigger
> Gliding at his feet.

These compact lines sum up the red-faced man's unnaturalness (he is strong in uprootedness, but a tree has strength in its roots), his challenge to the forms and limits of the past (the "west pillar" suggests the Pillars of Hercules, the limits to exploration set up by the Greek hero), and his exploitation of other men as well as his refusal to see his own mortality (the "long nigger/ Gliding at his feet"). The red-faced man has no more place in the world than the moving ox-cart or his own shadow.

The discontinuity that separates America from Europe is extended by the "cold northern track" of the "Absolute, steady sea." The sea stands not for history but for a reality beyond both time and history. The red-faced man cannot survive in these larger dimensions of space and time. He knows only the provincialism in time of a world that has rejected everything that came before it. He is absent from the Paris through which the speaker searches in hope of catching some trace of his existence:

> The man with the red face the stiff back
> I cannot see in the rainfall
> Down Saint-Michel by the quays,
> At the corner the wind speaking
> Destiny, the four ways.

Locked in the linear path of a one-dimensional quest for his own personal and private destiny, the red-faced man is ignorant of his own destiny; he does not understand the true forces, larger than his limited experience, that shape him and his actions. As a consequence, he cannot survive the voyage back to Europe and his image is "drowned deep" in the "dim foam" of the absolute. He has been absorbed by the "saltier oblivion of the sea," as Tate calls this impersonal natural force in "Ode to the Confederate Dead."

In the third section of the poem, Tate speaks of the pioneers as the "incorruptibles," linking them with those maniacal purists of the French Revolution, like Danton, whose abstract radicalism could not be compromised by humanity's concrete needs. They followed their vision of rejection to its limits, and now there is no permanent reminder of their achievements. If Europe has lost its soul, the fragments of the body are still extant to remind one, through skeletal monuments, of what greatness can be. But the abstract paradise of the American radical "rots." It is "out of date," passé, and detached from temporal reality, like their angry rejection. Their descendants have no access to what they said, thought, or felt day by day. They have left nothing to counter the overwhelming forces of an impersonal universe; and they are like Dante's damned shades, who can cast no shadows in hell or influence the living:

> The bent eaves
> On the cracked house,
> That ghost of a hound. . . .

The man red-faced and tall
Will cast no shadow
From the province of the drowned.

The fire that burns in the red-faced pioneer has been "drowned" in the bleak winter sea of forgetfulness. Ironically, the oblivion to which he will henceforth be confined is also a kind of hell, where a different kind of flame will consume him. Having rejected place and the settled land for most of his existence, the pioneer is given an eternity of static restlessness, tethered forever to the vast but empty halls of an Inferno he cannot escape.

Despite his overt condemnation of the ignorant pioneer, however, Tate does not offer an easy alternative to the death-in-life of a willed exile. In "Emblems," for instance, the way to recapture a lost identity demands a kind of death. The speaker muses on his loss of a sense of place and longs to belong, if only in imagination, to a region offering personal identity and public order. In his essay "A Southern Mode of the Imagination," Tate describes the kind of mind that is given understanding by a definite and visible attachment to place as "an extroverted mind not much given to introspection. (I do not say meditation, which is something quite different.) Such irony as this mind was capable of was distinctly romantic; it came out of the sense of dislocated external relations: because people were not *where* they ought to be they could not be *who* they ought to be; for men had missed their proper role, which was to be attached to a place."[4] "Emblems" interprets the buried city on a mythic level as a place in the memory and on a personal level as the realm of the buried fathers. It is a poem about submission to these forces.

Place exists in the mind as well as in the physical world, and it is informed and guarded by the memory. Through the memory, places are given a status that allows them to be elevated into meaning by the imagination. "Emblems" is composed of several sets of complementary themes: the masculine and the feminine, the hill and the river, the historical and the actual. All of these symbols are articulations of the need for attachment to something definite. The "Pent images in sleep" that open the poem are the names of places, but they are also the names of

4. Allen Tate, "A Southern Mode of the Imagination," in *Essays*, 581–82.

women: Mary, Virginia, Caroline. They are places with personalities, with the larger mythical properties that their feminine names suggest. These anchorings in mother earth conceal the hidden fathers, buried under the hills, but their spatial confinement is overcome to some extent by a temporal extension in their descendants:

> Out of that source of time my farthest blood
> Runs strangely to this day
> Unkempt the fathers waste in solitude
> Under the hills of clay.

The "pent images" are submerged in the unconscious, but the "breath" of living men keeps the spirit of the fathers alive, even after the descendants have "fled" from past woe to an "alien house" in another region.

The fathers, then, live on biologically and spiritually in the blood and in the memory. Despite his flight, the speaker has not allowed himself to forget them. Though he now resides by "a river in Tennessee," he knows that he must return someday to his source. In the second poem, the poet asks that he be buried in the East, "where life began," not

> By the far river (where never stood
> His fathers) flowing to the West.

He does not wish to be caught up in the pioneering push towards the West and all that it represents in the modern drive to conquer nature and space. The East is the traditional source of life; to strive for conquering the West is to attempt to overcome mortality itself. Life must come to an end, but death allows man to participate in other times and places through the flow of blood from one generation to the next and through the memories handed down by father to son. The river burial described at the end of the second section of the poem is a gesture establishing the speaker's willingness to yield and become a part of the flow of time rather than attempt a conquest of space:

> Men cannot live forever
> But they must die forever
> So take this body at sunset
> To the great stream whose pulses start
> In the blue hills, and let

These ashes drift from the Long Bridge
Where only a late gull breaks
That deep and populous grave.

The "Long Bridge" joins Georgetown and Alexandria on either side of the Potomac River. It stands as a bridge that faces Europe. By entering back into the peace of nature, the speaker will become a part of the anonymity of space, but he will not lose the particularity of time if he can drift with the "pulses" of this great stream of the Potomac back towards the European foundations of American civilization.

In the third part of the poem, the poet speaks of the founding that led the forefathers to carve out "Deep hollows of memory on a river isle/ Now lost." The "river isle" is like the bridge, in that it belongs to neither side of the river, but it remains a stable entity only as a place enveloped in the water's flow. The bridge, like the blood, connects place with place; the isle, like memory, preserves something stable in the midst of flow. The fathers learned to be satisfied with their human lot and to yield to "sunset by the cool river . . . And the long sleep by the cool river." Even as young men they were wise enough to know where to stop and settle. Their river isle, or settlement, is like the community which, though no longer in existence, still retains a sense of presence in the world through memory. The descendants have attempted to escape the past, to flee from the stability of an order founded long ago for the abstract future of a pioneer's land forever young and devoid of any history. But the presence of the fathers is evident in the very landscape. They are buried under its very hills and are part of its geography, having fostered the appearance it has today. The deep union of the masculine drive of the settlers with the feminine receptivity of nature is what creates place if that marriage is successful. To remain faithful to the land is to give it a name and a meaning in relation to men. The land becomes humanized and mythified simultaneously when man has his impulses satisfied by natural means. The creation of a place is the result of man's yielding to the landscape and becoming a part of it at the same time as he endows nature with new meaning through his presence.

The conclusion of the poem suggests both anticipation and dread. The cool repose of the fathers in their "Deep hollows of memory" is in contrast to the rapacious summer heat that is symbolic of the kind of chaos modern man has been committed to. Having failed to learn from his forefathers how to live, he has challenged rather than united with nature; and now he lives in continual fear of her powers. As "the air/ Waits twilit for their echo," the forefathers sleep "full and long" by the "cool river." But the descendants know no such repose; without this echo from the past, this memory that gives a sense of identity and coherence to man and his world, they must survive in the violence of a hostile environment where "the burning shiver/ Of August strikes like a hawk the crouching hare."

The winter twilight of "The Oath" is in sharp contrast to the fiery destructive power of August in "Emblems," but the two poems are linked by similar meditative themes. In "The Oath" a pair of friends, Andrew Lytle and, presumably, Tate, sit by a fire surrounded by the mementoes of family ancestors. Blood and fire are frequently linked in Tate's poetry; and as the two men draw closer to the warmth in the "blank twilight," it is evident that they are also trying to draw closer to the remaining icons of "Uncle Ben's" and "Major Bogan's" presence. The fire seems to make these mute objects speak: "There's naught to kill but the animated dead," they seem to say. The two friends remain in silence for the most part, recognizing that "There's precious little to say between day and dark." In this silence they both have time to meditate on the ends of things in violence and death. Tate wonders about "the implacable will/ Of time sailing like a magic barque," and Lytle probes for an answer to the question, "Who are the dead?/ Who are the living and the dead?"

The two men do not attempt to discuss their concerns together but explore the twin themes of nature and self in contemplative quiet. Tate tries to decide "what it is in time that gnaws/ The ageing fury of a mountain stream," but his meditation soon intersects with Lytle's. The darkness, which plays an active role in the scene, suddenly emerges in Tate's imagination as a frustrated being "pounding its head/ On a rock, crying: *Who are the dead?*" The men have received two complementary messages, one from the objects revealed by the fire and the other from the "old man's valedictory wheeze" that issues from the darkness. Both messages bring the silent men back from their meditations on time and identity to the injunction to kill "the animated dead." The chase is no longer pursued by the major, and the mountain stream has lost its fury. The energy that drove them forward has abated, and men of the present are at best only half-alive. The dead are not the vigorous ancestors whose memory is still alive but the "living" whose lives are without direction. The blood and fire of Uncle Ben and Major Bogan are still perceptible, but the two men who sit in the twilit room are part of a new chase of which they are the quarry. Lacking the kind of speech that would allow them to respond fully, the two friends are forced to answer in the frustrated verbal violence of an "oath" that provides recognition but not a resolution of their dilemma.

These strange images of entrapment in "The Oath" are given further elaboration in another poem written two years later—"The Ancestors." Again the setting is in a room and the hour is at twilight. Again the speaker meditates on the gnawing force of time:

> What masterful delay commands the blood
> Breaking its access to the living heart?

In the later poem, however, the poet is willing to hazard an answer to his own question:

> Not rudeness of time but the systaltic flood
> Of ancient failure begging its new start:
> The flickered pause between the day and night
> (When the heart knows its informality)
> The bones hear but the eyes will never see—
> Punctilious abyss, the yawn of space
> Come once a day to suffocate the sight.

If blood and the fire stand for the continuity of human energy from generation to generation, then the "systaltic flood" is a symbol of the discontinuity of all generations. History is not a straight line of progressive improvement nor an unrelieved decline. It is a recurrent confrontation within man between his desire to begin all over again and his certainty that the "ancient failure" of human efforts will be repeated:

> There is no man on earth who can be free
> Of this, the eldest in the latest crime.

In this poem, the human condition is affected by a fundamental disability that is like the theological concept of original sin, but human imperfection is not the main focus of Tate's insight. It is rather on the "flickered pause" of the instant of suspension or ambiguous twilight that separates heart pulse from heart pulse, high pressure from low pressure. The heart itself beats in a series of stops and starts, and this condition is one from which man cannot free himself without losing "the living heart" itself. The "masterful delay" that makes life possible is also a prelude to death.

An interesting parallel to both "The Oath" and "The Ancestors" occurs in *The Fathers*; the narrator, Lacy Buchan, engages at one point in a long meditation on night. He speaks of desiring the dark, of "days when we consciously guide the flow of being towards the night, and our suspense is a kind of listening, as if the absence of light, when it comes, will be audible just because sight and touch are frustrated." As so frequently happens in Tate's poems, sight in this passage is associated with spatial form and hearing with temporal form. More important, this access to the sense of the temporal given by darkness also frees the imagination from bondage to the literal world. As Lacy notes, these moments allow one to perceive the dark in a kind of synesthesia:

> And I think we do hear it; we hear it because our senses, not being mechanisms, actually perform the miracles of imagination that they themselves create: from our senses come the metaphors through which we know the world, and in turn our senses get knowledge of the world by means of figures of their own making.

But what does it mean "when we passionately desire to hear the night"? According to Tate's fictional protagonist,

> To hear the night, and to crave its coming, one must have deep inside one's secret being a vast metaphor controlling all the rest: a belief in the innate evil of man's nature, and the need to face that evil, of which the symbol is darkness, of which again the living image is man alone. Now that men cannot be alone, they cannot bear the dark, and they see themselves as innately good but betrayed by circumstances that render them pathetic.

In a later dream, Lacy hears the dark again as the water beating against a rock and as a panther screaming through the trees.

In these poems and in his novel, Tate introduces situations of confession and judgment that cannot be satisfactorily mastered by the personal will alone. One is inevitably reminded of still other poems—such as "The Wolves"—in which this strong sense of the evil within man is objectified in some beastly image. It is notable, however, that Tate's meditations on the nature of the self always include a sense of the past and of the community. Man can, indeed, attempt isolation, but he will never achieve it. Man is bound by his own analogical understanding, an essentially tragic perspective that views all things as inevitably flawed because incapable of standing alone. The tragic vision fixes no blame, but it does not absolve one from the necessity of acting, making connections, and distinguishing good from evil. Even so, judgment involves great risks, for it requires the embarrassingly personal revelations of one's own weaknesses. In *The Fathers* Lacy Buchan makes this very point:

> Doubtless we cannot help judging everybody a little, but if we judge one person we have got to judge all the others and to fix nicely the degree of personal within the common frailty, until in the end the judgments add up to a pharisaical jumble of ifs and buts. . . . But . . . it . . . is not only possible, it is necessary to say: that man is dishonest, or this other man is an honest man, for in so saying we are not judging an action or blaming or praising him for it; we are only distinguishing a quality of character. But if two honorable men kill each other—and it is possible for men of honor to kill without dishonor—and bring upon their families untold sorrows and troubles, what have we then? Who is to blame?[5]

Lacy's question is closely related to the query Tate addresses to Spengler in his review of *The Hour of Decision*: how should we act upon our judgments?

In confronting the extent to which a person participates in the very decadence that his civilization manifests, one is caught in the difficult distinction between personal and mythic action. In his "Sonnets of the Blood," a much-revised sequence of poems first published in 1931, Tate endows an extended personal confession with the elevation and rhythm of tragedy. It is an ambitious attempt to endow the private experiences of the poet and his family with a genuinely cosmic dimension without losing the confidentiality of an epistolary style. Reinforced with distinct allusions to the dark events of Greek myth, the sequence takes its

5. Tate, *The Fathers*, 217–19.

inspiration from several recent events in the poet's life—the death of his mother and a renewed relationship with his older brothers—but its primary concern is with the problem of broken bonds, both those which once united the human family and those which tied man to nature. The two themes are so intricately intertwined that they are often hard to separate in a given stanza. Each sonnet concerns the intimate drama of the family as it is played against the backdrop of a larger tragedy: the raping of *Natura* through the industrial lust for power of the modern entrepreneur.

The poems are closely linked to Tate's explorations of fundamentalism and agrarianism in his essays. In "The Fallacy of Humanism," to choose a particular example, Tate speaks of Irving Babbitt's "ideal of the man of action" and the "self-seeking industrialist who is *moved primarily by a regard for his own happiness.*" After quoting from Babbitt's *Rousseau and Romanticism*, Tate notes that this "man of action" is one "who, as a result of his moral choices based on due deliberation, choices in which he is moved primarily by a regard for his own happiness, has quelled the unruly impulses of his lower nature."[6] But since Babbitt and his fellow neohumanists advise man to adopt self-restraints yet never define them, Tate shows that their noble proposals can have no effect. They lack any authority other than the emotional appeal of their proponents. Though agreeing with the neohumanists in their reaction against a crude "naturalism," Tate finds that they have not managed to venture very far, if at all, beyond it. Unwilling to quantify morality, they are nevertheless incapable of giving it any other basis.

Tate never mentions Babbitt or his colleagues in his sonnet sequence, but it is clear that they represent the kind of minds he is arguing against. Theirs is a cast of thought that has its roots deep in the nineteenth century, and Tate's use of the familiar phrase "Captains of Industry" in his last sonnet suggests the stirring call to action of Thomas Carlyle in his *Past and Present*. Paradoxically, Carlyle demands a revival of such heroic leadership from the very men whose *laissez-faire* attitudes he held responsible for England's troubles. In the second part of his volume, the author asks for a new aristocracy: "The Leaders of Industry, if Industry is ever to be led, are virtually the Captains of the

6. Allen Tate, "Humanism and Naturalism," in *Memoirs*, 177.

World."[7] By using the phrase "Captains of Industry," Tate suggests that he is skeptical toward any such ill-defined vitalism or emotional appeal to the conscience of the modern industrialist.

"Sonnets of the Blood" is not, however, a treatise on the effects of capitalism on society. Its real subject is the futility of any attempt to "rectify" reality. The power of the blood is not simply a matter of simple heredity; it stands for the inescapable character shared by all human beings. Even the least significant human events are potentially tragic, but it is the individual who determines their meaning. Disaster or understanding are matters of judgment, not fixed impositions of an implacable and impersonal will. In speaking of his ignorance of his own birthplace and his father's revelation of it to him after his mother's death, Tate observes in his *Memoirs* that the "consequences of this confrontation were not as serious as the dire recognition and reversal undergone by a Greek when he learned that he had been born in Thebes and not as he had been led to believe, in defiance of the gods, in Corinth."[8] Yet one suspects that the self-understanding that emerged from the identification of his actual birthplace was no less important. In "Sonnets of the Blood" Tate does draw a parallel between Oedipus' fate and the condition of man in the twentieth century:

> Whether by Corinth or by Thebes we go
> The way is brief, but the fixed doom, not so.

Tate considers place to be of considerable importance as a link to the living community, but he recognizes that no attempt to falsify the past can be successful. He was more comfortable finding out that he was born in Kentucky than he was laboring under the burden of tracing his birthplace to Virginia and all that it implied for him. Blood is more a matter of memory and self-awareness than of heredity or a deterministic biology.

The brothers whose lives figure in "Sonnets of the Blood" share the burden of the past, but they also share those conditions of the present that involve the flesh and bones, the bounds of physical nature and its laws. Whatever it may mean for them to be sons of the same parents,

7. Thomas Carlyle, *Past and Present* (London, 1897), 271.
8. Allen Tate, "A Lost Traveller's Dream," in *Memoirs*, 5–6.

the brothers are made conscious of their common bonds only when those things they share are threatened. The death of their mother, who forced the bond of the past upon her sons, brings them closer together because it renders them siblings in a deeper sense, "brothers in mortality." Love, the only human bond worth considering as an absolute value, is intimately bound up with the "flesh-arguing crime" from the time of "the first settlers of our bone," Adam and Eve, to the present. If all men are brothers, it is only when confronted by death that they come to an understanding of what their "hard identity" signifies. Brotherly love is ultimately defined by human mortality rather than by shared existence. All of these themes are announced and explored in the first sonnet of the sequence.

The second sonnet introduces a new image, that of fire. In an earlier version of the poem, the opposition of the images of blood and fire is perhaps more evident. There the blood is described as "the long indentured slave" to the obscure flame burning within.[9] The blood cannot be a slave to itself; the fire must refer to something beyond it. Indeed, fire seems to stand in the sequence for that informing energy, at once identity and fate, which presides over each generation. The Greeks called it a "daemon." It is a fire of conflict as well as of unity, making for family strife as well as for family pride. Even the blood, with its burden of physical heredity, is subject to this overwhelming fire of family pride and tradition. Like the daemon that was for the Greeks both a guardian spirit and a terrifying ghost, the fire Tate speaks of brings both light and heat into the succeeding generations. It is the spiritual heredity that is the counterpart of the biological burden carried from father to son by the blood.

Throughout the sequence Tate seems to be identifying the hidden fire that has burned secretly within his ancestors with the fierce furies who guard the rights of mother earth. The tragic inheritance that has come to his family is countered by another family trait, a stoic bearing that he calls "a part so humble and so proud/ You'll think but little of it in your shroud." Even in birth the older brother had to struggle against mortality; yet the dignity through which he has continued to cope with straitened circumstances is not heroic but normal, deserving neither

9. Allen Tate, "Sonnets of the Blood," in *Poems, 1928–1931* (New York, 1932). The version published earlier in *Poetry*, XXXIX, 59–65, has significant variant readings.

praise nor criticism. It is an instinct that is deeply rooted within him. Nevertheless, this same instinct can be turned in other directions. What has been courage in the acts of one brother has emerged less positively in the other, who was brought back from the "cyclonic West." The same drive is embodied in different ways in Tate's two older brothers, but their common furies take a cue from the powerful matriarchal figure. In Sonnet VI Tate implies that the death of their mother has taken on deep implications for all three brothers, since hers was the most vigorous attempt to keep the furious flames glowing.

In Sonnets IV and V, Tate recalls two very different figures who show the conviction of their fire in opposing ways. One, presumably from their family's past, was a Virginian who cared so little for form and privilege that he freed his slaves to keep himself untrammeled by conventions. He bears a strong resemblance to George Posey in *The Fathers*:

> George Posey was a man without people or place; he had strong relationships, and he was capable of passionate feeling, but it was all personal; even his affection for his mother was personal and disordered. . . . In a world in which all men were like him, George would not have suffered—and he did suffer—the shock of communion with a world that he could not recover; while that world existed, its piety, its order, its elaborate rigamarole—his own forfeited heritage—teased him like a nightmare in which the dreamer dreams a dream within a dream within another dream of something that he cannot name. All violent people secretly desire to be curbed by something that they respect, so that they may become known to themselves.[10]

Tate finds his own generation to be in the same condition as George Posey and the Virginian, for neither the advantages nor the drawbacks of "the law of form" are available to them. The other figure—a bold contemporary one—is a football player whose extraordinary prowess cannot ensure that his team will win. He suggests a family courage that lies beyond the formal conventions of winning and losing. The brother to whom the sequence is addressed has had that kind of courage built into him from as far back as the impressive but ultimately fruitless

10. Tate, *The Fathers*, 179–80.

southern victories in the Civil War. Such courageous fire is not a matter of personal choice; it is given by the blood. Even so, the football player, like the tall Virginian, is an ambiguous figure; like Dante's Brunetto Latini, he has already lost, even though he seems to be winning.

The first six sonnets set the scene for the tragic drama that is sketched but never completed in the remaining poems. The poet knows that the daemon driving his family to achievement and, at the same time, to desperation, will perish with his generation. With the death of the mother, all the brothers will be changed as her flame subsides:

> Thank God the fuel is low, we'll not renew
> That length of flame into our firmament;
> Think too the rooftree crackles and will fall
> On us, who saw the sacred fury's height—
> Seated in her tall chair, with the black shawl
> From head to foot, burning with motherly light
> More spectral than November dusk could mix
> With sunset, to blaze on her pale crucifix.

The decline of a civilization will also mean the decline of this familial fire; here in this poem, as in "Emblems," Tate is aware that the blood will run out.

Although the death of the overbearing mother affords some relief from the tyranny of her expectations and faithfulness to family traditions, the loss of her commanding presence brings a new danger to the brothers, explored in the eighth sonnet. Every family has its sins, its ghosts, and its fears; but without the continuity of fire and blood, man has no identity at all in the face of death. To be brothers in mortality alone is not sufficient. In a direct allusion to Dante, Tate recognizes that a rejection of the limitations or evils of the past may also entail a rejection of order or life itself.

> I've heard the echoes in a dark tangled wood
> Yet never saw I a face peering within.
> These evils being anonymities,
> We fulminate, in exile from the earth,
> Aged exclusions of blood memories—
> Those superstitions of explosive birth;

Until there'll be of us not anything
But foolish death, who is confusion's king.

Because man is inherently sinful, he is always prone to tragedy; but few moderns have the courage to face the dark wood within their own souls. In the face of blind death, even evil has the power of preserving one's sense of reality and order. In their facile rejection of evil, modern men have become exiles from the world where good and evil mingle.

The ninth sonnet brings the sequence to its climax. No power on earth, the poet continues, "Shall keep us whole in our dissevering air." The dangers lie in pursuing extreme solutions. The brothers might attempt, mothlike, to fly directly into the flame and burn themselves out in the impossible pursuit of their family destiny; or they might turn, spiderlike, and destroy themselves in an attempt to escape it. Like the maddened and fury-pursued Orestes, last victim of the curse of Atreus, they must await the "lucid sieve" that will sort out "the appointed particles of time" in their blood and work out their fates. The best they can hope for is the understanding that comes from tragic acceptance of one's fate.

Call it the house of Atreus where we live—
Which one of us the Greek perplexed with crime
Questions the future: bring that lucid sieve
To strain the appointed particles of time!

Tate counsels his brother (and himself) to submit to destiny without attempting to reshape the circumstances that give rise to it. He does not offer any easy or even comforting advice. In a much earlier poem, "Elegy," Tate sees Jefferson Davis as an Orestes-like tragic figure; but he indicts the South that has sentimentalized the ambiguous statesman into a martyr. The harshness of the poem's assessment of Davis, like Tate's uncompromising sense of doom in "Sonnets of the Blood," is a vehement challenge to the "romantic traditionists" who would trivialize or attempt to escape their destiny.

The last sonnet is a kind of epilogue. It stands outside the more personal themes of the preceding sonnets, extending their substance into a wider realm. Addressing himself to his brother as one of the powerful "Captains of Industry," Tate warns that modern technology and the attack on nature have awakened self-deceptive desires for perfection in contemporary man. The quantification of nature—reduction of the mythical power of nature to an abstract set of numbers—will bring on "false division," destroying the wholeness of a world governed by "prime" numbers, indivisible by any number other than themselves. But it is the "inner mansion of the blood" that is most threatened, and once this blood-tide is unleashed, the blind forces of a dehumanized nature will "drown out him who swears to rectify/ Infinity, that has nor ear nor eye." This final sonnet ties all together by uniting the themes of the fury, blood, and the tragic-mythic order of historic Greece in the perspective of a declining present civilization. Beginning with the necessity of a confessional acceptance of one's own personal character and destiny, Tate moves to the necessity of applying that understanding to even larger concerns. The neohumanist and Carlylean optimism that would proffer some sort of emotional solution to the dark problems of humanity will result in greater disruptions than mere economic revolt. An arbitrarily supported power with no historical limitations and no cultural limits can only lead to an "unspeaking fury," an inhuman response to those guilty of assaulting nature. Without the essential bonds that are embodied in the family and symbolized by the blood, man cannot survive; and without the "laying on of hands from one generation to another," which produces a "sense of a past," as Tate later puts it in "A Lost Traveller's Dream,"[11] a culture cannot exist.

Two other poems are important complements to the tragic sense of the present depicted in "Sonnets of the Blood." The first, "Mother and Son," is an intense exploration of the themes of family destiny and death. The second, "To the Lacedemonians," examines the public and historical dimensions of cultural decline. The struggle between parent and child in "Mother and Son" is another dramatic presentation of the personal will imposed on a resisting reality. The mother attempts to turn decline and defeat into triumph and rebirth. She is locked in a death struggle with her moribund son; but it is she, "the fierce compositor of blood," who insists in a "harsh command/ That he should say the time is beautiful." The dying man knows that the tradition she is trying so desperately to save and impose on him is a wraith, a ghostly symbol of his own mortality:

11. Tate, "A Lost Traveller's Dream," 14.

> The dreary flies, lazy and casual,
> Stick to the ceiling, buzz along the wall,
> O heart, the spider shuffles from the mould
> Weaving, between the pinks and grapes, his pall.
> The bright wallpaper, imperishably old,
> Uncurls and flutters, it will never fall.

The man is mortal; his tattered culture, ironically figured in the vine-and-grape motif of the "bright wallpaper," has an imperishable quality that he cannot challenge. The room in which the son is dying is a symbolic reflection of the world he is rejecting by accepting death. Though the signs of decay are about him, evidence of the past still manages to hang on, like the wallpaper that only half conceals the wall whose decay it covers. The wallpaper and the wall seem to be analogous to the relationship between a culture and its supporting civilization. The culture never perishes, even if it is transformed by history into new forms; but civilizations rise and fall according to the material structures that constitute them. In a poem that seems to be exclusively concerned with a personal conflict, Tate has carried forward his reflections on the larger dimensions of history.

The locus of life and death in this poem is the bed on which the dying son lies:

> Where greed, avarice, anger writhed and slept
> Till to their silence they were gathered in:
> There, fallen with time, his tall and bitter kin
> Once fired the passions that were never kept
> In the permanent heart, and there his mother lay
> To bear him on the impenetrable day.

This unyielding son was born into an inescapable condition from which he can exit only in death. His "tall and bitter kin" have left nothing permanent from their own lives, except the bed where he lies. He is an Orestes, caught between the command to defend the honor of his forefathers and the "dry fury" of his mother's domination, summed up in the snakelike attack of the sun at the "black crucifix on her breast," a symbol of salvation but also a sign of death. There is no release from the struggle, except through mortality, which "will speak the victory soon." The poet does not attempt to resolve the tensions between mother and son, but he does suggest the despair and horror attendant upon a man whose honesty will not allow him to accept a false solution of his dilemma. The mother is more than the spectral fury of "Sonnets of the Blood." In this poem she seems to be the personal will itself, demanding that her son assume an optimism he cannot possibly believe in as a proper stance for transforming the times. The crucifix, which represents an alternative way of making the world beautiful, has no transcendent dimensions for him. Like Lacy Buchan, the dying man is listening for the night.

What Tate means by true history, as opposed to personal will, is described in an essay on Faulkner, where he explains that by *myth* he means "a dramatic projection of heroic action, or of the tragic failure of heroic action, upon the reality of the common life of a society, so that the myth *is* reality." The myth is imperishable, but the civilization is not. The South, for instance, "had to be destroyed, the good along with the evil." There are no perfect lives, no perfect civilizations. In seeking this abstract perfection, man sets himself impossible goals. In attempting to discover some system of superior benefit to mankind, he actively destroys those orders in the present which, like all earthly civilizations, contain both good and evil. In speaking of the "Southern myth," Tate offers a commentary on a historical situation that makes plain his own exploration in "Sonnets of the Blood" and "Mother and Son":

> The South, afflicted with the curse of slavery—a curse, like that of Original Sin, for which no single person is responsible—had to be destroyed, the good along with the evil. The old order had a great deal of good, one of the "goods" being a result of the evil; for slavery itself entailed a certain moral responsibility which the capitalist employer in free societies did not need to exercise if it was not his will to do so. This old order, in which the good could not be salvaged from the bad, was replaced by a new order which was in many ways worse than the old. . . . The cynical materialism of the new order brought to the South the American standard of living, but it also brought about a society similar to that which Matthew Arnold saw in the North in the eighties and called vigorous and uninteresting.[12]

12. Allen Tate, "Faulkner's *Sanctuary* and the Southern Myth," in *Memoirs*, 151.

In "To the Lacedemonians," Tate depicts through the ruminations of an old soldier a South that has lost its myth. The Confederate veteran rehearses the speech he is to give to a reunion of his colleagues. Through the reflections reported in his dramatic monologue, one is able to construct the main outlines of his impending address. The speaker appeals to the heroic sense that he and others knew in the past, but he does not exhort his hearers to revive it. What he sees, rather, is a complete contrast between the way of life he knew as a young man and the one he now witnesses. The "contraption" has replaced the "accomplishment," tempestuous motion the "bright course of blood along the vein." War has become terrible and meaningless because it is reduced to "a trade route, figures/ For the budget, reduction of population." The mathematical abstractions of Spengler's twilight age are everywhere evident.

The old soldier inveighs against the modern world, but he is aware that he must take some of the responsibility for its condition. The war in which he fought was itself a feature of the modern world:

> Waken, lords and ladies gay, we cried,
> And marched to Cedar Run and Malvern Hill,
> Kinsmen and friends from Texas to the Tide—
> Vain chivalry of the personal will!

Donald Davidson has published an excellent and very sympathetic reading of this poem,[13] but the difference between his and Tate's attitudes toward history may well be summed up in these lines. The old soldier sees the "chivalry" in which his generation indulged not as a viable preservation of the meaningful traditions of battle but as a disguised modernism. It was vain because it was powerless in confrontation with the chaos of real modern warfare, but it was above all an assertion of the "personal will," a product of the assertive imagination and not a genuine part of the society this chivalry was supposed to maintain and defend.

The men who went to war "to win the precincts of the light" did not recognize the signs of their changing history. They trusted history because they had known no other reality, higher or lower. They did not

13. Donald Davidson, "The Meaning of War: A Note on Allen Tate's 'To the Lacedemonians,'" *Southern Review*, n.s., I, 720–30.

understand, when they departed for battle, what the old man now knows: "There is no civilization without death." All civilizations must decline, however brilliant they may have been at their best. But the phrase may permit another interpretation: no culture can be sustained without personal and communal sacrifice. That is what the Lacedemonians, whose famous epigraph is paraphrased in the poem, stood for in their willingness to die. Today, the enemy is within:

> Soldiers, march! we shall not fight again
> The Yankees with our guns well-aimed and rammed—
> All are born Yankees of the race of men
> And this, too, now the country of the damned:
>
> Poor bodies crowding round us! The white face
> Eyeless with eyesight only, the modern power—
> Huddled sublimities of time and space.

The Dantesque conclusion of the poem, with its picture of the lost souls of the Inferno blown about by the wind, reveals the old man's secret, which he bears in the night. The damnation that he sees everywhere reveals that modern man is a denizen of Dante's hell.

The old man recognizes that he and his contemporaries who went "to win the precincts of the light,/ Unshadowing restriction of our day," have committed idolatry. As a boy, he "never knew cessation/ Of the bright course of blood along the vein." Now, however,

> Men expect too much, do too little,
> Put the contraption before the accomplishment,
> Lack skill of the interior mind
> To fashion dignity with shapes of air.

In their worship of power, they have lost the ability to imagine dignity. They have become Calibans, "hunched like savages in a rotten tree," waiting for "the thunder to speak." In this dual evocation of Shakespeare's *The Tempest* and Eliot's *The Waste Land*, Tate offers his most telling picture of the dying out of both fire and blood. In such a world, where men are no more than "echoes of a raging power/ That reared its moment upon a gone land," the heritage of the ancestral pioneers and their gift of exile has ended by "pouring a long cold wrath into the mind." The aimless destination of the wind, with which the poem ends, suggests Dante's infernal realm and the buffeting of its empty, bodiless souls from side to side as they swarm through the circle of lust. But it also suggests, through inversion and irony, the pentecostal fire that once brought inspiration to another group of men huddled in fear. In these dark and bleak poems of energy without control and blood without containment, there is a hint of Tate's persistent quest. The buried city cannot be willed back into existence as a means for overcoming cultural decline. The revival of manners or the privilege of form is meaningless in a society that has given itself to illusions. The old soldier recognizes in this "vain chivalry of the personal will" the same vampirism that prevails in "To the Romantic Traditionists." One cannot die fruitfully for a past that sucks all the lifeblood from the present.

Throughout these poems peopled by exiles, vanquished warriors, idiots, suicides, fiends, damned souls, or dead gods and pervaded by the imagery of broken visions, empty winds, stuffless rage, bodiless flesh, sullen thunder, dying fire, or the world's rot, there is an unmistakable vitality. The poet persists in searching for some revelation that will overcome the lust for vacancy he sees all about him. He refuses to yield up his soul to the night, preferring to find in the "tight, invisible lyric" of the owl, the tongue of the serpent, or even in the wolves and spiders one room away a natural order that will respond to his *horror vacui*.

Four

The Love That Hates Mortality

No person, made aware of the intolerable demands placed on the modern soul, could face them alone without despairing. Courage, sacrifice, personal honesty, and even the ability to "cull the act from the attempt," as Tate puts it in "Winter Mask," cannot suffice to deliver the good man from a meaningless world in which everyone lives by chance. Faith is a gift that cannot be willed into existence. The debasement of the earthly city into a provincial realm lacking symbolic dimensions removes the foundation of love as a way of life from the most sincere and resolute humanist. Fear without memory of man's response to terror in his most heroic moments destroys the ability to act. The modern world is filled with men of honesty and courage and love, but the fact of their existence is insufficient as a response to the question "How to live?" Even such seemingly severe projects as philosophic positivism are governed by this concern, as Raymond Aron has shown in analyzing a key nineteenth-century thinker, Auguste Comte, who "wanted men, though they are destined to live indefinitely in separate temporal societies, to be united by common convictions and by a single object of their love. Since this object could have no transcendent existence, was there any other solution but to imagine men united in the worship of their own unity by the desire to achieve and to love that which, regardless of centuries and cultures, transcends all particularity?"[1]

A crucial word in this description is *imagine*. The final justification of Comte's positivism is an idol created by the imagination and worshiped in love—that is, man's narcissistic affection for his own humanity—a value that is based not on fact or statistics but emotion. Despite Comte's manifest illusions about founding a secular religion, his hope

1. Raymond Aron, *Main Currents in Sociological Thought*, trans. Richard Howard and Helen Weaver (New York and London, 1965), I, 104–105.

of living without faith has not been lost on subsequent thinkers. One finds Walter Kaufmann, among many other contemporary writers, saying much the same thing: "I agree with Paul that love is more important than faith and hope; but so are honesty, integrity, and moral courage. The world needs less faith and more love and nobility."[2] Kaufmann's expressed hope for mankind may be elegant and courageous, but it is no more likely to be fulfilled than Comte's visionary society of love. The question to be answered is whether man can live at all without some form of faith. Tate would say that he cannot. In his poetry and prose he has recognized that men who attempt to live without a religious faith end by substituting for it a secular parody. Without belief in something higher than man, love can only mean self-love. Whatever others may claim to have experienced, Tate has confessed that he sees no other solution: "As I look back upon my own verse, written over more than twenty-five years, I see plainly that its main theme is man's suffering from unbelief; and I cannot for a moment suppose that this man is some other than myself."[3] What Tate the poet came to recognize was that the need for faith is inescapable and that without it love itself lacks a foundation.

Some of Tate's best-known poems are concerned with this very problem of a conflict between loves with and without faith. Perhaps the most familiar is "The Cross." As a dramatic portrayal of the situation of modern man, it moves swiftly and convincingly. The "last alternatives" that he faces are a choice between the faith and love demanded by the cross and the nihilism and narcissism inherited by the chaotic world of the present. This second way, Tate has demonstrated brilliantly, was given full expression by Edgar Allan Poe: "He is constantly telling us that we are all alone, that beauty is evanescent, that the only immortality may be a vampirish return from the grave, into which we must sink again through eternity."[4] The protagonist of "The Cross" knows that "turning back" will not spare him the necessity of choosing between the two ways. The last lines of the poem describe perfectly the fate of Poe's vampirish heroes; and the typical Poe-like themes of vortex, pit, and grave are unmistakable. At the beginning of the poem, the

2. Walter Kaufmann, *From Shakespeare to Existentialism* (New York, 1960), xii.
3. Allen Tate, "Religion and the Intellectuals," *Partisan Review*, XVII, 242.
4. Allen Tate, "The Poetry of Edgar Allan Poe," in *Memoirs*, 124.

abyss that threatens to destroy the self is accompanied with an illuminating fire

> Crushing the world with such a light
> The day sky fell to moonless black,
> The kingly sun to hateful night.

It is the kind of symbol Tate refers to in his essay on Poe that both illuminates and burns. The speaker, confronted with such knowledge, stands on the brink of the only truly heroic decision possible in the modern world: the decision to accept personal annihilation rather than vampiric immortality. The light of the cross that is revealed at the beginning of the poem is also the light of death.

Man has a natural resistance to mortality, whether it be expressed as self-love or love for another; but he cannot expect to save himself through it alone. The cross stands for a kind of death that leads somewhere, and its effectiveness as a symbol in this poem goes beyond traditional Christian associations. The cross is a much older icon; it stood in the pagan world for the belief in a world axis, for the crossroads that organize every human establishment of order and every choice of action. In other associations, the cross was the cosmic tree by means of which the soul reaches God, a point of intersection between earth and heaven. In Tate's poem it functions as the mediating image that brings together a great number of opposing motifs: flame (fire and life) and pit (earth, nothingness, and death); love and hate; immortality and mortality; the sun of rationalistic hope and the moon of irrational fear. The cross is also a symbol of agony and struggle. It is the paradigm for suffering carried out in a state of tension. It is also a symbol of destiny. No more apt commentary upon the action depicted in Tate's poem could be found than J. E. Cirlot's coincidentally appropriate description in his *Dictionary of Symbols*: "The basic idea behind the symbolism of crucifixion is that of experiencing the essence of antagonism, an idea which lies at the root of existence, expressing as it does life's agonizing pain, its cross-roads, possibilities and impossibilities, of construction and destruction. Evola suggests that the cross is a synthesis of the seven aspects of space and time, because its form is such that it both maintains and destroys free movement."[5]

5. J. E. Cirlot, *A Dictionary of Symbols*, trans. Jack Sage (New York, 1962), 68.

The violent oppositions so typical of Tate's poetry are aptly summed up in this central symbol. The poem is a powerful cosmic drama, played out on a stage where time and space are not specific or definite ("long ago," "a place that some men know") but remain, nevertheless, effective settings. The complexity of the poem lies in its oppositions as they occur on all levels, including the more intimate frame of reference of the human body (eye opposed to foot, head to heart) and the battleground of the psyche (wolflike aggression meeting staglike defenselessness). The success of the poem is doubtless a result of Tate's mixture of the very concrete and the very abstract. The symbol of the wolves is handled with particular brilliance. The young pups, weaned from their mother's milk to the taste of fresh blood, will no longer be satisfied with the blander nourishment. Man possesses a lust for life that drives him to seek something beyond death, but he has been "from all salvation weaned" and cannot go back.[6] Without religious faith, man will seek his salvation where he can; he will attempt to find it in the love that "so hates mortality/ Which is the providence of life," but he will find no peace there. The rending of the body, suggested in the image of the charged stag, is a destruction of the physical for the sake of the spiritual. It is the only alternative to the living death of a vampire immortality. It is modern man's cross that he cannot decide: he is crucified on the intersecting agonies of his dissociated condition and torn in two directions at once. Having encountered his dilemma directly, he knows that there is no turning back. Yet no secular form of salvation can save him from the wolf of death. He faces the fact of his own mortality without hope or faith and therefore without the benefit of love.

Though the poet obviously believes in the power of love, he cannot turn to it as a total solution, for desire to survive is greater than an understanding of the whole:

For love so hates mortality
Which is the providence of life
She will not let it blessèd be
But curses it with mortal strife,

6. Unpublished letter to the author from Allen Tate, November 18, 1972: "Wolves (so I've read somewhere), once they've tasted blood, will not return to mother's milk; men, once they have glimpsed salvation, will not accept death as the *end*. 'Being from all salvation weaned' means—or I intended it to mean—that men cannot be satisfied with secular or merely humanistic salvation."

Until beside the blinding rood
Within that world-destroying pit
—Like young wolves that have tasted blood—
Of death, men taste no more of it.

Occasionally, a poet's interpretation of the work of his colleagues may shed light on his own poems. Tate's reading of W. H. Auden's "Our Hunting Fathers Told the Story," which also deals with love and mortality in terms of hunting imagery, may be taken as a gloss on the lines about love from "The Cross":

> In this poem there is an immense complication of metaphor, but I do not propose to unravel it. I would say just this: that all the complications can be returned without confusion or contradiction to a definite, literal, and coherent field of imagery; that when the poet wishes to extend his meaning, he does it by means of this field of metaphor, not by changing the figure, which is: the hunter debases his human nature (Love) in his arrogant, predatory conquest of the world, and Love itself becomes not merely morally bad but evil. The field of imagery, to which all the implications refer, is that of the hunting squire, who by a deft ambiguity quickly becomes predatory man.[7]

This figure in Auden's poem may have caught Tate's attention because of his own use of similar images. In "The Cross" the love that hates mortality is human nature itself, and the fear of death makes man into a kind of predator seeking to destroy death. Once man has glimpsed salvation, he is like the young wolves who cannot return to their mother's milk. He can no longer accept death as the end. But the love that hates mortality must yield to a higher love that sees something beyond death. Tate's own field of imagery in this poem is the flight of the stag from the wolves; and, like Auden, he also depicts love the hunter turning into a predator first and then a victim.

This transformation of the predator of death into the prey of death is paralleled in two other poems of Tate's. In "The Traveller" he pictures a modern questor overcome by his own search for meaning:

7. Allen Tate, "Understanding Modern Poetry," in *Essays*, 168.

And a dark shift within the bone
Brings him the end he could not find.

In another poem, "Inside and Outside," he uses a figure like the hunter to show how hatred and fear of mortality turn on those who try to escape death:

There is not anything to say to those
Speechless, who have stood up white to the eye
All night—till day, harrying the game too close,
Quarries the perils that at midnight lie
Waiting for those who hope to mortify
With foolish daylight their most anxious fear.

There is a difference between accepting death as the end and seeing it as leading somewhere else. Love unassisted cannot triumph over death, for death is, after all, a part of nature. Only something above nature can transcend mortality, as Tate concludes in "Inside and Outside":

There is no word that death can find to say
Deeper than life, savager than their time.
When Gabriel's trumpet ends all life's delay,
Will crash the beams of firmamental woe:
Not nature will sustain the even crime
Of death, though death sustains all nature, so.

Man by nature bears the cross of his situation, and he can choose to accept what he is and come to understand his own nature or attempt to escape it without hope of success. Any solution that fails to recognize man's need to transcend his own nature will, Tate implies, lead to his ultimate destruction.

Other poems published at this time explore the same insight through different settings. "The Twelve," for instance, is an overt examination of the failure of belief. Though the poem appears to be about the apostles who followed Jesus, it is really about the modern man who has lost his faith but has not found an adequate substitute for it. Leaderless and solitary, the twelve come to prefer a vision of nothingness ("the mind's briefer and more desert place") to any substitution for faith. Without the "victor of Rome," they cannot bring the message of love to society. The "council of charity" is left to wander the "face of the earth a fatherless child." It is not the Christ of charity but the man utterly forsaken who remains to haunt them with "the fire of the wind, the thick and the fast/ Whirl of the damned in the heavenly storm." Unable to face either life or death, the twelve are caught in the hot wind of their own sterile desire. Nevertheless, they cannot remain in this condition long. Though the poem is clearly a description of lost faith in our world, the action it describes seems to take place between the time of the crucifixion and Pentecost, the wind of inspiration and rejuvenation. The apostles are not waiting in an upper room, however, but in a desert. Like the Christ who was tempted by Satan, they too are tempted by unbelief in an ambiance of "wrinkled stones round a leafless tree." The images remind one of the injunction to turn stones into bread or of the barren fig tree cursed for its fruitlessness in the New Testament. But they recall other symbols as well: the barren tree could also be the cross, and the rocks the foundation stone of the Church built upon Peter. Whatever meaning they had in the narrative action of Christ's life, in this setting they are blank and empty. The twelve have been challenged to follow the example of their master; but without some gift of grace beyond their own human powers, they will turn to inaction and despair. Their posture as they lie in the sand does not suggest an anticipation of the Holy Spirit; it is rather their embracing of a living death as the escape from the "inhuman ecstasy" of Christ's "last word" that "seared the western heart."

Human nature does supply one saving reaction to protect man from this kind of total nihilism, and even without faith man can still learn from fear to accept something beyond himself. In "Ode to Fear," subtitled "Variation on a Theme by Collins," Tate recognizes modern man's need to understand his own deepest terrors. His "variation" offers a more complex picture of fear than Collins' aesthetic *frisson*:

> Let the day glare, O memory, your tread
> Beats to the pulse of suffocating night—
> Night peering from his dark but fire-lit head
> Burns on the day his tense and secret light.

Night is a deeply buried part of the memory, inescapable and "firelit" in its uncanny secret light. Like the fire that illumines and consumes, it

Tate's Alice goes a step further than Poe's heroes, who are, after all, literally two. Hers is an even more intense incest, achieved in

> Love for herself who, as an earthly twain,
> Pouted to join her two in a sweet one.

Alice's divided self is united not by a return to the "world's entity" but by a peculiar geometric abstraction. She has become pure thought without content, gazing "At nothing, nothing thinking all the day." The stages of contemplation through which Beatrice led Dante have been collapsed into one. Alice is both Beatrice and Dante, beloved and lover. The beatific vision of the totally other has been replaced by Alice's demonic vision of the totally empty self. She has become all eye, concentrating her being in the "linear sight" of the highest organ of abstraction among the senses. Instead of the world, she dwells in a geometrical universe of pure forms. The Beatrice who expounded difficult theological matters for Dante has become as ignorant as the sinner who lost himself in the dark forest. The analogical mirrors that Tate discusses in "The Symbolic Imagination" as the eminently successful image of connatural knowledge in Dante's Paradise are reduced to tools of self-destruction.

The concluding lines of the poem show that damnation is worse in a world without faith than in a believer's world, for faith at least allows one to see more than a single level of meaning in the world. In rejecting all intermediaries, Alice has lost the ability to dwell in reality; as a consequence, she is neither damned nor saved—a figure akin to the indifferent shades Dante sees before the gate of Hell. Hers is not a unique dilemma, however, for it is shared by all moderns:

> —We too back to the world shall never pass
> Through the shattered door, a dumb shade-harried crowd
> Being all infinite, function depth and mass
> Without figure, a mathematical shroud
>
> Hurled at the air—blessèd without sin!

Although Alice has lost her being in a kind of self-violence, her example can be instructive to others if they can exercise a sense of analogy. The poet can speak imaginatively, even though Alice cannot. He asks at the end of the poem that man be given only a sense of his finitude, not a certainty of salvation. Unlike the condemned Guido da

Montefeltro, who told his tale to Dante because he could not believe that anyone would ever return from Hell to repeat his story of damnation, the speaker of the poem recognizes his plight and prays that man may be restored to the living world before it is too late. At the end of the poem Tate employs a device used by Baudelaire in "Au Lecteur" or by Eliot in his "Prufrock": the speaker suddenly addresses his reader as a denizen of the same hell as he himself occupies. The only way to beatitude that is meaningful is one in which man encounters difficulty and suffering, in which he must "falter on the stony path," for only through such a way can he learn to act out the meaning of his own fallibility and deserve the love of another.

"Last Days of Alice" is about a perverse love that is not of the body. In Augustine's time, the materialistic world of Rome threatened the spiritual dimensions of life; but in the modern era, there is perhaps not enough materialism in the proper sense to make love real. Modern man is more like a Manichaean than a pagan; he rejects more often than embraces the body. In the two parts of "Inside and Outside," already discussed briefly in connection with "The Cross," Tate gives a dramatic image of this temperament. The young woman who dies in the soundless room reveals nothing of her decease. There are strangely suggestive hints of vampirism in the scene. The "outside" of her appearance does not betray the reality of her "body's life," which

> deep as a foul well,
> Instinctive as the wind, busy as May,
> Burns out a secret passageway to hell.

She is like Poe's heroines in appearance, ready to rise from the coffin at any moment. Yet it is not the girl herself who is responsible for this vampiric appearance. It is those "who hold her pulses dear." The poem is not about the girl but about the effect of her death upon others. The onlookers, "speechless," "bloodless," and "white to the eye," do not fear for her so much as for themselves; and their hope is that daylight will somehow fight off the terrors of death. It is darkness and silence that they resist, knowing that their vigil is powerless to prevent either fear of death or inevitable mortality. They would "mortify" their fear—the verb suggests "control of the passions," "causing to feel shame," and "bringing about death and decay" as possible shades of meaning. Day, like a hunter, rounds up their fears for the attack; but the mourners are powerless. They cannot attack death with speech, and nothing that is said to them will ward off their terror. This play of inside and outside, darkness and light, vigilance and fear can be overcome only by a yielding to the human condition. As long as man is part of the natural world, he will know death. Only Gabriel's trumpet, the intervention of something above nature into time, can break the terrible silence and justify the existence of death in the world. Without the hope that the supernatural offers, death is an evil that the natural order cannot justify.

Seen in the context of these poems, "The Wolves," another frequently anthologized poem, appears to be more than simply a commentary on "those human situations from which there is no escape," though critics are certainly correct in seeing in it the nightmarish dramatization of just such a situation. Yet there is another motif hidden within the poem—the burden of a life without faith as expressed in fear. Without faith, man is always vulnerable, even when he possesses honesty, integrity, courage, and honor. Love that is not sustained by belief is often threatened by belief, for faith is like a beast of prey that threatens man's absolute existential autonomy. In speaking of the "tragic character" of his friend William Troy ("like a classical tragic man," he once noted sympathetically, "he had to explore his self-image at cost"), Tate describes this terrible dilemma: Troy's "uncompromising integrity" led to a "Pascalian pyrrhonism. He had lost his faith, which was nevertheless crouching in the next room waiting to spring upon him."[9] Tate's peculiar use of this image perhaps suggests that "The Wolves" is about more than simple animal fear.

The poem draws together many of the images and motifs that are prominent in other poems of this group: light, fear, archfiends, ravenous beasts, and mortality. Like them, it is a description of the divided psyche, separated into two parts by the "perilous gate" (in "Last Days of Alice") of a "white door patched with light from the hall." Like that threshold dividing man's identity from his self-consciousness, the mirror and the door outlined in light are Tate's images for a point of separation that must be acknowledged but never crossed. The wolf is on one side of the line, and his fearfulness is proverbial as an emblem of destruction. In Nordic mythologies, it is prophesied that he will break

9. Allen Tate, "William Troy: A Memoir," in William Troy, *Selected Essays*, ed. Stanley Edgar Hyman (New Brunswick, 1967), x.

free from his shackles and swallow the sun. The Romans, however, made the wolf an image of valor, and there is something about the wolves in this poem that suggests their own integrity as animals:

> the heart
> Of man has a little dignity, but less patience
> Than a wolf's, and a duller sense that cannot
> Smell its own mortality.

Compared to the animal, man is at a disadvantage, for he has the capacity to delude himself. He can try to calm his fears of darkness and night by looking for the evening star. He can pretend to ignore the scuffle of the wolves in the next room, even as he recognizes his claim to self-control as an empty ploy.

The starry heaven at which the speaker gazes is the traditional realm of order from Aeschylus to Kant, but Tate implies that there may be little moral order within the human breast. As the fearful man looks out the window, he sees two heavenly lights. The evening star is, of course, Venus; Arcturus is the brightest star in the constellation Boötes. Arcturus—Greek for "guardian bear" or "guardian of the bear"—and Boötes—Greek for "plowman"—suggest some mode of control over nature, as Venus suggests love. Yet the speaker does not expect to encounter any such transcendent powers: "The day will not follow night." He knows that his mind is already filled with thoughts of death:

> (This and other
> Meditations will be suited to other times
> After dog silence howls his epitaph.)

Even man's best friend is descended from the wolf; and his howl, like the wolves' scuffle, is inaudible to the dead in the grave. The dog and the wolf have an animal patience that will outlast man's fearful attempts at distraction; the dog has silence as his only epitaph—man needs words that give some meaning to his passing.

The confrontation in the concluding lines of this disturbing poem is a brilliant climax to Tate's earlier statements about the need for both fear and faith. Man must recognize that fear is spontaneous and always with him; it has the quality of the starlight outside his window. But courage is different; it must be summoned up through the memory of heroic action:

> Now remember courage, go to the door,
> Open it and see whether coiled on the bed
> Or cringing by the wall a savage beast
> Maybe with golden hair, with deep eyes
> Like a bearded spider on a sunlit floor,
> Will snarl—and man can never be alone.

Man's natural impulse to flee must be countered by all the models of heroism he can recall, yet even memory is not enough:

> no man has ever sat where the next room's
> Crowded with wolves, and for the honor of man
> I affirm that never have I before.

In other times, man had rituals and institutions to set a distance between himself and the demonic terrors that await one across the perilous threshold; but none of these forms is any longer available, and man must face his deepest fears alone. In the past, to cross that threshold would have been the act of extreme impiety and folly. Now it has become a necessity, and man must recognize that the only way back to the supernatural is through direct confrontation with his deepest fears. In this sense, then, faith and fear have become one. This unity, which is characteristic of the sacred sense wherever it appears, is suggested by the closing images of the poem. The wolf "coiled on the bed" like a snake and the "bearded spider" belong to both earth and air. The spider is a particularly striking image, and perhaps its link to the snarling mammals is conveyed by its beard, characteristic of the so-called wolf-spider, who bears mandibles for crushing victims. Even if this suggestion seems overingenious, one cannot fail to recognize that the spider is a menacing sort of creature like the beast "cringing by the wall" whose deep eyes cast a web that entraps before he devours. The key to this bestiary of fear—wolf, snake, and spider—is in the concluding phrase: "man can never be alone." To be trapped is to know that the attempt to live in isolation is both impossible and repugnant. Those moderns who would follow Poe in insisting that man is alone in his universe must reject both love and faith; for *alone*, as Tate has said, is a key term in Poe's definition of man that leads to "incest of spirit." Man will always be the prey of his attendant beasts, since, lacking a guardian angel, he will be quickly provided with a guardian demon.

In the secular schemes of salvation prevalent throughout the modern world, faith has been reduced to the subjective and the emotional. The honest man is right to reject such a faith, for without a basis in society and the physical world, belief is hollow. Such an insubstantial faith cannot save men; it only leads them to a further isolation. An example of the consequences for love in a world that consigns faith to the merely personal is the subject of "The Paradigm," a poem about the loss of affection between a married couple. While the passion of love draws one ever closer to the physical being of the one beloved, the passion of hate creates abstract caricatures of its object. Hatred expresses itself most vehemently in acts of revulsion toward the presence of another, as in this poem the couple who bore "pure passion once" toward each other have transformed it into "purest hate." Though there have been many metaphysical poems about love, Tate has written one of the few about hate.

"The Paradigm" treats the failure of erotic passion, unsupported by anything beyond itself, with the language of a seventeenth-century poet brought up to date. The globe, iron wedges, and parallel lines of Marvell's "Definition of Love," for instance, find their equivalents in this definition of hate as the poet compares his protagonists' emotions to steel wire, an iceberg, and a mirror. Hate, like love, can transform the universe:

> Love's but the echo of retreat
> Caught by the sunbeam stretched above
>
> Their frozen exile from the earth
> And lost. Each is the other's crime.

These former lovers play out their hatred in the emptiness of the air. The contact between them is never physical. Each reflects his hatred off the other as though the other were a hard mirrored surface. Donne shows his lovers reflecting their faces in each other's eyes. Tate's couple confront each other in a cold stare that

> Seals them up in their icy land
> (A few square feet) where into stone

The two hearts turning quickly pass
Once more their impenetrable world.

But air is not glass, and neither person can truly ignore the other. Thus each serves as the catalyst for the other's hatred. Their fate is to be bound together in mutual damnation; each is "the other's crime."

This is their equity in birth—
Hate is its ignorant paradigm.

Though their love has been unassisted by any outside forces, their hatred is more than personal. It goes back to the Original Sin that both shared in birth. Without a world to sustain them, they had nothing to believe in but each other. When they failed each other, the whole world failed them. "The Paradigm" might well be called "Dover Beach Fifty Years After."

Fear of the world is fear of the body, Tate implies in poem after poem. The true lover knows that his vulnerability is centered in his body, even when he claims to care most for the spirit. What the true lover must learn to accept is the body with all its defects. Tate encountered a powerful vision of the two loves in Baudelaire, and even the great French poet's near Jansenism could not overcome his determination to see man as necessarily composite and contradictory. Tate's translation of "Une Charogne" as "A Carrion" is a version of another poet's insight, but it is pure Tate in its own way and deserves some attention. As an interpretation of a great modern poem, the translation provides a key to the themes it bears in common with Tate's original poetry.

The word *charogne* is feminine in French, but it does not necessarily convey the sense of a feminine body. Nevertheless, Tate's translation gives the "carrion" a distinctly feminine character. He also heightens the sexual implications of the original poem, perhaps recalling Hamlet's "god kissing carrion" and the Elizabethan pun on the verb *to die*. The sun is a hot lover, and decomposition is compared to the sexual act. Death is a kind of love in nature, for the rotting body is a profitable return for all she invested in its form. Heaven looks down upon the carrion as though it were a blooming flower with soporific powers. The old poetic comparison of fragile feminine beauty with a fading flower is given an ironic twist in this comparison of the decaying carcass with a poppy. Indeed, the body is ambivalent in relation to the universe around and within it:

> One would have thought the corpse was held a slave
> To living by the life it bore!

The body becomes a world of its own in death, with its own music, its own feelings, and its own harvest season. The love that nature bears toward all created things will cause her to reclaim "all forms," but she will also embody them into "a perfect art." Yet one must not overlook the "restless bitch," another rival awaiting her turn to tear into the skeleton. The body's shame is not its absorption back into the desiring largess of nature but its desecration by a jealous animal life of carnivorous beasts and "the worm that shall kiss [its] proud estate." Man is the prey of a life lower than his own. He will lose his ascendance over the beasts as they repay him for his arrogant domination.

The poet's love for his "angel" and "passion" will be challenged by the larger "love" of the universe that holds the body as its slave

> When through your bones the flowers and sucking grass
> Weave their rank cerement.

Like the bodies of the soldiers lost in "acres of the insane green" in "Ode to the Confederate Dead," the carrion in this poem is given over to a strange and alien power. The ambiguous love nature offers to the body seems to exalt it, but also reduces it to the rank of "a courtesan." There can be no real comfort in knowing the body will give itself unselfishly to anonymous nature. The "queen of heavenly grace" who is the poet's love must learn to confront her body's destiny by recognizing that the poet alone has

> kept the divine form and the essense
> Of [his] festered loves inviolate.

Tate has added something significant to Baudelaire's last line. His version speaks of a "festered love." The "divine form and the essence" may remain virginal and "inviolate" in poetry, but the poet himself knows that he is part of the same nature which loves through process and change. The poet's attraction to beauty cannot be destroyed by the "rank cerement" that will eventually invest the body, for the ideal coexists with the "dire putrescence." Even in death they remain inseparable.

There is a beauty in mortality if it is seen as the threshold to a larger world of meaning.

Baudelaire's poem, as reinterpreted by Tate, is old-fashioned in its traditional insistence on the themes of *memento mori* and poetic immortality, despite its shocking realism and witty imagery. What Tate found most impressive about his French master was the refusal to see life as divided into two different essences, two different loves: "After reading Baudelaire I could no longer believe that romantic Beauty was the end of poetry; for in him the sordid and the sublime could be grasped in a single complex of experience; for that was the lesson taught by Baudelaire's great sonnet ['Correspondences']."[10] Both poems offer an alternative to misapplied romanticism of the kind that has become in the twentieth century a variety of contemporary Manichaeism. "Romantic Beauty" is a spurious version of the otherworldly, projected by the personal will but divorced from any analogical or real involvement with the lived world. As Tate has noted in summing up the thesis of William Lynch's *Christ and Apollo*, it is the case that "we are alienated from nature; that we circumvent the common reality and reach for transcendental meanings; that we use this revived Manichean heresy to justify our hatred of ourselves—a hatred that may express itself evasively in impossible attempts at human perfectibility, at the expense of human reality, or in disgust with the human condition."[11] For that reason, to place all value in love, courage, or honor alone, as vital as they are, is to ask them to bear too great a burden. As poems like "The Paradigm" show, love under such a strain very easily turns into hate and disgust of the sort that cannot cope with the carrion of the human body.

The alternative to Manichaeism is the "doctrine of analogy or connaturality," which "becomes in poetry the actuality of the identity of world and mind." Tate points out in "The Angelic Imagination" that this modern Manichaeism is a "perversion of man's nature" and demands "that external nature itself must be destroyed."[12] Baudelaire's "A Carrion" shows one side of the doctrine of connaturality through analogy. The universe knows only one love; it is man who tries to justify his own dissociation by pretending that there are two. In "Sonnet to Beauty," Tate opposes the world of modern aesthetics, which is a world

10. Allen Tate, "Poetry Modern and Unmodern," in *Essays*, 227–28.

11. Allen Tate, "The Unliteral Imagination; Or, I, too, Dislike It," in *Essays*, 460.

12. Allen Tate, "The Angelic Imagination," in *Essays*, 408.

of two beauties, to the world perceived as connatural. It is a theme that is evident in his earlier poetry, such as the sonnet "Art," where the poet is said to address a small, select audience for whom he can "let through" his "own vanishing slit of light." In the more mature poetry, he puts aside this youthful bravado for a celebration of those aspects of beauty available to all:

> The wonder of light is your familiar tale,
> Pert wench, down to the nineteenth century:
> Mr. Rimbaud, the Frenchman's apostasy
> Asserts the argument that you are stale,
> Flat and unprofitable, importunate but pale,
> Lithe Corpse!

During the nineteenth century something distorted man's perception of beauty. Rimbaud's disgust, like Hamlet's, was a rejection of the world—an apostasy from the example of his predecessor Baudelaire. Rimbaud, like Poe, was deficient in "philosophy," and the precocious poet who proclaimed that love had to be reinvented could not reinvent human nature. Beauty has not been stripped of its unity with truth, but we who are the descendants of nineteenth-century thinkers have lost the light: "Broken, our twilit visions fail."

It is in poetry and "the doctrine of the incorporate Word" that beauty's "fame" is conceived, for Rimbaud's poems at their best defeat his aesthetic claims. Beauty subsists in an art that is renewed and not corrupted by contact with the world, brought to life rather than to death. The flight of modern man from nature, "beak southward . . . like a bird," cannot destroy the "wonder of light" in its revelation:

> For often at Church I've seen the stained high glass
> Pour out the Virgin and Saints, twist and untwist
> The mortal youth of Christ astride an ass.

The last three lines of the sonnet suggest a comparison with the famous stanza in Shelley's "Adonais" that compares life to a "dome of many-colored glass." In an essay written a few years after his sonnet, Tate wrote of Shelley's lines that they "are not poetry; they express the frustrated individual will trying to compete with science. The will asserts a rhetorical proposition about the whole of life, but the imagination has not seized upon the materials of the poem and made them into a whole."[13] Though Tate as critic quarrels with the way in which the image is used in the poem, he does not argue about its truth or falsity as a proposition, for that is another matter. What he finds lacking is a concrete image of human action revealed by the light shining through the dome. The colors take on no shape that relates to humanity. What impresses the poet of "Sonnet to Beauty" about the images in the church is not simply the recognizable figures that the light creates but the twisting and untwisting of the light as it reveals the paradoxical image of Christ's dual nature in one person, the Son of God on a lowly beast of burden. The light moves through the colored glass with the same complexity, and the colors *are* what it reveals, not something that stains its purity.

One is tempted to ask concerning this poem whether or not the poet is referring to the "incarnate" as well as to the "incorporate Word." Is the poem a religious as well as an aesthetic statement? I think not. The church exists in this poem as part of a poetic image, even though it does have other inescapable associations. The stained glass is no more an evocation of theological doctrine than Shelley's dome. Both dome and church are symbols that evoke a sense of wholeness that man has lost, not a religious experience. The brief moment of encounter with the scenes in stained glass is a common, not a special, experience, available to anyone as a glimpse at beauty revealed. Without this ability to manifest itself in terms of ordinary experience, beauty is a "Lithe Corpse" that can be bent to any will. Beauty cannot be the creation of the will if it is to live; it must reside in autonomy from man's desire. Rimbaud's notion of beauty is "angelic." Only as revelation can beauty have any meaning for man, but that revelation must be made in terms of common human existence.

The doctrine of the resurrection of the body, referred to at the end of "Inside and Outside," is crucial, therefore, to earthly love, for it completes the order of the flesh. It is the reincorporation that proclaims the body as real and valuable, not the vampirism that comes from an attempt to avoid death.

In his elegy "The Anabasis," Tate offers an image of this tension between the need for incorporation and the inability of corporeal things to have full meaning in themselves. The dead woman, while alive, tran-

13. Allen Tate, "Three Types of Poetry," in *Essays*, 174. See also 183–84.

scended the conditions of her common existence. She was "Noble beyond degree/ In a democracy." Her attraction as a person was so great that her death has drawn her mourners into a conscious death wish. They are faced with a vision of nothingness that has abstracted them from the physical world and are "now blinded quite/ By the grave's after-light." The poet calls for some sort of resurrection, if not in fact, at least in memory, to "Restore location" to the mourners whose grief has abstracted them from the physical world:

For unless it be done
The slave heart all alone
Strives timelessly
To go where you are gone.

There has been some change in Tate's depiction of the bereaved from the mute and frightened automatons of "Death of Little Boys." These mourners are tempted not to flee death but to seek out those "regions that are fair/ Beyond heart's mastery" and "imitate mortality" in joining "before our place,/ Death's long anabasis." The military maneuver from the coast to the interior of a country is a march into the heart of darkness, but it is not man's "place" to relinquish his "living's pace," even in pursuit of the loved one ravished by death. One must continue to march, even as a member of a "blind race" of enslaved hearts, through a world of ordinary, daily actions. It is only through the evoked memory of the woman's form, as she used to stop upon the stair in a gesture of transition between high and low, that the imagination can recorporate its image of the beloved.

The ritual of the funeral is a means of bringing together the necessity of accepting the natural order of death with the need to foster the memory of the person who has died. In a unified love, both the acceptance of nature and the image of the person in memory are part of a harmonious social act. The modern, by seeing nature as a force to be conquered, has caused the beauty of the person in memory to be lost in the struggle against mortality. In "Unnatural Love," Tate argues with Shelley's contemporary Walter Savage Landor about the ability of any modern to be faithful both to nature and to art. Tate has provided an interesting commentary on his epigrammatic answer: "Landor's 'nature,' a benign and responsive mother, had undergone, since 1850, a portentous change: had changed, or been changed by man, from the

Latin *natura* (feminine noun), mother nature, into an aggressive and destructive creature so vaguely human as to cease being a *Thou* and to become an impersonal *It*." Nature, in Tate's brief poem, is turned into a rapacious *He* who rapes beauty in the person of Helen and destroys her. The shutting of Helen's eyes at the end of the poem with pennies "is a symbolic act," Tate notes, "the final shutting of the king of the senses. Beauty thus becomes blind and incapable of projecting herself upon nature, or may one say of seeing herself in nature?"[14] Helen, then, is beauty transformed into Rimbaud's "lithe corpse." The failure to maintain an understanding of the natural world has driven men to a lust for nothingness as well as a lust of power.

Nature, as both Tate and Shelley would agree in opposition to Landor, does not sustain art, beauty, or love. The natural world appears to be oblivious to the works of man. Human love, unsupported by anything other than some form of grace, cannot last long against the challenge of nature, for nature's love embraces and reduces all things back to their components. This confrontation of the force of nature and man's physical desires is the theme of all of Tate's love poems. Like "A Carrion," they all show that what was once a comfortable relationship between man and his world has turned into a hopeless struggle for survival. "The Robber Bridegroom," for example, presents a naïve girl whose marriage night will be her encounter with mortality, rather like Walter Scott's "Proud Maisie." She is warned by a bird, but she ignores its message. Nature herself offers man the evidence of his condition, but he refuses to listen.

In another poem that takes its setting from a traditional motif, the ironic love verse "Pastoral," the poet himself is poised between two views of the relationship between man and nature. The traditional pastoral world, which is friendly to man, consists of "enquiring fields, courtesies/ And tribulations of the air" that the poet asks to "be still" so that the lovers may have peace. The couple who recline in clover lie motionless. By their side is a willow tree growing on a river bank. The young man is tall and green, like the tree, and he attempts to stop time for a while with his words, "Let time be quiet as a mile" and "Time, be easy and cool." His words are like the leaf whose "light interval" rings "the deep hurrying mirror" of the river. As in Tate's earlier poem

14. Allen Tate, "A Sequence of Stanzas," in *Memoirs*, 211–12.

"Idiot," the young man tries to reduce time to space (measured as "a mile") and counter its threat with clichés: "Time is love's fool." But the river's flow is the mirror of his own natural destination in death, and the result of his meditation on time is a paralysis of the will rather than an intervention in temporality. As evening arrives, neither man nor woman—though different in their individual resolves—finds fulfillment in love:

> She, her head back waited
> Barbarous the stalking tide;
> He, nor balked nor sated
>
> But plunged into the wide
> Area of mental ire,
> Lay at her wandering side.

"Shadow and Shade" is a more difficult love poem than "Pastoral," but it recalls some of the urgency and metaphysical anguish of "To His Coy Mistress" and "Dover Beach." A paraphrase of the poem might read as follows: man attempts to overcome his fear and uncertainty through erotic passion, but passion is eventually overcome by death. Nevertheless, passion at least gives man a relief from the terrors of his isolation in the universe:

> Companion of this lust, we fall,
> I said, lest we should die alone.

If the "shade" of passion cannot extinguish, though it can disguise for a while the "shadow" of fear, it does provide a perspective from which man can view those forces that will finally "assail the wall" of his resistance to terror. Shadow and shade are the feminine and masculine forces that confront man in nature, one threatening him, the other offering relief. They are, in fact, the masculine and feminine sides of man as well, and their conjunction is both creative and destructive. Man must fall, for if he does not, he will die "alone," isolated in time and space from his own nature in a Poe-like solipsism. Better to yield to the destructive element in some form of companionship than attempt to escape it alone, Tate suggests; and like the speaker in "Dover Beach," he does not argue that love will solve all man's dilemmas but only that it will at least keep him human. To acknowledge the shadow is to confront and accept one's own human fears; in this, more than in any other of his love poems, Tate makes a clear distinction between physical lust and the personal will. A person who yields to the desire of the body has perhaps failed to resist the animal appetite, but he has stayed within the realm of nature. To seek power over nature is to be guilty of a far more serious kind of lust, even when the natural world seems as mechanical and impersonal as Arnold's grinding pebbles on the wave-torn beach.

Nevertheless, the dilemma dramatized by "The Cross" is not to be resolved by natural love. The facile vitalist philosophy that Venus represents in "Seasons of the Soul" cannot compensate for the loss of faith. Tate recognized early "that nature could not more refine/ What it had given in a looking-glass," as he puts it later in "The Buried Lake." The violence of a love without faith leads only to a terrible nihilism. Yet the buried city of the memory and the buried lake of the heart can continue to sustain the human order, even when they remain submerged. By bringing them to the surface, the imagination can begin to recover that sense of time and history which restores the understanding.

Five

The Historical Imagination

IT WAS Nietzsche, in *Beyond Good and Evil*, who first recognized that the historical sense had emerged in "the wake of . . . the democratic mingling of classes and races." As Christopher Dawson has noted, such a "distinct consciousness of the essential characteristics of different ages and civilizations" is "above all the product of the Romantic movement which first taught men to respect the diversity of human life, and to regard culture not as an abstract ideal but as the vital product of an organic social tradition."[1] It is this "sixth sense," Nietzsche maintained, to which Europeans may lay claim as their specialty, but its emergence in the nineteenth century was possible only because Western man has become, as he puts it, "a kind of chaos." As Spengler, influenced by Nietzsche, was later to show, this historical awareness is both a positive virtue and a sign of the loss of a certain order. Spengler's relativism, which some would criticize as self-contradictory, is a conscious response to this paradoxical situation. His focus is the "West-European–American" culture that he wishes to analyze in detail and whose "still untravelled stages" he attempts to predict. He is truly interested only in the Western world, the only culture of our time and on our planet which is actually in the phase of fulfillment. Therefore, when Spengler claims to have transcended the narrow limits of all previous historical points of view, he is really celebrating the historical imagination.

In an essay Tate himself cites with approval, Philip Rahv has described the historical imagination as both an "analytic instrument and a tonic resource of the modern sensibility."[2] This ambivalence is obvious

1. Christopher Dawson, "The Kingdom of God and History," in *The Dynamics of World History* (New York, 1956), 270. The citation from Nietzsche is in *Beyond Good and Evil*, # 224, in *Basic Writings*, trans. Walter Kaufmann (New York, 1968), 341–43.

2. Philip Rahv, "Art and the Historical Imagination," in *Literature and the Sixth Sense* (Boston, 1969), 360. Tate calls attention to this essay in "Is Literary Criticism Possible?" in *Essays*, p. 37, n. 3.

in Spengler, whose *Decline of the West* is therefore a vast work of fiction that asserts the reality of its claims while, at the same time, drawing attention to the limits of its point of view. It is important to recognize the peculiar position of the sixth sense between science and religion or myth, for it represents a fruitful tension between the mechanism of nature and the perspective of the self.

Tate's reflections on the historical imagination are to be found in a number of essays published between 1930 and 1940. Although he never ceased to meditate on the problem of history, this decade was one of particularly intense contemplation of its "tonic resources." It is a period that begins with Tate's contribution to the cultural criticism of *I'll Take My Stand* and ends with his call for a reassessment of the current academic approach to history and literature in "Miss Emily and the Bibliographer." It was during this time that Tate was most inclined to accept the solution to his personal dilemma that the historical imagination seemed to offer. Even in the fifties, when his perspective had changed considerably, he continued to make important statements about the need for this special talent of modern man.

The most revealing of Tate's analyses of the sixth sense is in his 1936 Phi Beta Kappa address, "What Is a Traditional Society?" In it he gives his fullest attention to the ambivalence of the historical imagination:

> I use the term [historical imagination] not in a strict sense, but in a very general sense, and perhaps in a somewhat pejorative sense. I mean that with the revival of Greek studies men in Europe began to pose as Greeks. After a couple of centuries, when the pose, too heroic to last, grew tired, they posed as Romans of the Republic. There we have a nice historical dramatization of the common sense of the eighteenth century.[3]

In an extended discussion of this phenomenon, Tate offers a broad scheme of the development of the modern mind:

> First, there is the religious imagination, which can mythologize indiscriminately history, legend, trees, the sea, animals, all being humanly dramatized, somehow converted to the nature of man. Secondly, there is the historical imagination, which is the religious imagination *manqué*—an exercise of the myth-making pro-

3. Allen Tate, "What Is a Traditional Society?" in *Essays*, 549.

> pensity of man within the restricted realm of historical event. Men see themselves in the stern light of the character of Cato, but they can no longer see themselves under the control of a tutelary deity. Cato actually lived; Apollo was merely far-darting.
>
> The third stage is the complete triumph of positivism. And with the complete triumph of positivism, in our own time, we get, in place of so workable a makeshift as the historical imagination, merely a truncation of that phrase in which the adjective has declared its independence. Under positivism we get just plain, everyday history [which] must be written by men whose minds are as little immune to prejudice as to the law of contradiction. . . . [It] is true that any sort of creative imagination is, on principle, eliminated. Yet in recognition of history's impotence to bring itself into being, the historians give us a new word: method. We live in the age of the historical method.[4]

Tate is careful to indicate that this "chart" is not history but a modest "device to ease the strain of the idea" he is delineating. What is noteworthy about it, however, is the shift Tate's thought has taken from an opposition of religion and science to an opposition of imagination and method.

Though Tate sees little possibility of restoring the mythic sense, he does defend the "makeshift" solution of the historical imagination against the pseudo solution of the scientific method applied to history. What Tate finds most objectionable about the "method" is a procrustean tendency on the part of its practitioners to study only those phenomena that fit into its categories: "The historical method then may be briefly described—by one who does not believe in its use—as the way of discovering historical 'truths' that are true in some other world than that inhabited by the historian and his fellow men: truths, in a word, that are true for the historical method." The result, Tate shows in "Miss Emily and the Bibliographer," is a total separation between the historian and the thing he studies, "for under whatever analogy we employ the historical method—organism, mechanism, causality—it has the immediate effect of removing the historian himself from history, so that he cannot participate as a living imagination." In this essay, Tate makes

4. *Ibid.*, 551–52.

an important point about the mode of historical imagination he is defending:

> We must judge the past and keep it alive by being alive ourselves; and that is to say that we must judge the past not with a method or an abstract hierarchy but with the present, or with as much of the present as our poets have succeeded in elevating to the objectivity of form. For it is through the formed, objective experience of our own time that we must approach the past; and then by means of a critical mastery of our own formed experience we may test the present and the value of form in the works of the past.

Though he speaks in this passage of the application of history to the study of poetry, Tate is also making an important point about all historical thought. The attempt to separate judgment from history through the insulation of a method or the imposition of the romantic will results in rendering the present—and hence ourselves—unimportant. Tate remarks ironically, "If we wait for history to judge [the worth of the present] there will be no judgment; for if we are not history then history is nobody."[5] The positivist historian has, through the logic of his own method, refined himself out of existence. He refuses to acknowledge the role his own imagination plays in creating the order that he is supposed to be describing "objectively."

Past and future exist only in the imagination. The attempt to make history predictive—the ideal of a scientific method—is mistaken, for, as Tate puts it, we then "ignore the present, which is momently translated into the past, and derive our standards from imaginative constructions of the future."[6] The imaginative writer, on the other hand, has a different kind of standard for judging his times, which Tate calls "a rational insight into the meaning of the present in terms of some imaginable past implicit in our own lives." The poet depends on a certain aspect of the past that he absorbs but cannot will into existence. The background on which he depends is a responsibility that he accepts; its source "lies back of the paraphernalia of culture, and not all the historical activity of an enlightened age can create it." In the paragraph follow-

5. Allen Tate, "Miss Emily and the Bibliographer," in *Essays*, 151–53.
6. Allen Tate, "Emily Dickinson," in *Essays*, 281–82.

ing this assertion, Tate makes an important statement about the way a poet perceives history:

> A culture cannot be consciously created. It is an available source of ideas that are imbedded in a complete and homogeneous society. The poet finds himself balanced upon the moment when such a world is about to fall, when it threatens to run out into looser and less self-sufficient impulses. This world order is assimilated, in Miss Dickinson, as medievalism was in Shakespeare, to the poetic vision; it is brought down from abstraction to personal sensibility.[7]

Few poets are granted this felt involvement with the past, and a realization of the consequence of historical events for the present is difficult to achieve. Yet Tate could appreciate this achievement in Shakespeare, Donne, and Dickinson because he himself had known what it means to be balanced upon a moment when "a world is about to fall."

Tate has spoken of his own personal encounter with history—the sense of separation and detachment from the past that requires an imaginative effort of identification with it—in a memoir-essay describing his first reception of the news that World War I had broken out:

> What effect could a war in Europe have on me? No more than the news of a thunderstorm over at Deer Park. I could not know that August 5, 1914, was the end of the nineteenth century, and that four years later, when I entered college, I would be in a new world so different from the old that I would never quite understand it, but would be both of it and opposed to it the rest of my life.[8]

These "four years later" are caught with hallucinatory clarity in the poem "Records," which articulates the terrible burden of the past in the face of a coming chaos.

The first section of the poem, "A Dream," tells of a child's nightmare that looks both forward and backward in time. He is at once the "man he was to be" and the "grandfather of his mother." It is a situation much like the one Tate later describes in his memoirs as "a glimpse of

7. *Ibid.*, 293–94.

8. Allen Tate, "A Lost Traveller's Dream," in *Memoirs*, 17.

the past that reversed my stance at the time it happened. Instead of looking back, I felt that I had been shifted into the past and was looking into a future that nobody but myself at the end of the eighteenth century could have seen."[9] In the poem, after a long and relentless walk along a cracked road, the "boy-man" comes to a gate and meets "a tall fat man with stringy hair." What he tells the boy is not reported, but the effect of his message is devastating.

In a letter to Tate, Davidson mentions the relationship between "Records I" and Lacy Buchan's vision in Part III of Tate's novel *The Fathers*. Though Tate's reply ("In a sense that early poem was the spring-board for The Fathers") is of interest for an interpretation of the novel, this genetic relationship reveals little about the meaning of the poem. Of greater assistance in interpreting "Records" are those essays of Tate's in which a figure similar to the "tall fat man" also appears. In a commencement address, "Several Thousand Books," Tate describes him as one of the few truly educated men he had met, a man who knew of no separation between vocation and avocation.[10] Likewise, in "What Is a Traditional Society?" he speaks of "a special tradition of realism in thinking about the nature of tradition" that was alive in Thomas Jefferson:

> The presiding spirit of that tradition was clear in his belief that the way of life and the livelihood of men must be the same; that the way we make our living must strongly affect the way of life; that our way of getting a living is not good enough if we are driven by it to pretend that it is something else; that we cannot pretend to be landed gentlemen two days of the week if we are middle-class capitalists the five others.[11]

The man who speaks from within the "dog-run country store fallen-in,/ Deserted" is both "innocent of sin" and "gravely learned." He is traditional man still residing in the wreck of traditional society but capable of seeing the coming chaos. His way of life is being destroyed, and the "man in breeches" who hears him has encountered a moment where past and future have intersected in a point of consciousness. What the sleeping boy has peered into may be a fever-provoked night-

9. *Ibid.*, 12.
10. Allen Tate, "Several Thousand Books," *Sewanee Review*, LXXV, 377–84.
11. Tate, "What Is a Traditional Society?" 547–48.

mare, but it is also "the deep coherence of hell." He has stared at the entrance to the Inferno, in the guise of a "two-barred gate" that divides the traditional past from the chaotic present and future, and has received the revelation that he is among the damned. Events beyond his knowledge and control have suddenly caught up with him as he walks back through time on "the old road cracked and burned" that leads him in his quest through a near wilderness to an image of a decrepit civilization. As he moves "steadily with discipline like fate/ Without memory, too ancient to be learned," he finds this lone survivor of a whole way of life in the wreck of the present. Something larger than the boy's personal memory has spoken to him in this dream, and its impact seems to be the result not so much of an unconscious fear as of large, uncontrollable historical forces.

The only historical event of sufficiently great impact to have occurred at the time of Tate's great-grandfather was the Civil War. In *The Fathers* the revelation Lacy Buchan receives is the secession of Virginia from the Union. In his biography of Jefferson Davis, published a few years before he wrote "Records," Tate makes an important point about the global meaning of that war:

> The War between the States has a remote origin, and it cannot be understood apart from the chief movements of European history since the Reformation. It was another war between America and Europe, and "America," in the second great attempt, won. The South was the last stronghold of European civilization in the western hemisphere, a conservative check upon the restless expansiveness of the industrial North, and the South had to go. The South was permanently old-fashioned, backward-looking, slow, contented to live upon a modest conquest of nature, unwilling to conquer the earth's resources for the fun of the conquest; contented, in short, to take only what man needs; unwilling to juggle the needs of man in the illusory pursuit of abstract wealth. . . . The War between the States was the second and decisive struggle of the Western spirit against the European—the spirit of restless aggression against a stable spirit of ordered economy—and the Western won.[12]

12. Allen Tate, *Jefferson Davis, His Rise and Fall: A Biographical Narrative* (New York, 1929), 301.

The first part of "Records," then, is a small, ailing boy's unconscious awareness of being doubly trapped in his own personal mortality and in the dying stages of Western civilization.

In the second part of the poem, which is set eleven years later (the protagonist is twenty), the record of the past returns as "A Vision." The boy is no longer "sickly"; he is "strong" and "Most fashionably dressed in the deserted park/ At midnight." Confident in himself as he returns home from seeing his "girl, who had sat silent and alone," he suddenly begins to hear "some old forgotten talk/ . . . And was afraid of all the living air." The same figure who emerged in "A Dream" now appears once more. He has grown thin, and his sight is as devastating to the protagonist as the apparition in the dream had been:

> Now between steps with one heel lifted
> A stern command froze him to the spot
> And then a tall thin man with stringy hair,
> Fear in his eyes, his breath quick and hot,
> His arms lank and his neck a little twisted,
> Spoke, and the trees sifted the air:
> "I'm growing old," he said, "you have no choice,"
> And said no more, but his bright eyes insisted
> Incalculably with his relentless voice.

The identity of the strange man is never established; but he is clearly a remnant of some dying past, a stern Virgil for this modern Dante lost in the dark forest of cultural disorder. The world has fallen twice in recent history, and the young man has been born into a dilemma that he cannot escape. The "dream" he has had is connected with the collapse of values that followed the Civil War; the "vision," with the world which fell as a result of the First World War. Impelled without choice into an era of disorder, the young man must gather up what the dying generations know and try to carry the remnants of a shattered past into the future, like Aeneas with the "old man my father" upon his back, saving only, as Tate puts it later in "Aeneas at Washington," "a mind imperishable/ If time is, a love of past things." The "tall thin man" has placed this burden on the young man's shoulders with "a stern command" that speaks both of heroic duty and tragic destiny. Whether he be a father or simply an acquaintance, his urgent insistence will not allow for personal choice or comfort, not even the consolations of female companionship. In "A Vision" Tate recognizes that romantic dreams of love and security are impossible in times of collapse. Instead of them, one must accept the responsibility of living in a disordered world and attempt to bear the essential things into the uncertain future. Among them are those truths preserved by memory and love; but the mind itself is bound to the temporal order, and love of the past is as fragile as the fading world that is its object. History appears in "Records" more as the past felt than the past understood, more as inescapable commitment than as nostalgic desire.

Tate once said that he often thought of his poems "as commentaries on those human situations from which there is no escape."[13] Tate sees the present world as suffering from a loss not only of ritual but of civic form; for "men who have lost both the higher myth of religion and the lower myth of historical dramatization have lost the forms of human action." If, as Tate claims in the "Horatian Epode," "the form requires the myth," the historical imagination is a crucial mainstay against total disorder. Yet it also represents a tacit acceptance of the condition of permanent exile. The lower myth may save men from immediate destruction, but it cannot halt the sense of distance from past and present that its very drama portends.

Tate's awareness of this dilemma separates his biographies of Stonewall Jackson (1928) and Jefferson Davis (1929)—the first a study in personal integrity, the second in personal divisiveness—from the attempted analysis of Robert E. Lee that Tate never finished. His difficulty, he wrote to John Peale Bishop in 1932, was that "the facts have got into an emotional association with a certain conception of his character which will be very difficult to break down."[14] Tate found impossible the task of presenting the facts dispassionately, not because he lacked sufficient detachment, but because his audience did. His own insights, supported by argument rather than by palpable evidence, were not adequate to overcome southern piety about Lee's valor. Bishop encouraged him to ignore this difficulty: "Proceed with your Lee! If it is not true to the facts of Lee's life, it will be true to you. And that is more important. You are, alas, a poet. . . . So, if you write the life of

13. Cited by F. O. Matthiessen, "Fragmentary and Whole," *New Republic*, CXII, 233.
14. Allen Tate to John Peale Bishop, October 19, 1932, in *Letters*, 64.

the Southerner (yourself, myself, all of us) in terms of Lee, so much more it will be than a life of Lee. I feel this now as a moral problem."[15] Despite such insistent advice, the project was dropped. Nevertheless, Bishop shrewdly pinpointed the source of the dilemma as a moral problem. Tate could not complete the biography without a proper view of the poet's responsibility to his society. If the modern southerner, a "romantic traditionist," cannot be persuaded of his historical fallacies by the poet, what serious role remains for the man of letters in the modern world?

During the thirties, even as he was probing the tragic collapse of southern culture, Tate was also seeking a means for viewing the past with detachment. The impasse that he reached in writing about Lee raised serious doubts concerning the practicality of the historical imagination as an alternative to the historical method. The first is unacceptable to the positivist because it seems to neglect the facts. Yet the champions of the second mode, in failing to see that their facts are colored by emotional associations even when they claim to be objective, are methodologically naïve. One of Tate's main criticisms of the historical method is that its practitioners fail to recognize the limits of their own point of view. Thus, because the historical method imposes a "fixed hierarchy" on all it examines, in literary studies it makes for the belief

> that the great writers of the past occupy a fixed position. If we alter the figure slightly, admitting that History has frozen their reputations, we must assume also that the position from which we look at them is likewise fixed; for if it were not we should see them in constantly changing relations and perspectives, and we should think their positions were changing too. If you will now see this same figure as a landscape of hills, trees, plains, you will quickly become fearful for the man who from a fixed point surveys the unchanging scene; for the man, the only man who cannot change his position is a dead man. . . . And so . . . we must conclude that the great authors are dead, too, because there is nobody to look at them.[16]

15. John Peale Bishop to Allen Tate, October 19–26, 1932, in *Letters*, 65.
16. Tate, "Miss Emily and the Bibliographer," 153–54.

If the great authors—or simply the great men of the past—are the figures to whom Tate is referring in "To the Romantic Traditionists," then what he is urging in all of these poems concerned with history and the imagination is the necessity for judging both past and present and constantly altering the perspective from which judgments are made.

Participation and empathy are essential tools for understanding the past. The provincial in time has no means of entering into the wholeness of past events, for the past he studies is fixed and dead, like a laboratory specimen about to be dissected. Tate accuses modern literary critics, for instance, of having never "considered critically the relation of their points of view to what they are looking at." They analyze the technique of the novelist in fine detail without reflecting on their own perspectives.

> In writing criticism they forget that they occupy "posts of observation," that they themselves are "trapped spectators." If what the novelist knows . . . is limited to what his characters see, hear, do, and think, why is the critic not similarly confined to place and moment? The answer is that he *is*. But the critic does not see himself, *his* point of view, as a variable in the historical situation that he undertakes to explain: as one motion of the history he is writing.[17]

This critique of literary methodology is obviously congruent with Tate's complaints against the historical method. For all its makeshift nature and inadequacies, the historical imagination is preferable to historical positivism because it emphasizes the narrative character of history. The writing of history, like the writing of a novel, is the creating of a story through the use of symbols and analogies. Submerging or neglecting their presence does not change the fact of their existence in all coherent narrative.

This awareness of point of view is what Tate means by "relativism," and he praises historian Carl Becker's *The Heavenly City of the Eighteenth-Century Philosophers* for its awareness of point of view as well as for its urbanity of style.[18] Now Becker was something of a pioneer in the development of the relativistic approach to the writing of history; his

17. Allen Tate, "Modern Poetry," in *Essays*, 213.
18. Tate, "Miss Emily and the Bibliographer," 150–51.

earliest essay expounding the author's overt recognition of his own perspective dates from 1910. Relativism is central to the historical imagination, for total detachment from the conditions of time and space that govern the historian is impossible. Even Spengler sees the detachment he adopts in the development of his grand cyclical theory as a characteristic aspect of his own Faustian point of view.

It may come as a surprise, after all that has been said of Tate's concern with value and judgment in history, to find him ranked among the relativists, but his statements about his own position are unambiguous. In an essay on the work of Donald Davidson, Tate distinguishes his attitude toward history from that of his old friend and fellow Fugitive-Agrarian: "The region that Mr. Davidson occupies, and that I do not see myself in, is one in which historical relativity seems to have little play."[19] He goes on to speak of his own "relativism—historical only, not philosophical and moral"—in terms that can leave no doubt.

By taking his own point of view into account, the knower acknowledges his essential condition as time-bound, and he comes to see that poetry and the imagination, far from avoiding temporality, plunge one more deeply into it. The twenties and thirties were filled with speculation and discussion about time and space. Besides Einstein's momentous contributions, there were the philosophies of Bergson, Whitehead, Husserl, and the young Heidegger. Wyndham Lewis was driven to devote a rather polemical book, *Time and Western Man*, to what he considered a widespread modern obsession. Tate, as we have seen, was no stranger to these topics.

Typical of the literary preoccupation with time and space is an essay by Charles Mauron that T. S. Eliot translated and published in the *Criterion* in 1930. Tate probably saw it, for he was both a contributor to and avid reader of Eliot's quarterly at this time; but even if he did not, Charles Mauron's reflections on the impact of Einstein's theories are relevant to the concept of historical relativism and imagination. Mauron begins by distinguishing two modes of understanding, one which "holds that any profound knowledge of any reality, implies an intimate fusion of the mind with that reality; we only understand a thing in becoming it, in living it"; and a second, which "holds that this mystical knowledge is meaningless, that to try to reach a reality in itself is vain, in-

19. Allen Tate, "The Gaze Past, the Glance Present," in *Memoirs*, 36–37.

asmuch as our mind can conceive nothing but relations and systems of relations."[20] Mauron notes that both types of knowledge are still in coexistence, but constantly confused in everyday thinking, "which as a matter of fact is nothing but a muddle of the two kinds of knowledge."

The two modes may be identified with the temporal and spatial or intuitive and analytic ways of approaching reality. They are like Tate's historical imagination and historical method. Mauron emphasizes the necessity of recognizing which point of view is truly one's own. He offers an example:

> When I say, "I know this path well," that evidently means that I know ahead all its twists and turnings, that, if asked, I can even sketch a map more or less in detail. But after sketching this map, I am well aware that I have not told all I know about that path: within myself I have my own impression, personal, useless, and incommunicable; and this impression also went to the making of my phrase, "I know this path well."

By coincidence, Tate uses the same image in a poem written several years later. In "The Trout Map" he dramatizes the modern attempt to live the present as though the future were assured by a plan as abstract as a chart.

Fishing is a familiar analogy for the search after knowledge, and the protagonists of the fishing adventure in this poem are intellectuals. Maps are predictive devices, corresponding to Mauron's second mode of knowledge—they tell one what to expect. They do not offer images of things in space but relationships between boundaries. By divorcing the experience of space from the desire for fish, the map creates a kind of "positivistic" sportsmanship. Now though the scientist often thinks in as intuitive a fashion as the poet, what he seeks to know is not the same. The irony in "The Trout Map" is that the intellectual fishermen are attempting to turn recreation into an exact science.

> The Management Area of Cherokee
> National Forest, interested in fish,
> Has mapped Tellico and Bald Rivers
> And North River, with the tributaries
> Brookshire Branch and Sugar Cove Creek.

20. Charles Mauron, "On Reading Einstein," *Criterion*, X, 24–25.

But is fishing like scientific discovery? Can one predict when and where he will make a catch? The attempt to offer rules for catching fish produces a "fishy map for facile fishery/ In Marvel's kind Ocean." Tate is referring to Andrew Marvell's "Mind, that ocean where each kind/ Doth straight its own resemblance find," but the spelling of the poet's name with one "l" also suggests that this is a fairyland body of wondrous waters, a fisherman's dream of fulfilling his desire for unlimited catches. Perhaps "kind" is also a pun, implying that the mind both contains an ocean of types and is also unduly flattering for man's hopes. For the most part, Tate is posing an unstated question: "Can intuition and opportunity be mapped?"

For much of their journey, the fishermen hold "map and scene" to be "one/ In seen-identity." However, the correspondence between them is purely visual, and there is little visual about the catching of fish. The eye and the foot are dissociated by the map. The foot is led one way by the actual road, but the eye is deceived into a different route by the map:

> The river, right, tumbled into a cove;
> But the map dashed the road along the stream
> And we dotted man's fishiest enthymeme
> With jellied feet upon understanding love
> Of what eyes see not, that nourishes the will.

What eye has not seen, in St. Paul's words, must be taken upon faith or known through Mauron's first kind of knowledge. An enthymeme suppresses or merely implies one of the conditions or the conclusion in an argument. The fishers believe in their knowledge of the way fish are caught, but they have gone wrong in trying "to fish/ The egoed belly's dry cartograph." The mind and the personal will have obscured what the heart knows. There is no water on a map, and the fish that are charted by it are virtually in the employ of the government which assigns them their places. The artificiality of the situation, with its predictive measurements, suggests a hoax or charade. The fish know their element better than government or fishermen with their abstractions can ever fathom. They "lie down and laugh" at the plight of the lost sportsmen.

Though the poem is about the modern will and man's attempt to support his "understanding love" with "jellied feet," it concerns more than the attempt to engineer the fisherman's dream. It is about the historical exploration of the world. Water is represented on the map

in two
Colors, blue and red—blue for the hue
Of Europe (Tennessee water is green),
Red lines by blue streams to warn
The fancy-fishmen from protected fish;
Black borders hold the Area in a cracked dish,
While other blacks, the dots and dashes, wire
The fisher's will through classic laurel. . . .

The poem ends with two images: Magellan "idling with his fates" as he explores the unknown world, and the angel from *Paradise Lost* who slides down a sunbeam to visit the "new world." The map divides the will from memory and understanding, America from Europe. It falsifies the cultural past by imposing the blue waters of European tradition on the green (and hence fresh or new) waters of Tennessee. The fishmen are fancy or precious intellectuals trying to use the latest scientific knowledge for up to date angling, but they are also fishing only in the fancy. The "mapless" mountains that the lost fishermen face at the end of the poem leave them confronted with a sightless world that is all "dream." They have lost both the ability to use the map and the skill of their own intuition.

By mistaking one kind of knowledge for the other, the predictive for the dream, modern man has lost all ability to know reality. As Mauron puts it,

> A man of science who has dreams at night and who spends his days in writing out chemical equations will tell you that the equations are *true* and the dreams illusory, and on that point he will be wholly in accord with his doctrine; but he will admit, nevertheless, that the dreams give him a much stronger impression of reality than the formulae; for the latter are relations which may well serve for prediction, but have not, like dreams or any other sensation, the flavour of immediate experience.[21]

If history has any meaning, it lies in this "immediate experience" and not some set of predictive formulae. Such an order can be lived

21. *Ibid.*, 25–26.

through, but it cannot be charted or visited by a "mind with tidy scorn." An attempt to codify it will lead, like the trout map, to disorder and directionlessness. "The Trout Map" presents two ways of approaching the knowable: through acceptance of the past, with all its imperfections, from the standpoint of men living in the present; or through "methods" that are supposed to refine and improve it to a schematic and bloodless ideal.

In "Religion and the Old South," an essay published in the same year as Mauron's, Tate calls these two ways of looking at history the "Short View" and the "Long View." The first mode envisions "a concrete series that has taken place in a very real time . . . a time as sensible, as full of sensation, and as replete with accident and uncertainty as the time they themselves are living in, moment by moment." The second has as its model "the physicist's concept of natural law. There is then ideally no accident or contingency; for accident and contingency are names for our insufficient information."[22]

Tate's most complete examination of the historical imagination, its dangers as well as its positive uses, is not in his poetry or criticism but in his single novel *The Fathers*. Though aspects of it have already been discussed and a full analysis would be out of place here, some further account of the book as a reflection on history is important; for this story of a young man who witnesses the collapse of a civilization comes closest to answering Tate's urgent questions about the proper kind of action to take in a period of crisis. The narrator, Lacy Buchan, thrown from the familiarity of a personal but highly formal world into the alienation of an abstract and chaotic one, asks himself:

> Is it not something to tell, when a score of people whom I knew and loved, people beyond whose lives I could imagine no other life, either out of violence in themselves or the times, or out of some misery or shame, scattered into the new life of the modern age where they cannot even find themselves? Why cannot life change without tangling the lives of innocent persons? Why do innocent persons cease their innocence and become violent and evil in themselves that such great changes may take place?[23]

22. Allen Tate, "Religion and the Old South," in *Essays*, 563–64.
23. Allen Tate, *The Fathers*, 5. Subsequent page references are given in the text.

The novel is about the collapse of a civilization and its reflected consequences in the lives of two families, the Buchans and the Poseys. The narrator points out that "excessively refined persons have a communion with the abyss; but is not civilization the agreement, slowly arrived at, to let the abyss alone?" The excessively refined Buchans, no less than the grotesquely isolated Poseys, are representatives of a society that has lost the balanced conventions of a stable order.

The novel, divided into three sections ("Pleasant Hill," "The Crisis," "The Abyss"), shows the effects of attempting to confront the abyss directly rather than seek detachment from it. It shares, as has already been noted, various scenes, images, and motifs with Tate's verse. The Posey mansion, where everyone resides in a separate compartment behind closed doors, casts back to the scene in "A Pauper" and forward to the empty hall of "Autumn." Many of Lacy Buchan's comments are paralleled by passages in the author's prose essays, though one can never say for sure that the fictional character is a totally reliable representation of Tate's point of view. Yet even after making allowances for the dramatic setting of these utterances, one finds in them important reflections on history that are surely consonant with the larger implications of Tate's work. What Lacy possesses to a high degree is not simply a historical imagination but an awareness of the need to transcend it.

Lacy Buchan is not, then, simply the point of view of the novel. He is also conscious, as the good historian must be, of his own post of observation:

> In my feelings of that time there is a new element—my feelings now about that time: there is not an old man living who can recover the emotions of the past; he can only bring back the objects around which, secretly, the emotions have ordered themselves in memory, and that memory is not what happened in the year 1860 but is rather a few symbols, a voice, a tree, a gun shining on the wall—symbols that will preserve only so much of the old life as they may, in their own mysterious history, consent to bear. (p. 22)

In this passage the narrator touches on the essential shaping power of memory. One does not choose what one remembers; the "few symbols" remaining long after the event preserve only that part of the past still truly significant for the present. These images are separate from, occasionally opposed to, the will of the person who benefits from their illumination. In a later passage, Lacy recognizes the concrete, almost autonomous nature of what is given in remembrance: "Memory is all chance, and I have learned that you remember things not because they are important; you remember the important things because they help you to fix in mind the trifles of your early life, or the trifles simply drag along with them through many years the incidents that have altered your fortunes" (p. 131). Thus memory offers judgments of its own, more fully shaped than anything the conscious mind can impose. Lacy speaks of "scenes that last a lifetime and remain the keys to the mystery of life: this was one of them but it survives for me through no act of understanding on my part, no judgment of motives. The meaning of what happens to us is never a phrase but lies rather in its own completeness" (p. 93).

So it is that memory serves to offer a sense of direction in life that the "ceaseless flow" of time does not in itself provide. Lacy Buchan has moved a step beyond the protagonist of "Ode to the Confederate Dead" when he senses that, in his mother's death,

> the moment had come that all this waiting had been for, but it was lost in each new movement, each new step into our places in the melancholy procession. There was of course no one moment that it was all leading up to, and that piece of knowledge about life, learned that day, has permitted me to survive the disasters that overwhelmed other and better men, and to tell their story. Not even death was an instant; it too became part of the ceaseless flow, instructing me to beware of fixing any hope, or some terrible lack of it, upon birth or death, or upon love of the giving in marriage. None of these could draw to itself all the life around it or even all the life in one person; not one of them but fell short of its occasion, warning us all to fear, not death, or love, or any ecstasy or calamity, but rather to fear our own expectancy of it, good or ill, or our own lack of preparation for these final things. (p. 101)

This relativistic meditation on time and memory sums up almost all that Lacy learns about life. Though it is a negative lesson, it marks a necessary stage in the movement away from hope in history to faith in a supratemporal reality.

The narrator of *The Fathers* intuits that history has some kind of direction, even if it is not usefully knowable. He observes that "omens are those signals of futurity that we recognize when the future has already slid into the past"—in other words, after they are too late to be of use. Lacy learns how to act not through an abstract moral system but through meditation on the real, seemingly arbitrary events preserved in his personal memory and shaped by his imagination. What emerges is a larger pattern of importance beyond himself and the immediate present. Meaning is inherent in events, though they are independent of any man's will and endowed with an obscure purpose that is clarified only sporadically and without any warning by a sudden symbolic revelation.

The Buchans are characterized by their utter lack of historical imagination. Lacy alone achieves this "Short View" by being plunged into a crisis-ridden world and by coming to know George Posey. He is the only family member to survive. His sister is driven mad by the crisis; for, as he says, "people living in formal societies, lacking the historical imagination, can imagine for themselves only a timeless existence: they themselves never had any origin anywhere and they can have no end, but will go on forever" (p. 183). George Posey, at the other extreme, is an alien from any society. The typical modern who exists without the buffer zone of manners and civilization between himself and mortality, he is "a man who received the shock of the world at the end of his nerves" (p. 185). His marriage to Lacy's sister is symbolic of the clash that destroyed the old South.

What Lacy has to learn is how to sort out the inextricably mixed modes of good and evil in the world, judge them, and contrive to live properly in their midst. In "all highly developed societies," he tells the reader, "the line marking off the domestic from the public life was indistinct" (p. 125). But "the belief widely held today, that men may live apart from the political order, that indeed the only humane and honorable satisfactions must be gained in spite of the public order," is a Manichean rejection of the mixed condition of human life. Lacy's understanding is neither bound by the formal timelessness of his father's world nor subject to the excessively personal sensibility of the Poseys. In his situation he does not remain aloof but does all he can in an age of chaotic transition. He fights not for his father's cause but for a specific place that is part of his "individual quality." He chooses to act, acknowledging all the consequences of his participation in a morally ambiguous war. Unlike either his father or his brother-in-law, he has a true historical imagination, capable of detachment that allows him to control his life. His attitude toward history is totally unlike the Poe-like romanticism of Mr. Jarman, the Poseys' strange boarder who is "engaged upon a most interesting and illuminating work, the most ambitious work of the imagination." For Jarman is attempting to write "nothing less than a history of the struggle of man to build civilization upon the sterile wastes of the earth after the ice age" (p. 234). Death, for him, is "the sunderer, or time, or our enemy," but remains abstract in all its guises. Jarman is the intellectual counterpart of George Posey, clothed in the pretensions of both the romantic traditionist and the historical methodologist.

But if Lacy, in learning to cope with the catastrophes of a declining world, is the main protagonist of *The Fathers* as well as its narrator, he is nevertheless incomplete and has the honesty to recognize his own limitations. He is confined within what he calls his "Protestant ignorance of the mysterious Church that never changed for peace or war" (p. 196) and thus kept from going beyond the handful of symbols his memory can offer. A good man, he is like all moderns in being cut off from the truly mythical order that leads to transcendence. He thinks of the convent to which the unfortunate Jane is sent as a place for hiding one's sins and worldly disgrace. Yet he does begin at last to grasp what Father Monahan means when he says, "We've got to keep life simple. That is a practical reason for saving the human soul" (p. 236). Though attachment to place is a valuable means of keeping life simple, in the modern world such a choice is seldom available.

Nine years before publishing *The Fathers*, Tate wrote to Donald Davidson:

> All places are equally the wrong places. We are all at present doomed to live a harrowing life, and it may or may not be more harrowing than the lives of all men everywhere who have tried to find some ultimate discipline of the soul. It was just as hard to attain to salvation in the 13th century as it is now (perhaps harder), although the results of the quest in literature were grander and more coherent. That was largely because salvation was common, not personal.[24]

24. Allen Tate to Donald Davidson, February 18, 1929, in *Correspondence*, 223.

Though skeptical about the modern's ability to find an answer to his questions in a historic community, Tate was like his character Lacy Buchan in being equally skeptical of the things of the world. In his tribute to Davidson some twenty-five years after *The Fathers*, Tate saw his old friend as still limited by a trust in events: "Mr. Davidson long ago put his faith in history, and history in 1865 grievously let him down."

For Tate, however, the defeat of the South was a triumph of sorts, for "the South has enjoyed a longer period of identity in defeat than it might have been able to preserve in victory."[25] Only that aspect of the South which has remained present through a few symbols in the memory is very important. From that base alone can anything be constructed for the future. As early as 1936 Tate responded to the attacks of a Marxist journalist by asserting, "I do not want to restore the Middle Ages. I do not want to restore any previous age. I do not want to restore anything whatsoever. It is our task to create something."[26] A few weeks later, in his Phi Beta Kappa address at the University of Virginia, he extends this idea: "To revive something is to hasten its destruction—if it is only picturesquely and not sufficiently revived. For the moment the past becomes picturesque it is dead."[27]

By embracing historical relativism, Tate was assuming a stance toward the past that was consonant with the temper of his times without yielding to its more virulent fashions, for he recognized from the start that relativism is a dead end. Spengler's perspective, for instance, might satisfy secular man's longing for an ultimate order, but his large historical scheme is rather a parody than a substitute for a true teleology. Erich Heller has judged *The Decline of the West* sympathetically but severely:

> The image of man which lurks behind Spengler's vast historical canvas is perverted, and could only be accepted by a hopelessly perverted age. For Spengler has no idea of the true stature of the problem of human freedom. Therefore his historical vision is lacking in depth as well as in love, pity, and pathos. It is a worth-

25. Tate, "The Gaze Past, the Glance Present," 37.

26. Allen Tate, "Correspondence: Fascism and the Southern Agrarians," *New Republic*, LXXXVII, 75.

27. Tate, "What Is a Traditional Society?" 548.

> less and deeply untruthful sort of history which lacks these qualities, for they are the proper tools of human understanding.[28]

Tate understood this failure in Spengler, even as he must have recognized his philosophy of history as one of the great monuments of the historical imagination. For if nothing else, *Decline of the West* is "the massive concretization of a state of mind," as Stuart Hughes has said.

> It is as symptom, as synthesis, as symbol of a whole age that Spengler's book remains one of the major works of our century. . . . It formulates more comprehensively than any other single book the modern *malaise* that so many feel and so few can express. It has become the classic summary of the now familiar pessimism of the twentieth-century West with regard to its own historical future.[29]

In such a climate of opinion as Hughes sees reflected in *Decline of the West*, Tate could seek only two alternatives, neither satisfactory. In attempting to go beyond the limitations of the historical imagination, he could regress and become a romantic traditionist or try to move forward to some liberal scheme of social progress. Yet he knew from the beginning that neither alternative was satisfactory. To restore a picturesque medieval civilization was impossible and perhaps even, as an economic ploy, undesirable. In contrast, to adopt a liberal scheme of historical progress was hopelessly naïve. In the conclusion to "What Is a Traditional Society?" Tate recognizes the futility of any action not grounded in the world as we know it: "The higher myth of religion, the lower myth of history, even ordinary codes of conduct, cannot preserve themselves; indeed they do not exist apart from our experience. Since the most significant feature of our experience is the way we make our living, the economic basis of life is the soil out of which all the forms, good or bad, of our experience must come."[30]

The revival of the past, even through the refinements of the histori-

28. Erich Heller, "Oswald Spengler and the Predicament of the Historical Imagination," in *The Disinherited Mind* (New York, 1959), 193.

29. H. Stuart Hughes, *Oswald Spengler: A Critical Estimate*, (rev. ed.; New York, 1962), 164–65.

30. Tate, "What Is a Traditional Society?" 557.

cal imagination or a lower mythology, is a project doomed to failure. The simple adoption of the key beliefs of an epoch can hardly bring an entire culture back into existence. Tate's involvement with Agrarianism, as idealistic as it may have seemed, was a concern with physical means, not simply with lofty ideals. But Tate refused to rest even in the congenial doctrines of *I'll Take My Stand*. He knew that some truly vital model must be found for human action in a lost and declining age. In later years Tate wrote to Donald Davidson about their convictions of the late twenties, when they attacked modernism and "never got much further than Nostalgia because no historic faith came into consideration. . . . We were trying to find a religion in the secular, historical experience as such, particularly in the Old South. I would now go further . . . and say we were idolaters. But it is better to be an idolater than to worship nothing, and as far as our old religion went I still believe in it."[31] A historian whom Tate came to appreciate in later years, Christopher Dawson, has summed up the inadequacy of this "worship" in a single phrase: "If we rely on history alone we can never hope to transcend the sphere of relativity; it is only in religion and metaphysics that we can find truths that claim absolute and eternal validity."[32] Tate came to see himself as a "trapped spectator," limited by his "post of observation" like the narrator of a Henry James novel. Paradoxically, he was led to this awareness by his own highly developed historical imagination and was made to see, through it, the irreplaceable role played by a "historic faith."

31. Allen Tate to Donald Davidson, January 14, 1953, in *Correspondence*, 370.
32. Dawson, "The Kingdom of God and History," 273.

Six

The Augustinian Perspective

AT THE END of "Seasons of the Soul," Tate announces a stunning shift in perspective. Alluding to the famous scene in *The Confessions*, he imagines that St. Augustine and his mother have directed their gaze out the garden window at Ostia across fifteen centuries to the disorder of the modern world. In the concluding verses of the poem, he attempts to summon up a new beginning for a dying civilization. This new beginning is based on meditative silence, not on political upheaval or some hope for a return to the tranquillity of past eras. The changes that must occur, if the world is to be saved, will take place in the souls of individuals rather than in institutions. Tate has abandoned all notions of saving society by any means other than spiritual. The shift, moreover, is definitive. Henceforth, Tate's imaginative order is Augustinian in its essential nature.

Though Tate was to spend five more years bringing his new vision to fulfillment, he had already, in his previous work, laid the groundwork for a higher order of comprehension. The *via negativa* he followed in poem after poem rejecting the facile or misdirected solutions of his contemporaries allowed Tate to identify his goal with unusual clarity. It was entirely appropriate that he should turn, in mid-career, to the example of Augustine, for this great thinker had followed much the same path before his conversion as had the young Tate. More significant than this slight biographical parallel, however, is the order of Augustine's achievement. As the author of one of the foremost books on culture and history and the creator of the genre of confession, Augustine presents an historically accessible example of a man who, by speaking out and embodying his imaginative insights in masterful prose, brought the personal and cosmic realms into intimate conjunction. In addition, his main themes are Tate's as well. The inadequacy of makeshift conceptions of history, the chaos of a collapsing empire, the romanticism of a fading pagan culture, the loss of point of view, and the selfish willfulness of an increasingly desperate people—all are characteristic of both late antiquity and the world of late modernity into which Tate was born.

It is curious that the West has many examples of great eras, but only one prominent instance of decline. It is the fall of Rome that has most excited the historical imagination of Western man when he thinks of the ultimate catastrophe that can befall a civilization. Augustine's powerful impact can be traced in part to his way of responding to a historical moment that continues to haunt the modern world. R. H. Barrow has described this aspect of his achievement with admirable clarity:

> The world in which St. Augustine published his *De Civitate Dei* was a world disillusioned and bewildered and haunted by fears and uncertainties. It clung passionately to the past, for only the past offered any sure foothold in a changing world. Accepted values were challenged; institutions were tottering; yet the belief rightly dominated men's minds that in the values of the past lay a wealth of effort and achievement which was of vital and permanent significance. With this belief St. Augustine was in profound agreement; he did not propose a clean break. But he read history differently. . . . History could be read aright only by the standards of Christian insight into values. Thus read, history gave no support to despair; sure confidence awaited those who had the eyes to see.[1]

Augustine forged out of his historical moment a vision of things that was not simply a response to his own times but a far-reaching program for the future. In finding solutions to his personal problems, he showed how men can build a life that is not a nostalgic restoration of a fading past but a genuinely new kind of existence that draws on yet does not fear to leave behind what is dying. Augustine did not hesitate to accept the decline of Roman civilization. His version of history was written out of a sweeping imagination that was capable of engaging the past in argument and dialectic as though it were still present. Certainly he did

1. R. H. Barrow, *Introduction to St. Augustine, "The City of God," Being Selections from the "De Civitate Dei" Including Most of XIXth Book with Text, Translation and Running Commentary* (London, 1950), 260.

not view the past as irrelevant to the world of the living, but he was unwilling to sustain the memory of events for the sake of a purely antiquarian passion. Arnaldo Momigliano has shown that pagan historians, like their modern counterparts, "were not concerned with ultimate values in their elementary teaching. Their main concern was to keep alive a knowledge of the Roman past."[2] The Christian historians of Augustine's era "could not avoid touching upon the essentials of the destiny of man. The convert, in abandoning paganism, was compelled to enlarge his historical horizon: he was likely to think for the first time in terms of universal history." Augustine saw the antiquarian approach to history as irrelevant to life, as devoid of significance because it seals off the past from the present. By refusing to take on a perspective larger than that of the events which they recounted, the pagan historians trapped themselves within their own times; they embraced the very historical "provincialism" that, according to R. A. Markus, Augustine saw as "the mark of a world in which there is *nihil solidum*, *nihil stabile*."[3] The pagan antiquarian, then, may be considered as both a kind of "romantic traditionist" and a precursor of the modern positivist, skeptical about ultimate values and locked into a nostalgia for Rome's past glories. Sophisticated and cosmopolitan, the Roman historian was nevertheless a provincial in time.

The starting point of Augustinian thought is not in this tenuous realm of historicity but in the immediate truths that are evident to the self. Yet this point of departure is far from being a solipsistic rejection of the world and experience; it is rather a radically new acknowledgment of the role that perception plays in reality as man knows it. By recognizing the limits of one's own viewpoint as a human being, one is forced to acknowledge an incompleteness and dependence. In *The Confessions* Augustine is constantly contrasting his present understanding with his blindness in the past, the narrowness of his knowledge with the omniscience of a God who alone is beyond all point of view. This dual perspective is dramatized frequently in the narrative of his life. Augustine sees himself as an erring youth in the past, as a more know-

2. Arnaldo Momigliano, "Pagan and Christian Historiography in the Fourth Century A.D.," in *The Conflict Between Paganism and Christianity in the Fourth Century*, ed. Arnaldo Momigliano (Oxford, 1963), 83–85.

3. R. A. Markus, *Saeculum: History and Society in the Theology of St. Augustine* (Cambridge, 1970), 10.

ing but no less fallible person in the present, and as an object of God's plan in the future.

Point of view and the consciousness of self in Augustine's writings are closely linked with a sense of time and history. He was the first thinker in the West "to discover the meaning of time . . . to take time seriously," according to Herman Hausheer.[4] The Greeks thought of time as cyclical, objectivized in space by the rotation of the planets and stars. But Augustine was original in analyzing time as perception and progression: "It is in thee, my mind, that I measure times . . . the impression, which things as they pass by cause in thee, remains even when they are gone; this it is which still present, I measure, not the things which pass by to make this impression." The measurement of time is possible because experiences are remembered as actions with beginnings and ends. Memory and the present act of attention are the key to man's perception of time. Thus it is the poem, rather than moving bodies or a fixed point in space, that embodies the structure of time within itself and shows that time can be measured without resort to physical means. In the course of reciting a psalm, one has a memory of what has been repeated and an expectation as to what will be repeated. Furthermore, "this which takes place in the whole Psalm, the same takes place in each several portion of it, and each several syllable." But the recitation is itself but a portion of history, and so "the same holds in the whole life of man, whereof all the actions of man are parts; the same holds through the whole age of the sons of men, whereof all the lives of men are parts."[5] This example demonstrates the ease with which Augustine moves from personal experience to history, from perception to order. As a possessor of a point of view, man shares his perspective with the universe of which he is a part. Joseph A. Mazzeo has pointed out that time occupies a special position in Augustine's philosophy: "Time is more of an image of eternity than space. Further, it is a kind of distension of the soul, its very dimension of life." Thus for Augustine, "memory is not of the past but is synonymous with the divine, present within, the inner teacher."[6]

4. Herman Hausheer, "St. Augustine's Conception of Time," *Philosophical Review*, XLVI, 512.

5. Saint Augustine, *The Confessions*, trans. Edward B. Pusey (New York, 1949), 267.

6. Joseph A. Mazzeo, "St. Augustine's Rhetoric of Silence: Truth vs. Eloquence and Things vs. Signs," in *Renaissance and Seventeenth-Century Studies* (New York, 1968), 27.

The importance to both Augustine and Tate of these common themes of time, memory, and perception is considerable, but they constitute a point of departure, not of conclusion. Their ramifications extend to include further theories of civilization, history, and the structure of the soul. Augustine's famous concept of the two cities, for instance, begins not with a reflection on past cultures but with mental experiences. Both reside in the present, but the City of Man exists above all as a rhythm in the memory and the City of God as an image of things unseen but hoped for. They meet in every individual, where their conflict is played out in terms of the bonds of love. At the center of Augustine's philosophy—and Tate's poetry—is the conviction that what is to be transformed is the individual rather than the mass of men. Yet only by transcending himself and his personal will can the individual be transformed. He does so not by absolutely rejecting the one and embracing the other but by recognizing their proper order. R. H. Barrow points out that Augustine "did not parcel out man's world between Church and State. He did not counsel men to escape from the realities of this world into a dream existence or to turn their backs upon the responsibilities of daily life in pursuit of a fugitive otherworldliness." Instead, he urged men to "recognise a higher loyalty which should inform the manner of the discharge of lesser loyalties."[7]

Barrow goes on to show that Augustine did not invent the notion of this double allegiance, though his contribution to it was certainly original. It is to be found in the writings of Plato, Zeno, Marcus Aurelius, and Cicero. Nevertheless, the difference between the "City of Zeus" they describe and Augustine's City of God is paramount, for the Augustinian city is accessible to all mankind through love and not restricted to the few who can attain it through knowledge or philosophy. Augustine's citizen belongs to this higher community because he clings to God through a will to do good. Not self-sufficiency or sophrosyne but a confession of utter dependence upon the divine will admits man to its membership. In Book XV, Chapter 2 of *The City of God*, this deep relationship of the two cities is explored:

> One portion of the earthly city became an image of the heavenly city, not having a significance of its own, but signifying another city, and therefore serving, or "being in bondage." For it was

7. Barrow, *Introduction to St. Augustine*, 261.

> founded not for its own sake, but to prefigure another city; and this shadow of a city was also itself foreshadowed by another preceding figure. . . . In the earthly city, then, we find two things—its own obvious presence, and its symbolic presentation of the heavenly city. Now citizens are begotten to the earthly city by nature vitiated by sin, but to the heavenly city by grace freeing nature from sin.[8]

The earthly city is both foreshadowing of and antitype to the heavenly city. It is not to be rejected totally, for it is a symbol that is the means by which the heavenly city is revealed. Yet it exists not in and for itself alone. When man recognizes only one city, he has mistaken the letter for the spirit.

In the late twenties Tate recognized a similar duality in his identification of the archetype of the city residing in "the heaven of man's mind" and his awareness of the "buried city" of the memory. Nevertheless, they are not opposed as are Augustine's two cities, for neither is simply to be identified with the City of Man or the City of God. The real opposition is between these two imaginative images of the city and the modern technological metropolis. Whether it be thought of as paradigmatic community or as buried culture, the poet's version of the City of God is present in Tate's work from beginning to end. He speaks of it movingly in one of his last prose essays, "A Lost Traveller's Dream": "The imaginative writer is the archeologist of memory, dedicated to the minute particulars of the past, definite things—*prima sacramenti memoria*. If his 'city' is to come alive again from a handful of shards, he will try to fit them together in an elusive jigsaw puzzle, most of the pieces of which are forever lost."[9] Tate's use of an Augustinian phrase—"The first remembrance of the mystery"—clarifies the relationship between the buried city and Augustine's heavenly city. The shards of the past are both remembrances and foreshadowings of the community that resides in human hope and the spirit, the "sacrament" of communion in a society.

Tate's "buried city" is the precursor, then, of the heavenly city, much as Virgil's Rome is the prefiguration, to some extent, of Augustine's heavenly Jerusalem as goal and image of divinely ordained

8. Saint Augustine, *The City of God*, trans. Marcus Dods (New York, 1950), 480.
9. Allen Tate, "A Lost Traveller's Dream," in *Memoirs*, 12.

community. Indeed, Tate honors Virgil often in his poems and sees him as a great mentor who was the first European to understand the basic actions that underlie the two cities. In an essay on "The Pietas of Southern Poetry," Louise Cowan has emphasized the Virgilian basis of the southern myth of order. She speaks of the southerner's ability to

> find in *The Aeneid* a correlative for the Southern situation. Just as Aeneas and his men thought of themselves as Trojans all the more as they were forced to leave their burning homes, so the Southerners identified themselves in the instance of defeat. But, as Aeneas's concern was more with continuity than with the ashes of the old Troy, similarly, the impelling quest of which Davidson speaks is the joint enterprise of "building a city." . . . If we explore the indicated parallel further, we shall recall that Aeneas's mission was not only to found a city but to introduce his gods into Latium. At the base of the Trojan—and Southern—attitude toward history, we see, was a sense of sacredness connected with their cultural traditions, those local and familiar manifestations of the universal and mysterious.[10]

This reverence, which the Romans called *pietas*, is not to be confused with "the pietism by which a given society equates itself with the kingdom of God," she claims. It is a respect for those things which must be preserved and fostered as part of a community.

There is, however, another side of Virgil's achievement that must also be taken into account. St. Augustine recognized in Virgil's poem the dedication to a goal higher than oneself which leads Aeneas to found a new city. Virgil, Augustine, and Dante are the major sources for an understanding of the two cities. As John O'Meara has rightly pointed out, the Christian saint and the pagan poet are the great twin sources of the mainstream of Western culture:

> Augustine shares from time to time with Vergil the title of "Father of the West"—but Augustine's must surely be the greater claim. He was, of course, himself profoundly affected by Vergil. In the pages of Vergil's *Aeneid* he had learned of Love and Mis-

10. Louise Cowan, "The *Pietas* of Southern Poetry," in *South: Modern Southern Literature in Its Cultural Setting*, ed. Louis D. Rubin, Jr., and Robert D. Jacobs (Garden City, N.Y., 1961), 98.

> sion—of Dido and Aeneas. The struggle in the heart of Vergil was the struggle in the heart of Augustine: love appeared to be the only and all-conquering value. It was also self-indulgent and destructive. Duty must transcend it—obedience to God and the service of his purpose with mankind. Augustine shows all the passion of Dido and all the temptations to weakness of Aeneas. But he follows Aeneas, and consciously. . . . This was an intellectual struggle for Vergil. It was "real" for the character Aeneas. It was real also for Augustine.[11]

In all his writings, Augustine remains more affectionate toward Virgil than toward Rome itself. If Rome has often been characterized by the appetites proper to the City of Man, Virgil has shown that there were higher impulses at work in its founding.

The other side of Virgil's achievement in the light of Augustine's transformation is carried on by Dante. However, as Christopher Dawson has pointed out, "Dante's view of the Empire is entirely opposed to that of St. Augustine."[12] For the medieval poet, Virgil is the co-founder of the unified world that has become Christendom. Dante's is the ideal of an earthly city that has been transformed by faith, and Virgil himself is honored in *The Divine Comedy* as the bearer of a magnificent tradition, a pagan Moses who could enjoy a Pisgah-sight of the new era he had foretold in his Fourth Eclogue but who had to remain behind in Limbo without entering the Promised Land. Virgil becomes for Dante the founder of a great city and the prophet of the emergence of the City of God. Tate also speaks of Virgil's decisive importance in his later writings: "Dante's guide was not just 'another poet' who had lived in the past, thus providing a merely literary tradition; Vergil represented the utmost reach of the secular imagination as reason; and this rational, secular imagination had, for Dante, found its limit in the idea of Rome, or the City, which was to be transcended but not abolished by the superaddition of the City of God."[13]

Among Tate's highest tributes to Virgil is "The Mediterranean,"

11. John J. O'Meara, "Introduction" to *An Augustine Reader* (Garden City, N.Y., 1973), 22.

12. Christopher Dawson, "The Christian View of History," in *The Dynamics of World History* (New York, 1956), 244.

13. Allen Tate, Review of Edward Dahlberg's *Can These Bones Live*, in *Sewanee Review*, LXIX, 316.

after "Ode to the Confederate Dead" one of his most frequently discussed poems. The large meaning of the poem, in its exploration of the sense of history, has seldom been in doubt, and its allusions to the *Aeneid* and the original event which inspired the verses, a picnic on the shores of southern France, are well known.[14] Yet the poem continues to fascinate because of the tantalizingly suggestive resonances of its language. One dimension of the poem that has been overlooked is a possible second level of allusion beyond Virgil to a modern counterpart of Aeneas' voyage—the colonizing of Virginia. Tate uses Michael Drayton's "To the Virginian Voyage" in his satiric "Ode: To Our Young Proconsuls of the Air" and has stressed the relevance of Drayton's poem to another satirical piece, "False Nightmare."[15] There may also be echoes of it in "The Mediterranean."

The relationship between the two poems is made plausible by certain close parallels in imagery, concept, or even sound: "Atlantis howls but is no longer steep" ("The Mediterranean") recalls

When Eolus scowles,
You need not feare,
So absolute the deepe,

from "To the Virginian Voyage."[16] Two rhyming pairs, "howl"/ "scowl" and "steep"/"deep" suggest a verbal inspiration as well as a conceptual one. Furthermore, the last line of Drayton's stanza also resembles "How absolute the sea!" from "Message from Abroad." Yet another verse—"They, in a wineskin, bore earth's paradise"—reminds one of "Virginia,/ Earth's onely paradise" in Drayton's poem. Virginia is the destination of the voyagers in both cases, but the New World has changed from "earth's paradise" to a "tired land" in Tate's verse. Finally, in still another passage, neglect and rot replace an effortless harvest in this "paradise,"

where tasseling corn,
Fat beans, grapes sweeter than muscadine
Rot on the vine.

14. Allen Tate, "Speculations," *Southern Review*, n.s., XIV, 226–27.

15. Allen Tate, "A Sequence of Stanzas," in *Memoirs*, 214.

16. Michael Drayton, "To the Virginian Voyage," in *The Works of Michael Drayton*, ed. John Buxton (Cambridge, Mass., 1953), 123–24.

Tate's unstewarded landscape reflects ironically on Drayton's cornucopia of natural goods in a land

Where nature hath in store,
Fowle, venison, and fish,
  And the fruitfull'st soyle,
  Without your toyle,
Three harvests more,
All greater than you wish.

The optimism of Drayton's ode, an exhortation to the voyagers as "brave heroique minds,/ Worthy your countries name," is a remarkable expression of the spirit of adventure and national destiny that led the Renaissance voyagers to the New World. Tate has called it "the ignorant Edenic *enthusiasm* of Michael Drayton."[17]

At least three of Tate's poems (and possibly a fourth, "Message from Abroad") are related to Drayton's, then, and they help define one of his principal themes: the "ignorant Edenic" vision that is fixed on the "ignis fatuus" of modern utopia, the secularized version of the City of God. "The Mediterranean" opposes two poets and two voyages—Virgil's narrative of the carrying of Troy to Rome and Drayton's celebration of the new colonization of America by Europe. But the difference between them is considerable, despite the heroic cast and national fervor that Drayton tries to lend to the Virginian voyage. Both poets see their heroes as driven by the divine will, but the modern attributes an economic rather than a spiritual destiny to the venture:

And cheerefully at sea,
Successe you still intice
  To get the pearle and gold,
  And ours to hold,
Virginia,
Earth's onely paradise.

Aeneas' quest for a new home was hard and fraught with difficult decisions. Drayton's Englishmen "Let cannons roare,/ Frighting the wide heaven" as though they were traveling without barriers. It is this too

17. Tate, "A Sequence of Stanzas," in *Memoirs*, 214.

easy and irresponsible conquest that has led modern man to crack "the hemispheres with careless hand."

The main theme of "The Mediterranean" is the reality of place and the respect for limits. The epigraph, slightly altered from the *Aeneid*,[18] speaks of a limit (*finem*) to sorrow, but the word is ambivalent and also allows the interpretation "What goal is made possible by our suffering?" The sufferings and labors of the voyagers are meaningful because they will come to a conclusion in some permanent community. Man is limited by his sufferings, but he is also defined by them. They serve to counter his appetite, which left unchecked would devour everything. The balance between appetite and limits, between what nature offers and man truly needs, creates a proper sense of place. It is a mutual relationship between the land that man inhabits and his own spirit that leads to a respect for the character of place.

"Mediterranean" means "middle of the earth." In Tate's poem it also stands for the center of Western experience. The action that is embodied in the poem is the return to the center, the recovery of origins that gives a fresh perspective and new life to an old world. The "landless wanderers" who picnic on the coast are no longer men whose city was destroyed—they are not tied to any land at all. Their picnic is an "affectation" of a "day of piracy," not the fulfillment of a prophecy. Yet they can achieve something like Aeneas' mythical voyage in their imaginations. The opening lines of the poem echo Virgilian phrases. It is through the historical imagination that the wanderers rediscover the meaning of "antiquity's delay" and "time's monotone." Their picnic is a communion with, not simply a vision of, the past. The imagery of feasting in the poem suggests that taking "that sweet land in" is a sort of communion, even in affectation, with eucharistic meaning. The past is tasted, not simply visualized in the imagination:

> We for that time might taste the famous age
> Eternal here yet hidden from our eyes
> When lust of power undid its stuffless rage;
> They, in a wineskin, bore earth's paradise.

18. Tate emends the epigraph to read correctly (*laborum* instead of *dolorum*) in the Yale Series recording *Allen Tate Reads from His Own Works* (Decca DL9130; Carillon Records YP300, 1960).

The return to the center is a ritual undertaken through the concrete participation in a meal. Eden is held in a wineskin and consumed only "in our secret need." Such is Tate's and Virgil's understanding of the way the City of God resides in the hearts of men. The "green coast" can be reached only by drinking and eating, for that is man's only genuine access to any paradise on earth—through his body's limits. The "stuffless rage" of the modern mind is unleashed by "lust of power" (an Augustinian phrase, from Book XV of *The City of God*, that has become part of contemporary language). The paradise that the Virginian voyagers first encountered in the New World was a place where nature sufficed to fill the body's desire. The abundance of fat beans and sweet grapes that "rot on the vine" in the land where Americans were born and live has been neglected for an appetite that lusts after power. Man learns to locate his blood, found his traditions, and become part of a place where he can establish a new center of tradition only after he has settled into a life that is a "modest conquest of nature," as Tate says elsewhere.

In contrast to the Virgilian fable of the refounding of Troy is the modern exploration of the universe for its own sake. The Gates of Hercules were the natural limits beyond which the Greek world felt it should not venture. But now that "We've cracked the hemispheres with careless hand," there is no longer a sense of time and place in our experience. Reality is no longer accessible to man unaided by his mediating technology. Places are no longer a "slingshot" or "a month" wide. They are mere abstract points on a map, neither fearful nor impressive. Only in the imagination can we return to the state of things that characterized Virgil's world, but that return to the remembered center is of primary importance:

> Let us lie down once more by the breathing side
> Of Ocean, where our live forefathers sleep
> As if the Known Sea still were a month wide—
> Atlantis howls but is no longer steep!

The unknown no longer frightens modern man, but he has lost the power of keeping his known world alive. Only through the remembered image of all cities, mythical or real, can he know how to settle down and foster his own.

This symbolic stratification of cities is the focus of Tate's companion piece, "Aeneas at Washington," usually printed after "The Mediterranean." It reverses the situation of the first poem. Instead of dramatizing the discovery by a modern American of the scenes where the Trojans might have landed, Tate imagines Aeneas discovering the shores where the Americans have landed and settled, carrying his Rome to other shores. Aeneas speaks and compares his own actions during the fall of Troy with the motives of the men who have made Washington what it is; he looks back on his flight from the burning city without self-recrimination:

> In that extremity I bore me well,
> A true gentleman, valorous in arms,
> Disinterested and honourable.

After he has done all that can be achieved for his stricken city, Aeneas turns to those things that matter to him personally—his wife and the "old man" his father—and leaves for a new world after taking up "cold victualing" (for eating also has a great prominence in this poem). But the crisis is not simply a matter of foreign invasion; there has been an internal change as well: "civilization/ Run by the few" has fallen "to the many." Aeneas knows that only two things can survive the collapse of a civilization: "a mind imperishable" and "a love of past things." Aeneas hastily gathers up the few definite things about him—the household gods (his *prima sacramenti memoria*)—and hoists his father, symbol of the living past, onto his back. All that remains of the particular Troy he was a part of is his love of it, "tenuous as the hesitation of receding love" symbolized by the fading ghost of his first wife Creusa.

Although Aeneas is aware of the divine origins of his conquering energies, he recognizes that his chief responsibility lies in exercising them with prudence and restraint.

> (To the reduction of uncitied littorals
> We brought chiefly the vigor of prophecy,
> Our hunger breeding calculation
> And fixed triumphs.)

The words that play against each other are all Latin-derived—"reduction" is tempered by "vigor," "calculation" by "fixed." The behavior common to ravaging conquerors has been muted and softened. The point of the aside is that any human community is a matter of compromise between good and bad elements, but exaggerated Latinisms like "littorals" also remind the reader that "reduction" (*reductio*, a "leading back") and "calculation" have neutral senses. Aeneas, like other men, has lust for power, but he has learned to control and contain it because he has the knowledge of his city's destiny that will limit his ambitions. In fact, Aeneas alone possesses the controlling detachment that is possible when life is informed by a myth; he can "see all things apart." The proper human proportion of desire is, after all, related to reasonable fulfillment. There is no lust for power in Aeneas' meditations:

> Now I demand little. The singular passion
> Abides its object and consumes desire
> In the circling shadow of its appetite.

Unlike the modern explorer or pioneer, Aeneas can be satisfied because his desire does not stray from its object and is eliminated once his appetite is satisfied.

What Aeneas sees, however, has certainly been swollen out of proportion to the needs of refounding a fallen city. Looking at Washington, the first city in the world created specifically for government, Aeneas must admit that his original motives for building a new community have become unrecognizable: "The city my blood had built I knew no more." Washington is a city built not with blood but with geometric abstractions and disembodied ideas. Washington is the symbol of what Spengler calls "infinite relations, conceivable only in pure Space" by the Faustian imagination. The Greeks, according to Spengler and others,[19] abhorred the "desensualized idea of infinity of the Unextended," or "Time actualized as infinite Space." The great dome of the Capitol is a new symbolic center of the universe, but the light that plays about it suggests the enlightenment of the abstract will for power rather than a return to a traditional cosmos, and this city of Faustian men has been created through the imposition of a geometric pattern on the "wet mire" of the world. Aeneas finds himself at an enormous distance from "the ninth buried city" of his homeland, and his alienation is created by a disjunction of both time and space.

The darkest image in the poem, however, is the screech-owl's whis-

19. Oswald Spengler, *The Decline of the West*, trans. Charles Francis Atkinson (New York, 1939), I, 67–73; F. M. Cornford, "The Invention of Space," in *Essays in Honour of Gilbert Murray* (London, 1936), 215–35.

tle, a sound that in "Ode to the Confederate Dead" evokes the fury of battle. In this poem it may represent another allusion to the *Aeneid.* The owl is, of course, Athena's bird and a symbol of wisdom; but in oriental and middle-eastern mythologies, it symbolizes "death, night, cold and passivity," according to J. E. Cirlot. Since confronting the dark and coming to a deeper understanding are not opposed in Tate's other writings, it may be that the owl stands for both. Cirlot says that the owl symbol "pertains to the realm of the dead sun, that is, of the sun which has set below the horizon and which is crossing the lake or sea of darkness."[20] Associated with twilight, the owl can be seen as the harbinger of Spengler's final phase of civilization. Certainly Tate uses it as an image of falling time and twilight:

> I stood in the rain, far from home at nightfall
>
> . . . .
>
> While the screech-owl whistled his new delight
> Consecutively dark.

But even more suggestive is the Virgilian parallel that occurs toward the end of the *Aeneid*, when Megaera in the form of an owl causes Turnus to recognize the inevitability of his fate:

> She beholds the Trojan armies and the troops of Turnus, having suddenly contracted into the form of the little bird, which sometimes sitting by night on graves, or abandoned roofs, untimely sings her late strain among the shades.[21]

The sight of the dome and all its pretensions to permanence is challenged by the sound of the bird; once again Tate opposes the visual and the aural to suggest transience.

Two related poems of lesser importance are concerned with a more topical application of these themes. In "The Ivory Tower," Tate attacks the contention that science will eventually solve all problems because all evils are ultimately social. The poem is an indictment of the provincial ignorance that thinks "Everybody but us is an example of capitalism" and a warning that man needs more than "Beef and cheese washed down by Pilsen" to "adjust the sexual act/ To truth of economic fact." If

20. J. E. Cirlot, *A Dictionary of Symbols*, trans. Jack Sage (New York, 1962), 235–36.
21. Virgil, *The Aeneid*, XII, 874–80 (my translation).

sex and economics are the two common elements of man's psychic dilemma, why cannot the stomach and the prostate be satisfied at the same time? Love, it seems, "engenders" an "uneconomic woe" that has crushed mankind since Adam and Eve. The true artist knows that his hunger drives him to communion, not to commodity—to the darkness and light of human relationships. The poem is an attack on the position taken by Tate's friend Edmund Wilson in his book *Axel's Castle.* Tate sums up Wilson's argument in one of his essays: "Modern symbolism is a method, invented by the poets, of evading the problems of modern economics: our belief in the inferiority of our own age to the past is due to the palsied irresponsibility of the Ivory Tower." Tate's response is that "this belief is the fundamental groundwork of all poetry at all times. It is the instinctive counterattack of the intelligence against the dogma of future perfection for persons and societies."[22] The poet does not reside in an "Ivory Tower" by choice. He is placed there by a society that is more intent on adjusting economics than promoting communion.

The other poem is an attack on the contrary point of view, expressed in a poem by Archibald MacLeish, another of Tate's friends. It appeared under the title "Aeneas at New York" as a letter to the editor of the *New Republic* in response to MacLeish's "Invocation to the Social Muse," published October 26, 1932. According to MacLeish, the poet should not take sides; he is a camp follower who must sleep with both contenders, choosing neither Marx nor Hoover and remaining naked of ideology. His true responsibilities are to speak of man and love. The poem ends with a question, "Is it just to demand of us also to bear arms?"

In light of the seeming reversal of their positions during the Second World War, this difference between the two poets may seem to be of little account. But while MacLeish did change his mind later and take the opposite point of view, Tate managed to be consistent on both occasions. (He attacked MacLeish's call for a politically conscious war poetry in a later poem, "Ode to Our Young Pro-consuls of the Air.") In

22. Allen Tate, "A Note on Elizabethan Satire," in *Essays*, 260. Spengler (I, 155) has a similar comment: "Hunger and Love thus become mechanical causes of mechanical processes in the 'life of peoples.' Social problems and sexual problems . . . become the obvious themes of utilitarian history and therefore of the corresponding tragedy." The ideas and phrases are curiously close to the main lines of Tate's poem.

"Aeneas at New York," Tate has the Roman hero object that poets are priests, not whores:

> We are those who have arranged the auguries
> And in dangerous youth made the good battle.

There are precedents for the fighting poet in such men as Sophocles at Salamis, but this actual engagement in warfare is not what Tate has in mind:

> The poet is he who fights on the passionate
> Side and whoever loses he wins.

The poet must fight battles, but they are not political or military ones. He must defend the traditional society that is present in "Penates," "altars," and "your great-great-grandfather's breeches," those emblems of the great actions of the past that the present is in danger of forgetting. It is the "passionate side" that the poet must take, for "when he/ Is defeated it is hard to say who wins." The poet is not the person who defends the City of God against the City of Man but the one who is responsible for distinguishing them. The battle is within each man; it is the struggle between the two cities for mastery of the individual. Even when one is convinced that he is on the just side, he is in danger of losing himself to the "lust of power." In "Ode to Our Young Proconsuls of the Air," Tate warns, against a MacLeish who is now blaming the poets for the present condition of the world, that it is not the political enemy—the Germans or the Japanese—whom the poets must fight but man's own destructive hatred within. Tate continued to sound the same warning later during the Cold War, when the Soviet Union had become the new adversary. In "Christ and the Unicorn," he cautions his audience against neglecting the fight against the real spiritual enemy by attempting to project all evil onto the Russians.[23] In times of war, when intense patriotism and national self-righteousness are demanded, this kind of detachment seems scandalous; but Tate felt that it was the only honest posture the poet can take in a world where even the visible enemy changes every decade. In "Ode to Our Young Proconsuls of the Air," Tate dares to insist on the humanity of the enemy. It is the Lama, who appears at the end of the poem, that is doomed to

23. Allen Tate, "Christ and the Unicorn," *Sewanee Review*, LXIII, 175–81.

extirpation as priest and leader. By comparing him to a "dying swan," Tate points to his priestlike identity with the poet, a notion sketched out in the earlier "Aeneas at New York." If the City of God resides partly in the "heaven of the mind," then it is the survival of the imagination itself, in its full integrity, that is at stake. Though the imagination can never be totally destroyed, it can be perverted to produce dangerous forms, like the utopian world of pseudo perfection satirized in another poem, "Jubilo." To behold the heavenly city in the imagination and to expect to realize it on earth are two different impulses. As in an earlier poem, also addressed to Edmund Wilson—"Epistle: To a Syracusan Too Much of Late at Rome"—Tate sees the quest for building the perfect city on earth as turning into an attack on nature. The result, as it is depicted in "Jubilo," is to suck all the blood from man and replace it with a "salt serum." The consequence of an attempt to construct a utopia is that man is left sterile and mechanically subservient, like the slaves in the original song parodied in Tate's poem.

Tate's two cities, then, may be understood as interpretations and adaptations of Augustine's. The City of Man is that condition of narcissism, lust for power, and abstraction that has become increasingly prevalent in a declining world. The City of God finds expression in the heart and mind as a sense of transcendence, an instinct for limit and restraint, and a sacramental anchoring through memory in the real world. It is available to the poet through the symbolic imagination, just as the City of Man finds its aesthetic counterpart in the angelic. Tate's famous essays on "The Angelic Imagination" and "The Symbolic Imagination" are his fullest attempt in prose to give the Augustinian dualities contemporary articulation. But long before he wrote them, he had probed the Augustinian theme of the two cities in less direct fashion as a poet.

A pair of companion poems—"The Meaning of Life" and "The Meaning of Death"—illustrates the way these oppositions are embodied in imaginative images. The first poem, subtitled "A Monologue," ironically shows a greater sense of community than the second, styled "An After-Dinner Speech." The two poems suggest the opposition between spirit and letter, for meaning implies some sort of interpretation. The shared images of both poems—particularly the eye and the cave—are given life or death according to the way they are read by the speaker. Both poems recount childhood memories, and both speak of time and darkness. Nevertheless, the meaning of these things is utterly different in each poem. The speakers' individual backgrounds seem to be divergent. One is rural, the other urban; one was exposed early in life to the ambivalence of the world in its mixture of good and evil, the other brought up in fear of the "mixed modes."

"The Meaning of Life" begins with a short meditation on exegesis:

> there is that
> Which is the commentary; there's that other
> Which may be called the immaculate
> Conception of its essence in itself.
> It is necessary to distinguish the weights
> Of the two methods lest the first smother
> The second, the second be speechless (without the first).

Meaning comes as a result of the interplay between the two interdependent "methods" or ways of approaching life. One way of viewing life sees it as self-sufficient, self-explanatory. Another sees it as requiring explication, unfolding through commentary, even though "one's sense of the proper decoration alters" and the commentary must be rewritten again and again. The poet moves immediately to an example:

> When I was a small boy I lived at home
> For nine years in that part of old Kentucky
> Where the mountains fringe the Blue Grass,
> The old men shot at one another for luck;
> It made me think I was like none of them.
> At twelve I was determined to shoot only
> For honor; at twenty not to shoot at all;
> I know at thirty-three that one must shoot
> As often as one gets the rare chance—
> In killing there is more than commentary.

In his memoir "A Lost Traveller's Dream," Tate mentions an event in his life that throws further light upon this unusual passage:

> One September day in the valley below Sewanee, twenty-five years ago, I shot a dove that fell into the weeds, and when I found her she was lying head up with a gout of blood in each eye. I shot her again. Her life had been given to my memory;

> and I have never hunted from that day. . . . The feminine memory says: Here is that dying dove; you must really kill it this time or you will not remember it from all the other birds you have killed; take it or leave it; I have given it to you.[24]

"Killing," when part of the kind of ritual that is the hunt or the maintenance of communal order in rural Kentucky, is "more than commentary" because it is part of that sacrificial moment that engages the memory—the *prima sacramenti memoria*. Ritual and blood sacrifice, as René Girard has argued in his book *Violence and the Sacred*,[25] are the means of forestalling universal disorder and violence. The attitude of the speaker in the poem comes full circle from a repugnance for shooting to a recognition that there are special moments when life can have meaning only if one is willing to take the ultimate responsibility for it. Shooting is a metaphor for attention and commitment, a means of concentrating in the memory a focused image of the preciousness of life and the necessity of taking risks to preserve its essential values. By shooting "at one another for luck," the old men in the mountains kept constantly alive their awareness of what it means to live in a community.

The concluding lines of the poem move into the realm of pure life, the unchanging and eternally earthbound "lust" that is proper within its own domain because, like Aeneas' "circling shadow of its appetite," it "feeds on itself." Both self-renewing and self-consuming, like the ouroboros, it is an image of pure flowing that is nevertheless pregnant with the future and "heavy with spawn." The darkness of the river and blindness of the fish in this passage stand for that ineffability beyond expression that commentary can point to and only partly reveal. They are an image of that "passion for time/ Longer than the arteries of a cave" held in the memory when the commentary is forgotten. If shooting is an act of exegetical attention that relates human action to the essence of life, then the cave is the great unconscious repository of life-blood that can be elevated to the level of the explicit only through the proper commentary executed in an act of total attention.

"The Meaning of Death" is spoken by a man of modern temper who is unaware of the irony of his own words. He speaks in a "twilight" that for him points towards the fulfillment of civilization even as the reader

24. Tate, "A Lost Traveller's Dream," 12.

25. René Girard, *Violence and the Sacred*, trans. Patrick Gregory (Baltimore, 1977).

recognizes its decline. He fears time as a threat and speaks, like Tate's romantics, of an "eternal light" that "shall on our heads be worn." His notion of the good is couched in utterly spatial terms. His eye commands and selects from the scenes before it a "useful view" that includes more water towers than churches, more churches than rivers. The landscape he sees demonstrates the history of the elimination of natural force and sacred institution for the sake of a public technology. His commitment is to the coming utopia his ignorant faith in the future requires:

> Gentlemen, let's
> Forget the past, its related errors, coarseness
> Of parents, laxities, unrealities of principle.
> Think of tomorrow.

The solipsistic "roving eye" that creates the universe he wishes to see under the covers of a protection from unpleasantness will eliminate all ambiguity and all of life's "impurities." It will create pure love and a universe where only the most urgent material needs are satisfied:

> Make a firm postulate
> Of simplicity in desire and act
> Founded on the best hypotheses;
> Desire to eat secretly, alone, lest
> Ritual corrupt our charity,
> Lest darkness fall and time fall
> In a long night when learned arteries
> Mounting the ice and sum of barbarous time
> Shall yield, without essence, perfect accident.

Ritual, memory, and the past are the essence of that communal existence that the speaker would eliminate. Yet it is at a public dinner that he counsels his hearers to "eat secretly." "The Meaning of Life" is a defense of essence, out of which the indispensable commentary must grow. "The Meaning of Death" offers the ironic recommendation of "perfect accident" without substance, pure commentary without subject, killing letter without life-sustaining spirit. The speaker's last words, "We are the eyelids of defeated caves," echo the "arteries of a cave" that concludes "The Meaning of Life," but they also allude to Plato's cave, where appearance is mistaken for reality. The defeated cave is the world of the senses and the body. The modern thinks that he has triumphed over the ignorance of the past, but he has really closed his eyes to any reality other than the one projected by his own mind. His blindness is a self-imprisonment in the shadowy cave of death.

Tate's sense of detachment and perspective in these poems is evident even beneath his powerful irony and satire. He does not offer any schemes for improving the flawed world because he is painfully aware of participating in the evils he deplores. He does not exempt himself from guilt, for his poems are as much an indictment of himself as an attack on others. In one of the poems that allude to Drayton, the self-critical satire of "False Nightmare," he refuses to exonerate himself and places as much blame on himself as he does on those he is criticizing.[26] The poem combines terza rima from Dante with a short trimeter line that recalls Drayton's meter. In it Tate imagines Walt Whitman, the spokesman for self-love and rejection of all restraints, proclaiming his principles in a self-damning parody of barbaric yawp. But the poet admits that Whitman is no more than a straw man, for he too takes the same attitude that is being condemned. His is the obverse side of the obscene energy he attacks in Whitman. Both Whitman and the "mildly gloating" southerner who despises him participate in the mission to bind the new continent as their slave. Tate goes on to describe this condescending attack on nature as a rape. An exceedingly compact allusion to Zeus's bullish courting of Europa and its ambiguous consequences makes the point that this supposed "love" for the land is simply an excuse for ravishing it.

No one, no Yankee or southerner, can be smug about the role he continues to play in the destruction of his own land, whether he has stood by passively or promoted its downfall actively. The extraordinary complexity of Tate's figure, which unites Zeus's abduction of Europa across the waters with the colonizing of America, sums up the relationship between the two cities. The immoderate desire for conquest typical of modern man from Drayton's time to ours has been carried out in the name of a divine providence. We have entered the New World with as much confidence as Jesus entering Jerusalem in triumph. We have pretended to be Zeus himself in our designs on nature and culture. But

26. Allen Tate, "False Nightmare," in *The Swimmers and Other Poems* (New York, 1970), 62.

this belief in our own destiny has been based on self-love and destruction. We love only that which we have been able to conquer. Tate saw in Aeneas an image of the means for returning to the eternal things by carrying the past into the present, and he knew that the theme of the two cities predates Christianity. But he also knew that one could not overlook almost two millennia of Christian elaboration of this theme. Communion with the past and the "love of past things" in their tenuousness provide a way through memory to gain a glimpse of the heavenly city that is "eternal here, yet hidden from our eyes" by the immoderate desire for conquest typical of Western man from Drayton's time to ours. Yet even they are not enough. If there is a need for reform, it is less of institutions than of individuals. It is the nature of man's love that must somehow be set aright.

In his essay "The Man of Letters in the Modern World," Tate reveals his Augustinian vision in one of its most clearly articulated forms, providing his fullest statement of the relationship between the poet and the two cities. The long series of pairs that organizes the essay takes its origin from the notion of "society as the City of Augustine and Dante, where it was possible for men to find in the temporal city the imperfect analogue to the City of God."[27] No utopian blueprint, the City of God is a real, if mostly implicit, society of persons. The poet must somehow promote the ability of men to perceive it; for he, as spokesman for his culture, is responsible for bringing the hidden dimensions of the heavenly city into prominence through language. The literary person's duty, as the archeologist of memory, flows from his ability to perceive and make known the existence of this larger dimension.

The essay is an elaboration of the basic Augustinian dualism into further important distinctions. The first is a discrimination of "mere communication" from "communion." The difference between them lies in their respective purposes, which are "the control of other persons," on the one hand, and "self-knowledge," on the other. The hidden term that unites "communication" and "communion" is, of course, "community." "Communication" is the perversion of community into "the dehumanized society of secularism, which imitates Descartes' mechanized nature," but its contrary is "the eternal society of the communion

27. Allen Tate, "The Man of Letters in the Modern World," in *Essays*, 9. Subsequent page references are given in the text.

of the human spirit," which, like Augustine's City of God, is the "rule of love, added to the rule of law" (p. 9).

Like the City of Man, then, modern secular society that would "*use* communication" but cannot "participate in communion" is not so much evil as radically imperfect: "Communication that is not also communion is incomplete." Tate's dialectical opposition of the two terms emerges finally as a way of presenting two large complementary actions. It is only in the attempt to dissociate them that the two aspects become inhuman on the public scale and ineffective on the private one. The politician is a man who is unaware of the mechanistic nature of the world he governs; and the man of letters, who "sees that modern societies are machines, even if he thinks that they ought not to be," becomes "convinced that in its intractable Manichaeism, society cannot be redeemed" (p. 5). The public and private have become irreconcilable. The politician pursues public goals through amoral means that disregard private needs; and the man of letters "disdainfully, or perhaps even absentmindedly" withdraws from society. Neither the modern politician nor the contemporary man of letters is truly at the "moral center" of society. Neither is truly a participant in the "action of society" in the true sense, for what literary men "have been asked to support . . . is the action of society as *secularism*, or the society that substitutes means for ends." The result, as Tate puts it succinctly, is "an intolerable psychic crisis expressing itself as a political crisis" (p. 6).

Despite the terrifying pull of all these tensions, the ultimate problem modern man faces is his own disbelief, which deters him from positive action, for one must "believe in order to know, know in order to do." Without a belief in some kind of eternal society, the politician and his subjects are both equally subject to enslavement. In what Tate calls "gnostic arrogance and Augustinian humility," the modern man of letters is forced to recognize that the only important distinction is one between slaves and free men. His sole means of responding to this denial of a human destiny is to apply the critic's power of discrimination, asserting that the real choice is between the freedom that is love, on the one hand, and death, on the other. Yet this state of things cannot last long, for "man will never be completely or permanently enslaved. . . . If his *human* nature as such cannot participate in the action of society, he will not capitulate to it, if that action is inhuman: he will turn in upon himself." Solipsism is the inevitable reaction of modern man to his intolerable existence; and if he is honest about his situation, the man of letters may have no option except to withdraw from or reject his secular society. In any case, he should not be harshly judged for so doing, since if the man of letters "has not participated fully in the action of society," it is because "nobody else has either" (p. 8).

The man of letters, according to Tate, must recognize his limitations. He cannot resolve the split between self and society any more than he can revive the dead past. What he can do is convince men who have forgotten the eternal order that something is missing from their lives. He can cause them to remember the order that remains hidden from them because it is too deeply buried within their memories to be recovered except through some imaginative act of archeology. He must help them recover the meaning of action, for the "state is the mere operation of society, but culture is the way society lives." Yet the poet cannot address a faceless crowd; he must speak to a community of which he is a member. His powers of discrimination can be turned to the "letter," but it is the responsibility of the community to provide the "spirit." The poet is not the source of the order man needs. The true source is culture, the "material medium through which men receive the one lost truth which must be perpetually recovered: the truth of what Jacques Maritain calls the 'supra-temporal destiny of man'" (p. 16). Thus culture, according to Tate, is the nexus of the two cities, the meeting of the eternal with the temporal, of the free with the destined. Man is not meant to linger forever in the city of means but to keep his eye on the city of ends, for the "end of social man is communion in time through love, which is beyond time."

Thus the meaning of such terms as "buried city" and "heavenly city" resides in their embodiment of man's "supra-temporal destiny." They are poetic metaphors for culture, or "the way society lives" when mindful of dimensions beyond the merely social. But as Tate recognizes, the two cities are distinguished less by abstract ideals in the minds of their denizens than by the nature of their loves. The conclusion of Tate's essay on the man of letters is surely an echo of one of the most famous passages in *The City of God*:

> Accordingly, two cities have been formed by two loves: the earthly by the love of self, even to the contempt of God; the heavenly by the love of God, even to the contempt of self. The

> former, in a word, glorifies in itself, the latter in the Lord. For the one seeks glory from men; but the greatest glory of the other is God, the witness of conscience. . . . In the one, the princes and the nations it subdues are ruled by the love of ruling; in the other, the princes and the subjects serve one another in love.[28]

In another passage Augustine analyzes the mystical meaning of the biblical figures of Sarah and her slave Hagar to clarify his symbolic interpretation of the two cities. After speaking of Sarah's barrenness and her exacting of "her due from her husband . . . by another's womb," Augustine shows that those things which cannot be accomplished by nature must be achieved through a grace that is not due to any natural course.

> This nature, so constituted that offspring could not be looked for, symbolized the nature of the human race vitiated by sin and by just consequence condemned, which deserves no future felicity. Fitly, therefore, does Isaac, the child of promise, typify the children of grace, the citizens of the free city, who dwell together in everlasting peace, in which self-love and self-will have no place, but a ministering love that rejoices in the common joy of all, of many hearts makes one, that is to say, secures a perfect concord. (p. 481)

The love in the two cities is conveyed in this passage through the image of childbearing. Sarah's unselfish action is the antithesis of romantic love, for it has no roots whatsoever in passion. Nevertheless, the physical body is not to be despised, for it is both real in itself and the means to an end, the symbol of something greater than itself. Earthly love is imperfect only becuase it is half of a greater whole. The body is not evil, but it is subject to strife because its incompleteness keeps man from attaining peace and harmony. For Augustine, who refuses to separate the collective actions of man from the private ones, love in its essential unity is the primary aspect of human order. He makes it a pivotal part of his definition of a people in *The City of God* (XIX, 24): "A people is an assemblage of reasonable beings bound together by a common agreement as to the objects of their love, [and] in order to discover

28. Saint Augustine, *The City of God*, 477. Subsequent page references are given in the text.

the character of any people, we have only to observe what they love" (p. 706).

Although most historians recognize that Christianity introduced a new concept of love to the West, they have often been in violent disagreement about the nature of Christian love itself. In his provocative study *Agape and Eros*, Anders Nygren discriminates between Christian and pagan notions of love, but he goes a step further to make vigorous claims for the originality of Augustine's contribution: "After Augustine the Christian idea of love is no longer the same as before. Further, Augustine's view of love has exercised by far the greatest influence in the whole history of the Christian idea of love. . . . Ever since his time the meaning of Christian love has generally been expressed in the categories he created, and even the emotional quality which it bears is largely due to him."[29] Nygren credits Augustine with the formulation of a synthesis of the anthropocentric love, *eros*, and the theocentric, *agape*. Augustine fused them in a vigorous hybrid that he called *caritas*. For all the theological controversy generated by Nygren's book, his insight into Augustine's contribution is sound.

Though he drew on Platonic and Plotinian concepts as well as Johannine and Pauline doctrines of love, Augustine was no detached theorist. He had a full and direct experience of the whole range of love, from physical passion to spiritual ecstasy. Romano Guardini has claimed that Augustine attempted "to make love the determining element of existence in general,"[30] but he did not attempt to reduce it to a single variety or even to a duality. Love for him is, first of all, the will itself. It is like the Aristotelian notion of weight, a kind of inherent gravity in things that draws physical bodies to their resting place. Ultimately, it moves toward God, who is the final locus of repose for all things. Love seeks its own completion and satisfaction as part of that force by which all things are drawn to God. On a less exalted level, it is "a kind of life which joins, or seeks to join, some two things," whether they be physical bodies or spirits, Augustine explains in *The Trinity* (VIII, 10).[31]

29. Anders Nygren, *Agape and Eros*, trans. Philip S. Watson (New York and Evanston, 1969), 450.

30. Romano Guardini, *The Conversion of Augustine*, trans. Elinor Briefs (Westminster, Md., 1960), 61.

31. Saint Augustine, *The Trinity*, trans. Stephen McKenna (Washington, D.C., 1970), 266.

All things are subject to and motivated by love, but in the human order love takes on a special significance as part of the movement to action. Etienne Gilson sums up this view: "Man's love never rests. What it does may be good or bad, but it is always doing something. Crime, adultery, homicide, lust; love causes all of these as well as acts of pure charity or heroism. For good or ill, its capacity is unfailing; for the man it drives, it is an inexhaustible source of action."[32] Love is not simply a weight; it is an action. Until love has been completed in action, it cannot reach its end, whether that goal be physical or spiritual, good or evil.

Augustine sees love, then, as one, not two. Yet the West has been dominated by the notion of the dual loves at least since the time of Plato. How can this tendency to divide love into a pair of opposed principles be reconciled with the unity on which Augustine insists? The answer lies in what Tate, following John Crowe Ransom, has called the "mixed modes." Few men have been able to admit that love can be at once the highest of human values and a cause of evil. Baudelaire, for example, gives his readers a picture of man caught between two loves, one for God, the other for the abyss. Augustine's position is the more difficult to maintain. Love, as he sees it, emanates from and returns to God, even when it is turned to objects that are unworthy. It is what one loves, rather than love itself, that differentiates. Love is one; only its objects are opposed. Without some kind of transcendent faith, however, this unity is impossible to understand.

In his essay "A Reading of Keats," Tate lingers for a few pages over a curious passage that Keats scribbled in his copy of Burton's *Anatomy of Melancholy*:

> Here is the old plague spot; the pestilence, the raw scrofula. I mean there is nothing disgraces me in my own eyes so much as being one of a race of eyes nose and mouth beings in a planet call'd the earth who all from Plato to Wesley have always mingled goatish winnyish lustful love with the abstract adoration of the deity. I don't understand Greek—is the love of God and the Love of women express'd by the same word in Greek? I hope my

32. Etienne Gilson, *The Christian Philosophy of Saint Augustine*, trans. L. E. M. Lynch (New York, 1960), 135.

> little mind is wrong—if not I could . . . Has Plato separated these lovers? Ha! I see how they endeavour to divide—but there appears to be a horrid relationship.

Tate discusses this reaction as Keats's "reach towards and recoiling from the experience, greatly extended, which is represented by the ambivalent Aphrodite." He notes that Keats could understand the "immanence of the Uranian in the Pandemic goddess" intellectually, but not imaginatively:

> His pictorial and sculpturesque effects, which arrest time into space, tend to remove from experience the dramatic agitation of Aphrodite Pandemos, whose favors are granted and whose woes are counted in the actuality of time. . . .
>
> This "horrid relationship" between the heavenly and earthly Aphrodites had been in effect the great theme of St. Augustine, and before him of Lucretius; and it was to inform dramatically *The Divine Comedy*. It was perhaps the great achievement of the seventeenth-century English poets to have explored the relations of physical and spiritual love.[33]

The shock that Keats felt in perceiving the "horrid relationship" is typical of the divided modern sensibility, which severs space from time, physical from spiritual being, love of self from love of another. Even Baudelaire often comes closer to Manichaeism than to Augustine in such passages as the following from his intimate journal *Mon Coeur Mis à Nu*:

> There is in every man at every moment a dual and simultaneous drive, one toward God, the other toward Satan. The call to God, or spirituality, is a desire to climb the stairs; that to Satan, or animality, is a joy of descending. This latter must be related to the love for women and intimate association with animals, dogs, cats, etc.
>
> The joys that derive from these two loves are in conformity with the nature of the two loves.[34]

33. Allen Tate, "A Reading of Keats," in *Essays*, 277–79.

34. Charles Baudelaire, "Mon Coeur Mis à Nu," in *Oeuvres Complètes*, ed. Y.-G. Le Dantec and Claude Pichois (Paris, 1961), 1277 (my translation).

The two loves are an inescapable part of modern experience and a sign of social as well as psychic fragmentation. For poets like Keats and Baudelaire, the absolute division of love into two kinds is simply an extension into the modern world of Pascal's war between heart and head. Tate calls it an "intractable Manichaeism" that presents society as unredeemable: "The shadowy political philosophy of modern literature, from Proust to Faulkner, is, in its moral origins, Jansenist: we are disciples of Pascal, the merits of whose Redeemer were privately available but could not affect the operation of the power-state. While the politician, in his cynical innocence, uses society, the man of letters disdainfully, or perhaps even absentmindedly, withdraws from it."[35] The result of this withdrawal is a society "in which nobody participates with the full substance of his humanity."

Augustine's famous trinitarian psychology—which shows the mind as made up of memory, understanding, and will—helps in depicting this "full substance." "There is," Augustine says, "no love without hope, no hope without love, and neither hope nor love without faith."[36] Ultimately, the buried city and the heavenly city are made accessible to the poet through his faith in the efficacy of culture and its potential for transcendence. The recovery of love as the foundation of society cannot be achieved without some form of historic faith and a hope for the possibility of a new beginning.

Hannah Arendt, who has written on Augustine's concept of love, has seen the significance of this emphasis on beginnings as residing in the rejection of a history conceived without events, that sameness unfolding in time reflected by Lucretius' *eadem sunt omnia semper*:

> In its full significance, however, this was discovered by the one great thinker who lived in a period which in some respects resembled our own more than any other in recorded history, and who in any case wrote under the full impact of a catastrophic end, which perhaps resembles the end to which we have come. Augustine, in his *Civitas Dei*, said: *Initium ergo ut esset, creatus est homo, ante quem nullus fuit*. ("That there might be a beginning,

35. Tate, "The Man of Letters in the Modern World," 5.

36. Saint Augustine, *Faith, Hope, and Charity*, trans. Louis A. Arand (Westminster, Md., 1947), 17.

> man was created before whom nobody was.") Here, man has not only the capacity of beginning, but is this beginning himself.[37]

Arendt goes on to say that since the "essence of all . . . action is to make a new beginning, then understanding becomes . . . that form of cognition, in distinction from many others, by which acting men (and not men who are engaged in contemplating some progressive or doomed course of history) eventually can come to terms with what irrevocably happened and be reconciled with what unavoidably exists." It is through the gift of the "understanding heart," or, as she names it, "the faculty of imagination," that we are able to see things in their proper perspective and in "the particular density which surrounds everything that is real."

One of Tate's best-known essays, "The Symbolic Imagination," is a magisterial analysis of this vision. The commentary grows out of a brilliant explication of Canto XXXIII of Dante's "Paradise" in terms of its light imagery but ranges far beyond this immediate topic. Tate's deeper concern, as his title indicates, is with "the symbolic imagination," which he defines as a means of conducting "an action through analogy of the low to the high, of time to eternity." Nevertheless, its focus is always on active experience:

> Despite the timeless orders of both rational discourse and intuitive contemplation, it is the business of the symbolic poet to return to the order of temporal sequence—to *action*. His purpose is to show men experiencing whatever they may be capable of, with as much meaning as he may be able to see in it; but the action comes first. Shall we call this the Poetic Way? It is at any rate the way of the poet, who has got to do his work with the body of this world, whatever that body may look like to him, in his time and place.[38]

Tate does not propose in his essay to trace the history of the symbolic imagination. He is content to give a sketch of its character and provide a few outstanding examples of its operation. However, the

37. Hannah Arendt, "Understanding and Politics," *Partisan Review*, XX, 390. See her *Liebesbegriff bei Augustin* (Berlin, 1929).

38. Allen Tate, "The Symbolic Imagination," in *Essays*, 428.

most startling passage in the entire commentary comes at the end, where Tate suggests that *The Divine Comedy* "has a tragic mode" and continues by stating that

> perhaps the symbolic imagination is tragic in sentiment, if not always in form, in the degree of its development. Its every gain beyond the simple realism of experience imposes so great a strain upon any actuality of form as to set the ultimate limit of the gain as a defeat. The high order of the poetic insight that the final insight must elude us, is dramatic in the sense that its fullest image is an action in the shapes of this world: it does not reject, it includes; it sees not only with but through the natural world, to what may lie beyond it. Its humility is witnessed by its modesty. It never begins at the top; it carries the bottom along with it, however high it may climb.[39]

This "tragic" sentiment is the key to Augustine's thought as well, and it is intimately bound up with the dissociation of the contemporary mind and the consequent importance of the "Poetic Way." In a later essay, Tate has suggested that "what was dissociated—whenever it may have been dissociated—was not thought from feeling, nor feeling from thought; what was dissociated was the external world which by analogy could become the interior world of the mind. . . . The doctrine of analogy, or connaturality, becomes in poetry the actuality of the identity of world and mind."[40] Thus the way back to the unity of world and mind, a constant theme in Augustine's works, is through poetry, not through theology, politics, or nostalgic reconstructions of the past. Poetry provides modern man with an awareness of the unity of the world and mind along with a sense of their limitations.

Tate was fully aware that he shared with Augustine this recognition of limits as the ultimate means for understanding reality. As an epigraph to *On the Limits of Poetry*, he cites a phrase from the meditation on memory in Book Ten of *The Confessions*: "Therefore is the mind too strait to contain itself."[41] The mind has the power to contain all things,

39. *Ibid.*, 446.

40. Allen Tate, "The Unliteral Imagination; Or, I, too, Dislike It," in *Essays*, 460.

41. Allen Tate, *On the Limits of Poetry: Selected Essays, 1928–1948* (New York, 1948). The passage comes from Book X, viii. Tate is citing the Pusey translation.

yet it has its limits constantly tested by those things it would contain. The imagination is tragically bound in the moment of its greatest magnificence, for it can attempt to depict infinity but has not the power to become infinite. Both Tate and Augustine view the soul and culture as characterized by this paradoxical tension. They celebrate man's infinite range of possibilities while distrusting his pretensions to overcome his own nature. In his poetry Tate has embodied this insight in dramatic action and provided the connaturality he demands.

By approaching Tate through Augustine, one comes to recognize more fully the movement of his major poems without having to neglect the numerous other forces that accompany this powerful thrust. Yet this Augustinian matrix is not simply a means for assessing the poet's total achievement; it is also a major component of Tate's vision, one of the master themes of his mature work. Augustine's outlook makes apparent the ultimate harmony between culture and the soul that Tate claims as essential. The heavenly city is the paradigm toward which the soul aspires; the buried city is its cultural analogue in tradition. It is futile to speak of "the supratemporal destiny of man" without invoking its counterpart in the memory, just as it is impossible to discern the truth embedded in the material medium of social life without its heavenly paradigm.

Seven

Confession

THE TERM "confessional poetry" achieved some currency in the sixties and seventies as a description of a new style of poetic self-revelation. Typically, that style was meant to explore the meaning of subjective experience. Since all lyric poetry offers some access to the heart, one might claim that all poetry is confession, especially if the word is understood in its original Latin meaning, "to admit, to acknowledge formally, to proclaim," or, in a broader sense, "a stepping forth from the inmost reserve to the open, the public," in Romano Guardini's words.[1] But confession has meant something more specific for contemporary poets. It stands for that concern with the self which is the heritage of the psychoanalytical tradition, and it reflects a reaction against such early twentieth-century critical doctrines as Eliot's notion of the "impersonality of the poet." In addition to reflecting an attitude, it involves a definite language and subject matter, with claims to honesty and sincerity arrived at through the informal, simple style that presents a poet's most private, personal concerns to a public passionately interested in gaining access to the intimate life of the artist. In his aggressive self-presentation, the mid-century confessional poet would say, with Rousseau, "I want to display to my fellows a man in all the truth of nature; and this man will be I. I alone. I feel my heart and I know men. I am not made like any of those that I have seen; I dare to believe that I am not made like any of those who now exist. If I am not worth more, I am at least other than they."[2] Rousseau's emphasis on the unusual cast of his autobiography is not misplaced. Though far from being the first to offer his confessions to the world, he makes extreme claims for his own uniqueness that no writer before him could have as-

1. Romano Guardini, *The Conversion of Augustine*, trans. Elinor Briefs (Westminster, Md., 1960), 3.

2. Jean-Jacques Rousseau, *Les Confessions*, ed. J. Voisine (Paris, 1964), 3–4 (my translation).

serted. He gives a new sense to the word *personal* and transforms the meaning of the confessional mode.

Robert Lowell, whose later poetry is an important example of the modern confessional style, has called Allen Tate's work "terribly personal"; and the author of *Life Studies* has clearly acknowledged the influence of his older friend and mentor on his own poems. Nevertheless, those poems of Tate's that seem the most personal—such as "Sonnets at Christmas," "Sonnets of the Blood," or "The Swimmers"—are autobiographical in a radically different fashion. Though many of Tate's writings are correctly described as confessional, they are not simply transcriptions of the author's interior life without some larger formal purpose. Indeed, all contemporary poets are to some degree participants in the tradition of Rousseau, though such poets as Eliot and Yeats, by refusing to take themselves as their sole subject matter, have drawn the line between themselves and their more self-absorbed successors of the last two decades. But Tate is like these older poets he admired in that the end of his confession is illumination rather than self-justification.

Tate's confessions are written out of a vision larger than himself, a sense of history that makes his work an exploration of an age and a way of life rather than of an ego. Compared to Yeats's, Eliot's, or Pound's, his self-portrait is modest. He claims little for himself, is often self-deprecatory. He offers no schemes relating world history and the psychology of types, as does Yeats; nor comprehensive programs for the salvation of the world, as does Pound. He does not even advocate a return to some historically available "Christian society," as does Eliot. Yet he is aware that mere self-presentation will not suffice. Even the characteristic honesty that many have seen as the hallmark of Tate's personality would not, of itself, be sufficient to give his poems permanent interest. Yet what Tate has said of Emily Dickinson surely applies with equal force to his own work: "She exhibits one of the permanent relations between personality and objective truth, and she deserves the special attention of our time, which lacks that kind of truth."[3]

Yet there is something about Tate's poetry, in its frightening obliquity, its concrete density yoked with "fierce Latinity," and its demonic energy, that makes it stand apart from the work of other twentieth-

3. Allen Tate, "Emily Dickinson," in *Essays*, 297.

century poets. For that reason, Tate cannot be grouped with other moderns whom he resembles superficially. Always his own person, faithful to his vision of a world in need of true salvation from itself, Tate has never compromised or shirked the implications of his difficult situation. Therefore, his confessional posture is in some danger of being misunderstood by those who lack the perspective for seeing precisely what it is.

The key to Tate's confessional poetry is to be found in the tradition into which it fits. It does not belong with such writings as Rousseau's but with Augustine's. Tate returns to this source through a sequence of intermediaries that includes Baudelaire, Pascal, and Dante, but his ultimate inspiration lies in the figure of Augustine as it is revealed in *The Confessions*. In common with his great prototype, Tate possesses an imaginative fury and power that transcend a mere fascination with the psychological disarray of the contemporary soul. Like Augustine, Tate intends to guide his reader from the confrontation with the self to a confrontation with the world, from the fictionally personal to the historically public. Confession, like any other movement of the soul, serves poetry as an action to be imitated, as a fiction that points beyond itself analogically to something else.

Rousseau's confession points to no one but himself, for he claims to be unique. His autobiography is a matter of historical self-justification, of setting the record straight for future generations. Augustine's way is poetic, analogical, and typological. The story of his life follows the pattern of the scriptures, showing the fall from grace and the return to salvation. Like the Bible that Augustine read and the confessional poem that Dante, his greatest disciple, gave to the world, this revealing of one man's experience results not so much in a personal record as in a text with many levels of meaning.

It is not the poet's life that is opened to public view in such poems but that greater life of the memory that is sustained in culture. By seeing his own actions in relation to the past, the poet turns autobiography into the story of his culture's destiny. The accident of an individual's existence in space and time becomes a meaningful emblem of man's ultimate needs. In the elevation of his own experiences through poetry, Tate has been able to achieve that same double detachment that allowed Augustine to view both his own life and his era from a dramatic perspective. Tate's confessional poetry is a transformation of personal failings into deeper meanings; he moves from self-examination to history, from confession to memory.

Tate could not have evolved his kind of confessional poetry without the inspiration of Dante, for Augustine offers no specific model for the poet, even though he was himself a man of letters. It is Dante's depiction of the poet as protagonist that shows the special character of the artist in his quest for understanding. This dual inspiration of Augustine and Dante offers a richer dimension to Tate's meditations than he could have gained from either alone. Echoes of both writers appear in his mature poetry. The Augustinian parallels, however, are more basic to Tate's entire stance. At times he isolates incidents from his own life that, intentionally or not, have counterparts in Augustine's biography. A striking example is the episode of the stolen pears in Book Two of *The Confessions*:

> A pear tree there was near our vineyard, laden with fruit, tempting neither for colour nor taste. To shake and rob this, some lewd young fellows of us went, late one night (having according to our pestilent custom prolonged our sports in the streets till then), and took huge loads, not for our eating, but to fling to the very hogs, having only tasted them. And this, but to do what we liked only, because it was misliked. Behold my heart, O God, behold my heart, which Thou hadst pity upon in the bottom of the bottomless pit. Now, behold and let my heart tell Thee what it sought there, that I should be gratuitously evil, having no temptation to ill, but the ill itself. It was foul, and I loved it; I loved to perish, I loved mine own fault, not that for which I was faulty, but my fault itself.[4]

Man's perverse preference for his own damnation is a theme Tate takes up in "Winter Mask," but a more precise equivalent for the unaccountable sins of youth is in "Sonnets at Christmas" and "More Sonnets at Christmas." In the first of these, Tate recalls an event from his past:

> When I was ten I told a stinking lie
> That got a black boy whipped.

4. Saint Augustine, *The Confessions*, trans. Edward B. Pusey (New York, 1949), 29.

In his memoir "A Lost Traveller's Dream," Tate is more specific: "I had let a Negro boy, my playmate, take a beating from his mother, our cook Nanny, for a petty theft that I had committed. (Henry was killed in World War I; I never made it up to him for my cowardice.)"[5] The significance of this episode in the poems, however, has to do with the problem of forgiveness. Can there be any forgiving of sins in a purely immanent universe, where man alone is responsible for everything? For the implications of both the verse and prose versions of the story seem to point to a justice that demands retribution, even after there is no way to offer some redress to the injured person. If there can be no personal means of making up for a wrong against another, who has the authority to grant remission of the sin? In a world without faith, the answer is that no one can. There is only the convention that civilized people follow or the habit that remains from a childhood upbringing. A psychoanalyst could perhaps relieve the pressure of conscience on the sinner, but he could not forgive the sin. The act of forgiveness for an injury done to another requires the kind of enormous love that has authority in its own right. No man can command that kind of love in the modern world because no man is the spokesman for all of mankind, and men are rightly chary of allowing any one person to be their supreme spokesman in such matters. At best, our present world allows forgiveness to be dispensed through the abstract processes we call law.

But on a personal level, where the public law is inoperative, who can offer the comfort of remission? The answer is to be found only in religion, but a man who knows these things and yet is incapable of belief must suffer if he is honest. Therefore, Christmas in Tate's poem, as in Tennyson's *In Memoriam*, is a time of agony rather than a time of joy. The speaker may prepare his body and appetite for the season, but he cannot dress up his emotions:

> This is the day His hour of life draws near,
> Let me get ready from head to foot for it
> Most handily with eyes to pick the year
> For small feed to reward a feathered wit.

The ironic self-deprecation of this first poem in "Sonnets at Christmas" depicts a man whose head dominates his body—his eyes act as hands—

5. Allen Tate, "A Lost Traveller's Dream," in *Memoirs*, 7.

to no avail. He will be an observer, not a participant in the holiday. While others relax, eat, or hunt, he cannot take part in the festivity or see any "epiphany" in it. His meditations are unconnected with the half-secular, half-religious activities that stand for a presumably sacred moment of remembrance.

Yet I, stung lassitude, with ecstasy
Unspent argue the season's difficult case
So: Man, dull creature of enormous head,
What would he look at in the coiling sky?

The poet finds it curious that man, whose head has grown so large in his assertion of pride, should seek out anything beyond himself. Like the speaker in Wallace Stevens' "Sunday Morning," he is aware of the moral system of the past which, though no longer alive, still demands obeisance for social reasons: "But I must kneel again unto the Dead." The festivity is a decorative one; the paper bells are as silent as the God for whom they are supposed to be ringing, and man's fall has been reduced to a picture of children slipping off a sled.

The speaker's silence contrasts with the gaiety around him, but it is at least part of the "small feed" he has garnered with his eyes to sustain him. There are benefits in this silence that the boisterous celebration cannot confer. The meditation prompted by the ambiguous cries of "Ah, Christ, I love you" turns to the memory of past actions:

The going years, caught in an after-glow,
Reverse like balls englished upon green baize.

The act of remembrance is here conveyed in an unusual simile. To return to the past is to execute a clever shot, like a pool player who causes the ball to spin backwards as it moves forward. Christmas itself is such a memory, a casting back in time while life moves forward, but what emerges is the hope for some vision that will break the silence, a sight that has the impact of sound:

Let them return, let the round trumpets blow
The ancient crackle of the Christ's deep gaze.

The poet, who can neither hear nor see, asks that Christ return his attempted gaze into the darkness. The search through the memory is not simply a search for past crimes; it is also a search for God. But the secularization of the season, suggested in the activities of the first sonnet, is complete at the end of the second, for Christmas has become simply "late December." Gazing into the fire, the speaker knows that he is looking into the hell of a world where time is meaningless and where the fire that warms and lights the room in which he sits has no power to purge or enlighten him. He is permanently guilty of "crimes of which [he] would be quit."

In "More Sonnets at Christmas," the sense of failure is shifted from the personal and communal to all of civilization. It has been ten years since the first set of sonnets was published, and the poet's sense of crisis has deepened. The imagery has become more complex to reflect the desperate situation of the war. Now older, the speaker recognizes that age has produced a grey beard but without giving greater wisdom. The "native hour" of Christmas brings a relaxation of formalities but no relief from the terrors of the times. Christ's eyes, which the speaker longed to see ten years earlier, have now "pierced the close net of what [he] failed." The exchange of gazes in this spiritual badminton has become more intense. The "drift of cordial seas" that sustained the poet in the past has turned into a raging current of war leading toward the swirl of "the grave-clout." The net of the speaker's defenses has been deftly transformed into his winding-sheet. The birth of Christ is also a reminder of death, as the final image in the octave of the first sonnet—"mummy Christ, head crammed between his knees"—reminds him. Christ has become a mummy in time, even on the day his birth is celebrated. The end of civilization as we have known it in the West seems imminent, and the religion that gave it so much life has no power to revive.

The sestet of the first sonnet has worried some readers because it seems to be inconsistent with the imagery of the preceding octave. Yet it gathers together a number of images that are typical of Tate: the bomber in its blind arrogance, the eagle fleeing the earth to fly to the sun, the decapitated head of the man seeking to tear out all thought of death. Christ's birthday is "crucial" not only because it points ahead to the cross and death but also because it raises the question of the need for faith in the modern world. The "capital yoke" is not a reference to the crucifixion, however, but to the speaker. He cannot maintain the bond between body and soul. His temptation is to allow the head to soar beyond its bodily limitations and seek the light of the sun, "stroke by stroke." But the "sun-ghostlings," which whisper like Coleridge's phantoms "Death-in-life" and "Life-in-death," advise this dissociated bomber pilot to give up his fears by giving up his reason. Christ assaults the speaker through the eyes and ears. The only way to escape his "mummy" image is through self-destruction.

Christmas signals the end of the year, but there is, in addition, a possibility that this season points to the end of civilization itself:

> The day's at end and there's nowhere to go,
> Draw to the fire, even this fire is dying.

If the head cannot escape the body without severing its connections with reality, the body itself is incapable of meaningful action without the head. Empty ceremonies, vaguely disguised emblems of lust such as mistletoe, serve to pass the time. All that remains of Christmas is the speaker's childhood memory of a stuffed Santa. The future is summed up in a bleak picture of the inhuman subjugation of peoples from three continents—Asia, Africa, and Europe—for the sake of the "cold martial progress" of a nation given over to lust for power.

The third sonnet returns to the childhood scene of guilt recalled in "Sonnets at Christmas." The impersonal technological war in which America is trapped has been the product of the same false dream of progress that blessed the "lying boy of ten." Now America has ignorantly embraced the lie that hers is a national destiny—the same lie that drives her enemy Germany. With no real understanding of the complex issues at stake, the provincial American people "battle the world of which they're not at all." The young boy whose father held out a great political future for him must draw the conclusion that lying is good preparation for the presidency, for his "fall" evokes neither shame nor guilt. This arrogant belief in American superiority places its war morality on the same level as the enemy's. As the nation's "little boys go into violent slumber," America is threatened by the loss of its own soul.

Tate's constant warning is prominent in "More Sonnets at Christmas": the most dangerous enemy is the one within us. Modern men are trapped in Plato's cave of appearances without knowing it. They think to save themselves by simply turning to the light at the door but do not recognize, as Tate notes in "The Symbolic Imagination," that one cannot look directly into the light without being blinded. The difficult lines near the end of the fourth sonnet offer a bleak picture of the future. Men have traded the body for a skeleton, and they expect to escape the cave of existence without suspecting what might lie beyond it:

> Gay citizen, myself, and thoughtful friend,
> Your ghosts are Plato's Christians in the cave.
> Unfix your necks, turn to the door; the nave
> Gives back the cheated and light dividend
> So long sequestered . . .
> . . . .
> Thus light, your flesh made pale and sinister
> And put off like a dog that's had his day,
> You will be Plato's kept philosopher,
> Albino man bleached from the mortal clay.

These lines contain one of Tate's most compressed poetic figures. The famous discussion in Book Seven of *The Republic* is combined with the underground worship of the early Christians. Tate turns Plato's cave into a sort of parodic cathedral, penetrated by light but sealed off from the world outside it. Sheltered inside stone walls whose solidity has been all but completely whittled away, the modern Christian mistakes what he sees inside this cathedral-cave of the senses for the physical world. Inside this skeletal body of Gothic tracery that his past beliefs have become, man has refined himself into an albinolike translucence, discarding the flesh in a Manichean gesture. He has refined away the body to let the light of his soul shine through more clearly, but the result is that he has become a kind of prostitute to bad Platonism. Like Emerson, the "Lucifer of Concord," as Tate has called him, modern man has become "the light-bearer who could see nothing but light, and was fearfully blind."[6] It is not enough to turn from the wall of the cave to the light at the door. The capital yoke must be maintained at all costs; the spirit must remain embodied in living flesh if man is not to become a mummy in time or "a gossamer bone" that is only the skeleton of his being. Like the apple in "The Eagle," "wormed, blown up/ By shells of light," the cathedral-cave of the body has been eaten away from within. Modern man has not only turned to the door of the cave; he has tried to let the light in through every wall of the cave. But the concluding image of the sonnet shows the consequences of his remodeling. The natural

6. Tate, "Emily Dickinson," 284.

world is dominated by this grotesque yoking of a bodiless but squat sun with a sterile and formless ocean mass. The twilight of civilization, imaged in the graceless setting sun, is also figured in what has happened to the human person. Sun and sea are parallel instances from the natural world of this terrible distortion of the relationship between light and cave, spirit and body.

Fortunately, the unrelieved gloom of "More Sonnets at Christmas" is mitigated somewhat by the no less stark but slightly more hopeful picture of man in "Winter Mask." The poem was originally intended to be part of "Seasons of the Soul," and an early working title was "Dejected Stanzas."[7] It has certain features that recall Yeats's system in *A Vision* as well as Spengler's cycles. The mask, understood as Yeats used it, is an aspect of the personality, one of a great cycle of human appearances replicated throughout history. In this poem the cyclical philosophy of history of Yeats and Spengler is echoed poetically rather than intellectually in the structure of the verse. The title indicates that the poet has assumed an attitude; his confession is a dramatic expression of a mood, not a permanent posture.

The pattern of repetitions and variations in "Winter Mask" is complex. It consists of a series of six stanzas, each rhymed in such a way that the rhyming words are widely separated from one another, with the exception of the first pair. Though these five sets of rhymes are scattered over the ten lines of each stanza, other words are repeated from section to section, linking them through a kind of echo. "Thing," "worth," "living," and "life" are the key words. The result is a kind of theme with variations, a closing cadence for each stanza that suggests a return to the same central problem: what is the worth of life?

The most important of the repeated words is "sea," and the refrainlike repetition of this word at the end of each stanza emphasizes its allusive character. Both "Winter Mask" and "More Sonnets at Christmas" end with a vision of the sea, and they share this image with "Seasons of the Soul." The title of the volume in which all of these poems were published, *The Winter Sea*, suggests the central problem treated in them: "Why is it man hates/ His own salvation,/ Prefers the way to hell . . . ?" as Tate says in "Winter Mask." Even Yeats's poetic solution

7. Allen Tate to Donald Davidson, January 29, 1943, in *Correspondence*, 335. Shortly afterwards (February 3, 1943), Tate refers to "Dejected Stanzas" as "Winter" and to the whole poem as "Seasonal Meditations, To the Memory of W. B. Yeats" (337).

to this problem is not completely satisfactory; for he offers an elaborate symbolic vision of man's destiny, but he cannot provide "the sea worth living for." That sea could stand for a culture, like the "known sea" of "The Mediterranean," or for the anonymity and hostility of the northern winter sea. But in "Winter Mask," the alternative to Yeats's visionary system is obviously Dante's *Comedy*, where the sea stands for God's will and where history is not cyclical but leads to a transcendent goal.

Tate offers "two scenes of hell" in the poem, one a naturalistic, the other a poetic image. The rat in the first scene makes its home in the wall, but poison turns that wall into a prison. Driven by the thirst induced by the poison, the rat drinks water outside his hole and is killed by it. Man has been driven to thirst after salvation of a secular character by the poisons of his civilization, but to swallow that substitute salvation is to destroy one's humanity. The second scene is taken from Canto XX of Dante's "Inferno." Ugolino and Ruggiero, trapped "in eternal ice," are linked in eternal hatred. Ugolino gnaws on Ruggiero's skull, fed by hate, the food of the damned. Neither rat nor Ugolino can benefit from the water of salvation, but Ugolino's is the uglier picture—it points to human degradation and not simply a horrible death.

The alternative to these "human bestiaries" is to turn to "the sylvan door," where nature has been offered as the sole means of salvation. However, nature can no longer serve in this traditional role, for she has been turned into a commodity, purchased with the false coin of rationality. Ugolino's cannibalism is matched in the natural world by the carnivorous crows. Like the poisoned rat, man is doomed to die by the same instrument that is supposed to bring him salvation. The life he would seek to save "rattles" like the skeleton of a hanged man against the tree. Nature is no longer a mother to man but a double-dealer who will offer him an "uneven trade."

Great poet though he may be, Yeats has nevertheless failed to answer the most important question his contemporaries have posed:

> Why it is man hates
> His own salvation,
> Prefers the way to hell,
> And finds his last safety
> In the self-made curse that bore
> Him towards damnation:

The drowned undrowned by the sea,
The sea worth living for.

Like Spengler, Yeats has been unable to say why human beings take such comfort in the thought that man resides in a world of relentless cycles of growth and decay, captive of his own narrow subjectivity and victim of a declining civilization. Yeats, Tate feels, has evaded the problem of moral choice. Man would rather think that his failures are not his fault, that he has been condemned unfairly to a destiny he does not deserve. He finds Dante's "Inferno" more interesting than his "Paradiso." Having lost the sense of transcendence, man cannot afford to confess his failures. He would prefer to attribute them to a mechanism that will not allow him to act freely. In hating his own salvation, man is really refusing to act because he fears true freedom of choice. As a result, he prefers to accept the notion that he can avoid choice by creating systems like Spengler's in which he is the object of a "self-made curse." Drowned in the routine of a comfortable but mechanical existence, he can find refuge in a kind of anonymity that frees him from responsibility for his actions.

But there is another existence, demanding and unpredictable, that forces man to respond and to swim, to save himself even as he fails, to become aware of himself as more than a floating body in an ocean of repeated patterns. The sea worth living for is the dimension of transcendence in which man drowns in order to find himself. As long as one is "drowned" in the meaningless chaos of a purely secular order, he cannot be immersed in the waters of an existence beyond himself. The two examples Tate presents in "Winter Mask" are illustrations. The rat seeks out the wrong kind of water; Ugolino, frozen in the icy waters of his own ego, is trapped in the very element that could have saved him. The rat accepts the "water of life" too readily, and his failure to discriminate destroys him. Ugolino turns his back on God's will and is caught in the winter sea of his own hatred.

The essential anguish that modern man experiences, then, stems from his inability to confess—to believe in a transcendent dimension that gives meaning to his failures and to admit his failures in the first place. The theme of "Winter Mask" is amplified and given more convincing scope in "Seasons of the Soul," which developed out of Tate's metrical experiments. The stanza form and stylistic devices are not simply incidental. As in "Winter Mask," they are at the heart of the poem; by creating a longer poem in four parts, Tate managed to give an even greater sense of theme and variation, sharpening the oppositions and creating a work that sums up his major themes. The earlier title, "Seasonal Confessions,"[8] is an important clue to the stance Tate assumes in this poem. It is, in fact, his version of the first seven books of Augustine's *Confessions*, combined with Dante's journey to Hell and placed in the context of an era in which man seems bent upon his own destruction.

The poem shows a complicated interplay of progression and recurrence. The four elements of air, earth, water, and fire and the four seasons that accompany them are obvious features of the cyclical theme. They remind one of Spengler's philosophy of history, of course, and "Winter" is a presentation of that vision of life under the guise of Lucretius, whose materialistic universe can never escape the endless cycle of its monotonous sameness. Indeed, the "circular miles" and the "circular delay" that Tate refers to are evidence in the poem of this meaningless play of repetitive forces. The world has been given over completely to "lust of power." In a letter to Tate, Donald Davison describes "the *four* parts of 'Seasons of the Soul' as reflecting *throughout* the disastrous implications of World World II."[9] War is symptomatic of even greater disorders in man. As long as man must be condemned to live as an object among other objects, he cannot expect to escape from the cycle in which every season is destructive of life.

The correspondences between Tate and Spengler should not be pushed too far; much of the imagery connected with the seasons is traditional or obvious and requires no arcane source to explain its presence. Nevertheless, the imagery, like the verse form, does have an important role to play in the poem as part of a major motif. Both serve to point to one way of seeing the present in relation to the past. The organic cycle, as espoused by such thinkers as Spengler, or his master Nietzsche, is a more widely accepted tenet among modern intellectuals than is often recognized. The repetition of similar states that makes up the Nietzschean "eternal return" of things back to their original condition makes of matter a subjective form, opposed to time, which is conceived of as objective. These conceptions are familiar; they are part of

8. Allen Tate to Donald Davidson, March 21, 1943, in *Correspondence*, 338.
9. Donald Davidson to Allen Tate, December 21, 1962, in *Correspondence*, 387.

the symbolic system that comprises the historical imagination. But the real question that confronts a reader of Tate's poem is whether or not these physical states of recurrence are also to be attributed, in Spenglerian and Nietzschean style, to the soul. Is man irrevocably trapped in an historical cycle? Will the concluding poem, "Spring," be followed by the same "Winter" that preceded it?

A progressive theme acts as the contrasting motif in the poem, but this pattern is not a simple upward movement. It proceeds downward first, then upward to a level higher than its point of departure. It is the movement that William F. Lynch, in a book greatly influenced by Tate, has called "the Christian imagination."[10] In order to rise, a person must first submit, descend into experience, and accept his human condition. Only then is it possible to emerge and proceed to a higher order.

The interplay of cycle and progression is notable in Tate's poetry as early as "Ode to the Confederate Dead," where nature is simultaneously viewed as an eternal cycle of "casual sacrament" and as a realm whose "crazy fingers" and screech-owl's call point to something higher than nature itself. As in the "Ode," the conflict between cycle and progression is not definitively resolved in "Seasons of the Soul." Even "Spring," the last part of the poem, is about a descent into submission rather than a rise to glory. The images of entrapment—the wartime horrors of "Summer," the fall down the well in "Autumn," and the suicide victim of "Winter"—are echoed by Jack and Jill and Sisyphus in "Spring," figures who attempt to go up first and are driven downward instead. The sheep who have dropped to "their crooked knees" in "Spring" are, on the other hand, descending in order eventually to rise.

"Summer" is about the maturity of the physical body, the period of early manhood and energy.

> Summer, this is our flesh,
> The body you let mature.

The season is one that Tate describes later in the poem as "all space and no time," when temporality is arrested in an idyllic moment of light and things have reached the term of their natural growth. In an early poem, "Idyl," Tate calls summer the "eucharist of death," and he shows

10. William F. Lynch, *Christ and Apollo: The Dimensions of the Literary Imagination* (New York, 1960), Chap. 8.

the partaking of its seemingly eternal stillness as a means of bringing forth a vision of the arrested sun. It is the season of spatial clarity, freed for an interval from the demands of time. But in our era, summer has become sinister:

> If now while the body is fresh
> You take it, shall we give
> The heart, lest heart endure
> The mind's tattering
> Blow of greedy claws?
> Shall mind itself still live
> If like a hunting king
> It falls to the lion's jaws?

In time of war it is the physical body that is directly endangered, but the poet recognizes a greater peril: the loss of the heart to the narrowly rational mind. The intellect cannot stand alone; it will succumb too easily to the lion of physical violence it seeks to subdue. The mind's spatial clarity cannot be exercised properly when faced by the urgency of a terrible violence and a desperately accelerated rate of change. The contemporary soul is faced by two alternatives for keeping the reason whole:

> The soul cannot endure
> Unless by sleight or fast
> It seize or deny its day
> To make the eye secure.

One may plunge directly into the mad rush of time, *carpere diem*, or seek cover from the hot sun of violence by closing one's eyes to it. Neither alternative is satisfactory; the mind is trapped if it would attempt to preserve its spatial control over the soul and body.

The lion of violence is surely meant to recall Dante's encounter, at the mature age of thirty-five, with the three beasts in the dark wood. Yet Dante was able to pass by the lion and the leopard that confronted him, stopped only by the she-wolf of lust. Tate's world is assaulted by a new kind of violence at a level of intensity undreamed of by Dante. It is a war that both "dries and draws" the body toward a violent end, leaving a fasting from or grasping at time as respective reactions to each effect. Both body and soul are endangered by the "hot wind" of the modern hell earth has become.

In the third stanza of "Summer," the lion of violence has become a voracious army of mechanically driven insects. The body—attacked by the feet and jaws of two hungry varieties of insect—keeps the head from any hope of rest or coming to terms with its own rational needs. In Dante's Hell, men lost the good of the intellect. In Tate's world man has lost even more, for he can no longer bring senses, understanding, and will into a coherent relationship. The inner and outer man are divided by "war's usurping claws." The summer has become a twilight era, dominated by an abstract spatiality that turns all things into empty equalities. In childhood, the timeless world of the "become," the "liquid light" of a timeless world, was life-sustaining. Now summer innocence has been destroyed by a sort of time-driven plague. The green world has been eaten alive by the destructive caterpillars of the German appetite; France, the land of clarity and rational thought, has fallen to armies that combine the European caterpillar, devourer of the leaf, with the southern cotton weevil, devourer of the boll. Between them, these two varieties of insect—like the invading Nazis—destroy both outer and inner being.

The importance of the element of air in the elaboration of this invasion crisis is not immediately evident. The hot, desiccating wind of an infernal time is of course an allusion to Dante's underworld landscape. The lines on the southern summer sky remind us that the South also fell to an invading enemy and was ravaged by men pressing their own idea of morality on another people. Yet even beyond this historical allusion there lies a further concern with the terrors of invasion. The easy familiarity of the summer sky has become nightmarish, a realm to be watched nervously with "tired eyes" for signs of the enemy. It was in England especially that a whole population was forced to serve as sentries during the blitzkrieg and bombings. World War II was the first conflict to involve total populations. A deeper source of concern is hinted at by Davidson, who seems to have understood Tate's "sky of glass,/ Blue, empty, and tall/ Without tail or head" as an allusion to Major Alexander P. Seversky's *Victory Through Air Power*.[11] What Seversky

11. Donald Davidson to Allen Tate, March 21, 1943, in *Correspondence*, 339, referring to Alexander P. De Seversky, *Victory Through Air Power* (New York, 1942), 156.

insisted upon was the radical change in military strategy wrought by the airplane. America's once "impregnable ocean ramparts" are no longer an effective barrier against a massive air strike.

Seversky's predictions are now commonplace fact, and the terrors he evokes have been replaced by even greater ones. Nevertheless, the radical nature of this new means of warfare is too easily overlooked; it is an important part of what Tate is saying. What he evokes in "Summer" is a world that has been suddenly altered almost beyond imagining. The sky is no longer a comfort but a threat. The element of air is a new medium of destruction. The world is paralyzed; it has become a battlefield where all places are equally vulnerable. The sky no longer stands for transcendence or infinity; it has become a place of pure mathematical space

> Where burn the equal laws
> For Balaam and his ass
> Above the invalid dead,
> Who cannot lift their jaws.

The dead can no longer advise the living, through precept or exemplary action, how to face such terrors of total destruction. The same invasion that destroyed France can just as easily overcome the remainder of the world.

The allusion to Balaam in the Book of Numbers, at first glance a minor reference to a minor biblical event, is of great importance to the theme of "Summer." Its meaning lies in an implicit link with Tate's Virgilian poems of the thirties, for the Hebrews were landless wanderers driven by a prophecy, like Aeneas and his followers. The invasion of the Hebrews in their march toward the Promised Land is in sharp contrast to the German invasion of "Green France." The Hebraic sense of a historic destiny, the struggle to gain a national homeland, the journey filled with hardships, all of the search for a place where a society of men could find its proper identity—these the Jewish and Trojan experiences have in common. The earthly paradise of a "land of milk and honey" that the Israelites sought in Canaan has its parallel in the founding of Rome and the settlement of America, but the invasion of France in the name of an abstract Aryan destiny is very different from the appeal to transcendent destiny characteristic of these other invasions.

Balaam's story is a clear attempt to demonstrate the divine sanction of the Israelite march through Transjordan. Sent by their enemies to curse the Hebrews, Balaam is made to bless them instead. His ass sees the implications of Jahweh's command before he does, and the beast talks to his master as a sign of the miraculous disclosure of the divine mandate. But the modern sky "burns" with the terror of total war and an invasion not of men but of machines. Balaam prophesied an eventual Israelite victory. Now man and ass are equally helpless, equally inarticulate, equally blind. The unspeakable monstrosity of this false destiny of the Aryan race can be met by no power other than one equally hellish. The empty dome of the summer sky holds no promise of salvation from a divine presence, and whole cultures are menaced by the rapacious mechanized power of the modern invader.

Unlike the Israelites, the Trojans, and the exiles who sailed to the New World, the modern can find no refuge, no land that will shelter him from the threat of instant annihilation. The poet turns at this point to consider another "invasion," this time a descent into the abyss rather than an escape from it. He recalls the journey of Dante and Virgil, two men who descended imaginatively into Hell for a prophecy of the future. The "vast concluding shell" of Dante's Inferno, like the modern "sky of glass," presents a frightening spectacle; the two men can no longer confront the "liquid light" of the "summer world" they left behind. Instead, they watch their shadows "curl" as the light dies before them and "confound" (that is, either "curse" or "confuse") the region they have been permitted to enter.

> Stopping, they saw in the narrow
> Light a centaur pause
> And gaze, then his astounded
> Beard, with a notched arrow,
> Part back upon his jaws.

Several commentators have pointed out that the centaur is Chiron, the wise teacher of certain Greek heroes. In the context of Canto XII of the "Inferno," however, the allusion takes on an added dimension, for the episode occurs in the realm of the violent, presided over appropriately by centaurs. Chiron, the only one among these men-beasts in Greek mythology who could control the violent centaur nature, is astonished to see Dante in his domain, for no living person has ever descended there before. Dante's invasion of this part of the Inferno, even if divinely sanctioned, could not be carried out without valor. In order to emerge safely from it, he must learn, as Chiron once did, to escape the violence within himself.

Dante's journey takes him down into the depths that no living man had ever before faced. Like the protagonist of "The Wolves," he has crossed the threshold of fear. In some ways, Dante is alone, and his solitude seems to be underlined by the curious way that he appears in this canto ("Inferno," XII). In the entire section, Dante never speaks a word—an exceptional situation in a poem about a poet. It is Virgil, the voice from the past, who requests an escort from Chiron. Both the Roman poet and the master centaur are part of the understanding that is accessible through the historical imagination, but there is a knowledge beyond their classical wisdom. Dante's living presence, even in silence, is testimony to a world beyond their grasp. Nessus, their centaur-guide, leads Dante and Virgil past a blood-immersed group of murderous tyrants, petty princes, and highwaymen. The entire canto is given over to those who are guilty of violence against other men, but the majority of the damned are political figures. Tate's choice of this particular canto seems to indicate his judgment of the inhuman violence of modern politics. Virgil, Chiron, and Balaam stand as those voices of prophetic wisdom from the past that can no longer be redemptive for modern man. Like Dante, the contemporary poet is a silent witness of horrors he cannot control. He must attempt to conquer within himself the inhuman impulses to which he is often driven by the modern world.

"Summer" acts as a prologue to the other sections of "Seasons of the Soul." It is concerned with the public and the political as manifesting presences of a world crisis. This first part is unique, for it alone of the four is dominated by masculine figures. The kind of wisdom they represent, as masculine versions of the soul's self-understanding, has been severely impaired by the overwhelming violence of the world order. The feminine side of the soul, figured in the mother of "Autumn," Venus in "Winter," and the "mother of silences" in "Spring," shows a different response. These figures form a triad in a progression that dramatizes the various levels of spiritual understanding. They also stand as examples of the earthly mother, Mother Nature, and a mysterious spiritual mother who replaces Virgil and Chiron as preceptors at the end of the poem.

"Autumn" is about violence in the private world of familial memories. Dante's Hell finds its counterpart in the rabbit hole down which Alice plunges in Wonderland. Dante's silence in Canto XII of the "Inferno" is matched by the protagonist's silence in "Autumn." He sees the ghosts of his immediate past, but no one will speak to him or to anyone else. Time has become space—"I walked years down/ Towards the front door"—and space is time frozen by silence. The look of the father is Medusan; it petrifies the young man standing in the hall. One is reminded of earlier poems, such as "A Pauper" and "The Paradigm," where the mother and father cannot communicate with each other or where lovers are frozen into a spatially projected confrontation that never ends in a meeting. The gloomy hall with its opening and closing doors recalls the Posey mansion in *The Fathers* as well as the room in which Alice is trapped after her fall down the rabbit hole. It is a prison corridor, haunted by the abstractions of family life rather than by any love. Detail is vague—there is nothing the eye can focus on—but the senses of smell, taste, and touch are curiously heightened. The fleeting shades "raise their eyes and squint/ As through a needle's eye/ Into the faceless gloom." An allusion to Dante ("Inferno," XV), this simile gives an important clue to the nature of Tate's vision in "Autumn," for the person Dante meets in the dark realm is none other than Brunetto Latini, who was himself a poet and a mentor of the author of *The Divine Comedy*. The canto is disturbing for Dante, for it presents a moral ambivalence in the life of a man whom he held in great respect as a teacher. Tate's family, discovered at the bottom of a dry well, stands for a paternal emptiness that is a kind of violence in itself. It is not simply a literal allusion to an unhappy childhood; the nightmarish world of "Autumn" shows that violence and alienation have touched the very heart of the family, the foundation of all societies. Dante's horror at seeing his esteemed teacher among the damned is paralleled by the terrified vision of a man whose memory discloses the spiritual slaughter (the air reminds the speaker of "a butcher's stall") of his entire childhood household in a self-imposed, hellish family imprisonment. The fall into the dry well is a visit to the underworld and a descent into the grave.

The dried-up well of "Autumn" can offer no source of life to the poet, yet the cyclical energies of the natural world have even less power of renewal. In "Winter" Tate presents further evidence of the alienation of man from those larger dimensions that once sustained him. The myths that once ordered the universe for man have perished. Venus, the "goddess sea-born and bright," is implored to

Return into the sea
Where eddying twilight
Gathers upon your people—
Cold goddess, hear our plea!
Leave the burnt earth, Venus,
For the drying God above,
Hanged in his windy steeple,
No longer bears for us
The living wound of love.

Lucretius' "eternal wound of love" and his lovely invocation to *De Rerum Natura* are contrasted in this opening stanza with the decline of the West (Venus' "people" were, of course, the Romans) and the impotence of Christianity. What has been lost is any sense of the transcendent, and so the poet turns for a moment to entertain a naturalistic vision such as Lucretius presents. Nature has become "the tossed anonymous sea." It provides "shade for lovers," but it includes the shark of violence as well as the dove of peace. Tate may have in mind the example of Hart Crane, who celebrated the sea as mother and lover only to commit suicide by drowning. Crane's romanticizing of the sea lost sight of its destructive powers. The beautiful invocation of *alma Venus* at the beginning of Lucretius' poem cannot conceal the fact that for modern men, as Tate has noted, Mother Nature has become an "it." In attempting to remythify nature, the modern poet has chosen death over life. Having rejected historical religion as a means of salvation, he takes on a mystical naturalism, combined with a superficial form of depth-psychology as his guide:

And now the winter sea:
Within her hollow rind
What sleek facility
Of sea-conceited scop
To plumb the nether mind!

However, the poet who explores these depths finds a kind of damnation in love rather than a salvation. The images that characterize this sea-love remind one of a scene of punishment from Dante's "Inferno":

Eternal winters blow
Shivering flakes, and shove
Bodies that wheel and drop—
Cold soot upon the snow
Their livid wound of love.

The naturalistic attempt to find a satisfactory order for human desires produces an underwater form of "ignis fatuus," the "phosphor glow" of a goal deceptively glimmering in "the circular miles" of a purely cyclical reality. The "pacing animal" that would pounce upon his victim is trapped in a cage; the attempt to escape into the recurrent order of nature simply leads to another kind of trap. Indeed, man has become like the "rigid madrepore," the "mother-stone" of a petrified life-force that "gives the leaf no more." In his wild embracing of the cold sea, the modern poet who would choose this alternative becomes a kind of "headless, unageing oak" that reminds one of Dante's Pier delle Vigne in Canto XIII of the "Inferno." Because it is a rejection of all transcendent dimensions, this neo-Lucretian naturalism leads to a death of the self. Tate calls it a "stratagem" that leads to "suicide." But at the same time he recognizes his own implication in the same indictment; he, too, has become a victim of the same "self-inflicted woe" that led to the death of a Hart Crane:

I touched my sanguine hair
And felt it drip above
Their brother who, like them,
Was maimed and did not bear
The living wound of love.

The poet recognizes that he has not escaped the fate of others who have yielded to the deceptive allurements of a philosophy centered on nature or some immanent life-force. The vision of a Spengler, taken at face value, is a strange form of death wish, impressively elaborated in the imaginative presentation of a supposedly organic world.

The kind of love Tate rejects in "Winter" is not self-love. It is rather a desire to become part of something larger than the ego that leads to both self-denial and self-hatred. Pier delle Vigne wished to be loyal to his prince, and it was the thought that a false accusation had destroyed his honor that led him to his death. Such a love does not value the self sufficiently. It seeks to punish failure and has no place for self-forgiveness. By refusing to recognize any seed of transcendence within his own soul, modern man has condemned himself to an irrational grasping after any available means of restoring his integrity, whether in sex, nature, or death. The kind of violence that produces universal destruction is possible only because man has lost patience with mankind and wishes to impose perfection on the earth at once, even at the cost of annihilating himself. The invasion of France in "Summer" and the suicide of Pier delle Vigne in "Winter" are manifestations of the same self-hatred; they share in a thematic unity that organizes all four seasons of the soul.

The first three sections of the poem trace a downward movement that is a search for causes. The violence against a whole people can be traced back to violence against the family, and that, in turn, has its roots in violence against the self. It is in "Spring" that the poet attempts to see his way out of the cyclical trap that characterizes the first three sections. Through it Tate seems to be looking for some small but unmistakable sign of self-renewal. In this, the most Augustinian of all of Tate's poems before his conversion, there is a rich collocation of images that seem to come directly from the Augustinian tradition:

> Irritable spring, infuse
> Into the burning breast
> Your combustible juice
> That as a liquid soul
> Shall be the body's guest
> Who lights, but cannot stay
> To comfort this unease
> Which, like a dying coal,
> Hastens the cooler day
> Of the mother of silences.

Combining Sir Walter Raleigh's picture of the soul with Shelley's image of the mind as a dying coal, Tate sees the end of his quest in a light internal to himself, not in an "ignis fatuus" toward which he must strain. Nature can be the spark that will ignite a new understanding in the heart, but something greater is required to "comfort this unease." The hoped-for reintegration of the self will not come all at once; it requires a kind of patience that comes in wooing silence.

Thinking back to the days of his youth, the poet recalls "a pleasant land/ Where even death could please/ Us with an ancient pun." The remembered past includes a time when death and the act of love were associated aspects of a unified sensibility. The kind of death that will return one to the bosom of "the mother of silences" is also an act of love and a call for assistance, a yielding to powers beyond oneself. The "hand" of the lady is granted in a marriage of the two components of the soul that allow her to work her hand in gaining its salvation. But the real problem is not in knowing the idyllic past or in expecting some utopian future. It is a question of recognizing what is happening in the present, of interpreting events as part of a larger pattern:

In time of bloody war
Who will know the time?
Is it a new spring star
Within the timing chill,
Talking, or just a mime,
That rises in the blood?

In such terrible times, enlightenment is perhaps imminent for those who have the patience to explore and observe the events around them. The poet asks the crucial question that has run throughout "Seasons of the Soul." Does history lead somewhere, or is it, like the nursery rhyme, a pattern of blindly executed rises and declines of civilization? Is meaning revealed through events, or are they "just a mime,/ That rises in the blood," following the systaltic beat of the heart from high to low and back again?

The question is not answered in the poem itself. In the following stanza, Tate introduces a complex weaving of the vain efforts of Sisyphus with Plato's image of the cave to suggest that it is man himself who does not want to find meaning in the world he inhabits. He would use the earth, again and again, to block out all light of transcendence, even as he arrogantly attempts to assert his superiority to all natural limits. For the light of transcendence reveals the "slave" in man, his frailty and failings as well as his subordination to higher forces. Like Sisyphus, man attempts to go beyond the pull of the earth only to find himself obliged to begin his futile push all over again. He cannot escape from this gravity; his only hope is in submission, like the sheep who kneel on "crooked knees." Confession is not the arrogance of self-assertion but the humility of recognizing that one has "begun to die." Yet to confess is not to achieve salvation if the final result is mere self-abasement. Some model of transcendence must be present in man's meditations to lift him from his bestial humility. He must learn to join his will with another form of gravitational force.

Despite the wartime darkness that prevails in most of "Seasons of the Soul," it is the first of Tate's mature poems to end with an image suggestive of a resurrection. In the last two stanzas, Tate combines several figures—Venus, the Virgin Mary, Monica, and the Cumaean Sibyl who led Aeneas down to his underworld vision:

> Come, old woman, save
> Your sons who have gone down
> Into the burning cave.

They are clearly intended to suggest both the pagan and Christian figures of the holy mother; and their presence at this point in the poem is of great significance, for it evokes a neglected motif in Tate's poetry. In order to set these figures in perspective, it will be necessary to return to several earlier poems that have not yet been discussed.

Eight

Memoria

IN HIS MEMOIR "A Lost Traveller's Dream," Tate speaks eloquently of the figure that emerges finally as the ordering force in his quest for wholeness:

> Memory arrests the flow of inner time, but what we remember is not at the command of our wills; it has its own life and purposes; it gives what *it* wills. St. Augustine tells us that memory is like a woman. The Latin *memoria* is properly a feminine noun, for women never forget; and likewise the soul is the *anima*, even in man, his vital principle and the custodian of memory, the image of woman that all men both pursue and flee.[1]

Tate has in mind the notable analysis of memory in Book Ten of *The Confessions*, but he unites with it a picture of the soul that was already ancient when Lucretius, in Books III and IV of *De Rerum Natura*, distinguished a vital principle (anima, the cause of sensation in the body) and an intellectual one (animus, the mind, the seat of emotion and thought). C. G. Jung has revived this distinction, giving it a somewhat different psychological interpretation. Tate rather characteristically refuses to honor the division and broadens the feminine side of human existence to make it a poetic image of guardianship. By making the soul the guardian of memory, he brings to the forefront a new version of the once influential Augustinian psychology that made the soul not a duality but a trinity of memory, understanding, and will.

The famous analysis of memory in *The Confessions* is a key to Augustinian thought; for through the power of memory man can bridge the gaps that separate existence from non-existence, past from present, concrete from abstract. It is through memory that man achieves whatever salvation is available to him; and through this ability to remember

1. Allen Tate, "A Lost Traveller's Dream," in *Memoirs*, 12.

confession becomes possible. Without memory, man is fragile and ungrounded; with it, he can know himself and have a meaningful history. Romano Guardini has said of this great theme in Augustine's work that it makes the transitory permanent and man's longing for the absolute through the *beata vita* a meaningful enterprise. The poet who takes this as his major theme will be different from any who ignores it, for memory alone provides that double perspective on the world that can discover order in apparent chaos. Memory is not simply nostalgia; for Augustine it is synonymous with the divine, the transcendent presence within, the inner teacher. Guardini analyzes the impact of this dual perspective:

> The whole world, insofar as a man encounters it and has become the content of his life, exists twice: actually and in the memory. Twice, too, he himself exists, and everything that happens to him. In the second manner of being a man is not only "present," "here," but he exists intellectually and spiritually. It renders him conscious of himself and of all that has entered into his life; he is able to review that existence, to gather it together from the years and examine it in the present moment. Thus he is enabled to judge himself, to answer for his acts, and to place himself and his life before God. "Memoria," then, is the prerequisite of "confessio."[2]

The loss of memory, this dual perspective, reduces man to a being of only one dimension. When Tate speaks of the modern as a frightened hare, "scurrying/ Without memory" ("Message from Abroad"), he is also identifying the prime failure of himself and his contemporaries as a narrowness of vision. Modern man, as he notes from the beginning of his career, has become abstract, visually exclusive, and bound to the letter of the word. He is incapable of seeing beyond a single level of meaning because his imagination has lost this perspective that memory supplies.

Evidence of this blindness is prevalent throughout Tate's poetry, but it is especially prominent in "the image of woman that all men both pursue and flee." Feminine figures in his first poems—the Duchess of

2. Romano Guardini, *The Conversion of Augustine*, trans. Elinor Briefs (Westminster, Md., 1960), 15.

Malfi or the degraded women of "Bored to Choresis," "The Flapper," and "Hitch Your Wagon to a Star"—are ineffectual wraiths rather than images of hope. The woman who refuses to stoop to modern folly, like the young virgin of "Parthenia" or the older one of "To a Prodigal Old Maid," remains a puzzle rather than an inspiration. The girl in "Mary McDonald," "Resurgam," or "Credo in Intellectum Videntem" is mysteriously inaccessible. The poet may "take her Image to a secret place," as Tate puts it in "Eager Youths to a Dead Girl," but he can find no fulfillment, spiritual or erotic, in her person. Only in a translation of a fragmentary poem by Sappho, "Farewell to Anactoria," is there an image of femininity untouched by modern irony.

These negative or incomplete images of woman continue to appear in subsequent verse. "Inside and Outside," "The Robber Bridegroom," "Last Days of Alice," "Mother and Son," and "Sonnets of the Blood" offer weak, perverse, or overbearing and masculine depictions of women. With the exception of the dead woman in "The Anabasis," one looks in vain for a figure embodying positive feminine virtues. Two examples of the poet's inability to create such an image are particularly striking because, among the earliest poems, they represent fairly ambitious attempts at overcoming these failures. Tate tries to find in each of them some pagan image of life and fertility that remains meaningful in the modern world. In "Prayer to the Woman Mountain," he presents a sort of Earth-mother who is a massive bearer of memories.[3] Her face is pocked and pitted with stars and ruth, and her arms bear the remains of man's oldest curses. Her face is not beautiful, but it has a depth that reflects long experience of good and evil. Modern man, anxious to free himself from the bonds of the mother, is "unborn in living" and attempts to build rivals to the Woman Mountain. But the skyscraper-cities of his creation will desert him eventually, for these images of assertive power will not save him from destruction. Man is always tied to the Earth-mother in whom he is rooted. Yet if he is like a tree, he draws from her not the water of life but the "black blood" of petroleum that sustains his technology. Because the modern has never truly emerged from the earth's womb and brought up his eyes to the light, he remains bound to the earth as a prisoner, dependent on her like a perverse child.

3. Allen Tate, "Prayer to the Woman Mountain," in *Mr. Pope and Other Poems* (New York, 1928), 17–18.

To escape her, however, is to reject the body, that inescapable tie to the Woman Mountain which is only partly broken by the "different birth" of dying.

The poem bears as epigraph a stanza from the medieval Latin hymn "Dies Irae," and the plea at its conclusion is given a different sense by the apocalyptic verses of the dirge:

> Rex tremendae maiestatis,
> Qui salvandos salvas gratis—
> Salva me, fons pietatis!
>
> (King of fearsome majesty, who in saving save
> without recompense, save me, source of piety.)

"Prayer to the Woman Mountain" is about the vision of the last things. The Earth-mother must be accepted as the source and destination of our bodies, but she must also be transcended by the waters of the "fons pietatis" who is the source of salvation. The pagan figure of the Earth-mother is an insufficient, if necessary, step in coming to transcendence. For all her heights and depths, she cannot match the "rex tremendae maiestatis" to whom one must turn for help on the day of wrath. The prayer for release from the Woman Mountain is a recognition that man must yield to the earth but that he must also go beyond her and begin anew.

Tate has not reprinted "Prayer to the Woman Mountain" since 1928, but he has continued to reprint another poem from the same period. A longer poem with a mythical feminine figure at its center, the sequence "The Progress of Œnia," also argues the impossibility of recovering the imaginative world of the fertility goddess. At first the poem seems unaccountably ornamental in comparison with Tate's other work:

> Seed in your heart, warm dust transmuted
> Gold, blooms in flakes of radiance
> Arched in your face whereon my days,
> Brinks of silence, glance.

Œnia is a warm Primavera figure of awakening love and light, reminiscent of Swinburne's neopagan "maiden most perfect, lady of light" in *Atalanta in Calydon*, but her portrait is ambivalent:

How many winds forget the sea!
Your dubious intention I forgot
And look into the eager waste
Of your eyes unmemoried of yesterday.

She is opposed to the Woman Mountain, who is a figure of *memoria.* This radiant goddess is an emblem of the new, but like the Venus she partially resembles, Œnia leaves behind her only an "eager waste." She has no permanence:

Not now are you a whispered glory
Splendid of dreams from Baalbek;
You scattered in a highway dust
The loosed emeralds of a dream.

At the end of the poem, the poet admits that he cannot celebrate feminine beauty with the decadent poise of Propertius or Donne, for his only poetic subject is "the dry debility/ Of a spent wind in a winter tree." The ultimate focus of the poem is not the lady at all but the poet's inability to write convincingly about her. As an imaginative figure she cannot be taken seriously, and yet she is of interest because she is the first of Tate's versions of the lady of light.

The epigraph to the sequence is from Propertius, II, vi. The elegy from which the lines come is an attack on Cynthia for her loose behavior: "It was because of these vices, as they tell, that the world went to war; these were the beginning of the Trojan slaughter." In a lighthearted way, Œnia is made into a kind of belle over whom great battles might be waged.

Can more be said about her identity? One looks in vain to classical dictionaries, where her name does not figure; and it is probable that Tate invented her. "Œnia" would mean something like "she of the vine." In the first poem, "Madrigale," the speaker turns from the Beatrician lady of medieval and renaissance Europe back to this pagan figure:

Dream-emptied by some shifting
Monna Bice, you I resume:
Continually suffer the habitual
Cobra of my slightest gloom.

A complex combination of several figures, Œnia seems to be a sort of Alexandrian creation. She is associated with Cyrene in the fourth poem and therefore belongs among those nature goddesses who reign over farming and hunting. Cyrene was also the mid-summer bee goddess who wrestled a lion and had a son by Apollo. Her connection with Apollo and other characteristics make her into a sort of Artemis. But an allusion in an early version of Tate's poem to Baalbek[4] seems to place her as a combination of Bacchus and Venus with a temple in that city.

For all this splendor of association and light-handed classical pastiche, Tate cannot consider such a goddess as anything but an inaccessible ideal. However, in the early forties, Tate took up the late Latin "Pervigilium Veneris" and, after finally working out a satisfactory version of its refrain, translated it as "The Vigil of Venus." Though a pagan poem in the fullest sense, something of the religious fervor that is evident in its celebration of the erotic must have struck Tate quite forcefully. Indeed, as Tate points out in his introduction to the translation, it was Swinburne's neopaganism that kept him from appreciating it properly as a young man. Later he was particularly struck by the last two stanzas of the poem, notably by the "maid of Tereus," whose song does seem to introduce a new dimension in the poem. Up to this point, Tate says, the "Pervigilium Veneris" is moving "but it is not brilliant." The song of the violated girl comes out of the wisdom of suffering, and it is a challenge different from the hoarse cries of the "tall swans" on the lake. For she alone can speak out:

> She sings, we are silent. When will my spring come?
> Shall I find my voice when I shall be as the swallow?
> Silence destroyed the Amyclae: they were dumb.
> Silent, I lost the muse. Return, Apollo!

These lines lead straight into Tate's most magnificent poetry, from "Spring" in "Seasons of the Soul" to "The Buried Lake." Tate attributes the power of the stanza to the sudden appearance of the poet in his own voice. His commentary on it is a key to the poetry and prose that were to emerge in the next ten years:

> The symbolic power of the scene in stanza XXI is firmly grounded in the dramatic perception of the poet, whose person-

4. Allen Tate, "The Progress of Œnia," in *Mr. Pope and Other Poems*, 47.

> ality has not previously appeared. It appears explicitly in stanza XXII, where this long, gentle meditation on the sources of all life comes to a climax in the poet's sudden consciousness of his own feeble powers. When shall I, he says, like Philomela the swallow, suffer violence and be moved to sing? It is this unexpected and dramatic ending that makes, for me, what were otherwise an interesting ritualistic chant, one of the finest of lyric poems. Perhaps in the Amyclae, the people of the town of that name in Latium who were called *tacitae*, and who, when menaced by an enemy, could not speak for help and were destroyed, we may see an image of all "late" people. I like to think that the *Amyclae tacitae* were not Latians but lived in the Laconian town of that name, where Apollo was the tutelary deity under the surname Amyclaeus, and that having offended their god, the Laconian Amyclae were cursed with silence and died of their own emptiness of song. May we see something of this in the last stanza of the poem? If there is any external evidence for it I have not been able to find it. Yet is the poem not telling us that the loss of symbolic language may mean the extinction of our humanity?[5]

Whether or not Tate is right about the Latin original, he is surely correct about the meaning of the poem created by his own translation. The theme of silence is of pivotal importance in Tate's poetry, early or late, but it changes in significance as one moves towards "Spring." Love and language are closely linked in the kind of communion Tate insists is essential to man. The "lady of light" is the symbol of love and inspiration, and to lose her is to lose part of one's humanity. The Venus of "Pervigilium Veneris" is not a lady of light, but neither is she the violent goddess of "Winter." She is a figure of joy that presages the coming change in Tate's poetry:

> She shines the tarnished year with glowing buds
> That, wakening, head up to the western wind
> In eager clusters. Goddess! You deign to scatter
> Lucent night-drip of dew; for you are kind.

Through his work on "The Vigil of Venus," Tate found a more convincing image of the feminine.

5. Allen Tate, Introduction to "The Vigil of Venus," in *Collected Poems*, 148.

The climax of all these figures is the "mother of silences" in "Seasons of the Soul." As early as 1933, in an article entitled "Poetry and Politics," Tate refused to give up the figure of the Queen of Heaven, such as she appears in the verses of a medieval poet like Thibaut-le-Grand, and he described her as the kind of figure that a poet must have for his muse: "Our model is the Virgin if she will consent to instruct us."[6] The silence that is longed for in "Spring" is the ability to listen and confess to such a muse. She is superficially like Eliot's "Lady of Silences" in "Ash Wednesday," but as poetic images, they are different in kind. Tate noted, concerning this very figure in "Ash Wednesday," that in Eliot "there are images of his own invention which he almost pushes over the boundary of sensation into abstraction, where they have the appearance of conventional symbols."[7] But Tate's "mother of silences" cannot be pushed toward abstraction because she is grounded in an historical figure, Monica, the watchful guardian of a wayward son.

Monica is a paradoxical figure. In the pages of *The Confessions* she is consistently treated with great reverence, and yet one senses that she must have seemed to be both "terrible mother" and "blessed mother" to her tortured child. Though a gentle woman, she apparently possessed some of the determination that Tate depicts in the more imposing personalities of the mother in "Sonnets of the Blood" or "Mother and Son." For Augustine she was the source of his great dilemma. As Romano Guardini points out, she was for her son "the living representative of that demand which it is possible to fulfill only after first coming to grips with the all-essential (a circumstance, by the way, which does not prevent Monica from exercising also a negative influence)."[8] Thus his "mother, with all her worries, is burdensome to him," yet it is from her that Augustine learns finally how to live. The lesson of the mother, who "hovers over [him] with growing concern," is virtually a tyranny; and "regarding the manner in which all this takes place, we cannot shake off the impression of a certain ruthlessness on her part."[9] The powerful personality of Monica was one against which Augustine fought, even as he recognized his need for her influence. The greatest

6. Allen Tate, "Poetry and Politics," *New Republic*, LXXV, 311.
7. Allen Tate, "T. S. Eliot's *Ash Wednesday*," in *Essays*, 470.
8. Guardini, *The Conversion of Augustine*, 146.
9. *Ibid.*, 147.

thing she taught him, however, was how to die, and an important climax in *The Confessions* is the scene in which she so willingly accepts her death. In "Sonnets of the Blood," Tate has caught this same understanding, even if he does not have Monica in mind:

> Your blood is altered by the sudden death
> Of one who of all persons could not use
> Life half so well as death. Let's look beneath
> That life. Perhaps hers only is our rest—
> To study this, all lifetime may be best.

The paradoxes of Monica were not new to Tate, then, when he composed "Spring." The powerful influence of a mother to whom the son refuses to yield, presented in "Mother and Son," is reversed in "Seasons of the Soul," where the speaker has learned, as Augustine did, to accept the figure of the mother freely because he recognizes for the first time all that she stands for. If, as Guardini says, Monica took on a symbolic dimension in Augustine's mind that "was of utmost importance in his life, far outstripping the usual limits of maternal help, advice, and exhortation,"[10] then an understanding of the "mother of silences" as symbol is crucial to an interpretation of Tate's poem. Guardini describes her influence this way:

> His mother's influence on Augustine's life was of the spirit, or rather, of the Holy Spirit, an influence revealed most clearly later, in his image of the Church. She is the great holy Mother. It is she who draws the natural man into her inexpressible, only-to-be-believed depths that are at once grave and womb, bearing him through the already liturgically suggested act of baptism into the new Christian life. For Augustine, Monica seems to have been the representative, the living embodiment of the Church.

Guardini notes in Augustine's writings an interesting coming together of several images and several goddesses. Commenting on a passage in Book V, Chapter 8 of *The Confessions*, he elaborates on this complex image:

> The physical mother, longing to bear her child also into the new life of grace, pouring the water of her tears on the oldest mother

10. *Ibid.*, 150.

> of all, Earth, in the sight of the all-renewing God[.] Finally, now in apocalyptical dimension, the oneness of mother and Church at the end of Book Nine. In the place of the Earth-mother, a new maternal figure appears: the eternal, all-embracing abundance of the Heavenly Jerusalem, which is none other than the Church fulfilled.[11]

These parallels suggest a coincidence of vision between Tate and Augustine rather than a direct influence. The value of the Augustinian motifs in any consideration of Tate is that they reveal some important dimensions in his poetry where they might not otherwise be suspected. For like Augustine, Tate is concerned in his poetic quest with finding the right society. He saw glimpses of it in the vanishing Old South. In "Seasons of the Soul," faced with the imminent collapse of all human communities on the face of the earth, he is groping toward a new image of culture, one that is incorporated in the concrete experience of a spiritual family and a new spiritual mother. Yet he has not yet made the final decision to enter this new society; "Seasons of the Soul" does not describe a conversion but a threshold experience like that of "The Cross." The war has forced modern man to make an urgent choice. He can opt for the kind of natural cycle that the seasons and the four elements stand for, or he can look for some discipline that will show him how to approach death in a completely different fashion.

If the notion of the two cities can be extended to include the two mothers, it would seem that Tate's verse also demands a further discrimination of two silences. In all of his poetry up to and even including "The Vigil of Venus," Tate sees silence as an inability on the part of the modern poet to speak out. "Spring" offers a sudden revaluation of the meaning of silence. Tate has moved to an appreciation of the contemplative mode of speechlessness; and in so doing, he has returned to yet another Augustinian theme. Joseph A. Mazzeo speaks of Augustine's great originality in adapting the language of rhetoric and eloquence to his metaphysics and theology and shows that a "movement from words to silence, from signs to realities is the fundamental presupposition of Augustinian allegorical exegesis." Thus "the world that Scripture described was itself a further silent, wordless allegory of the

11. *Ibid.*, 151.

eternal. The whole created world is a set of symbols of the divine, a sublime poem whose words are things, whose silent voice is the voice of its creator." For Augustine, "true rhetoric culminates in silence, in which the mind is in immediate contact with reality." This is the kind of silence, Mazzeo goes on to show, that dominates the crucial events of Augustine's autobiography, where silence is "nothing else than listening to the instruction of the inner teacher," and to move through love "to that silence from which the world fell into the perpetual clamour of life as fallen men know it."[12] It is of primary importance that Tate came to renounce the strain of trying to speak out to an uncaring world and sought in silence the perspective he needed to recapture those lost dimensions of myth and imagination whose lack he so insistently deplored.

The specific reference to *The Confessions* in "Spring" comes in the penultimate stanza of the poem:

Come, mother, and lean
At the window with your son
And gaze through its light frame
These fifteen centuries
Upon the shirking scene
Where men, blind, go lame.

Monica's sibylline vision of what is to come reveals, fifteen centuries later, a dismal scene. Man has lost both his intellect, in a spiritual blindness, and his body, in a lameness of his own physical nature. As Augustine reports, in his moving account, mother and son sit in a window overlooking the interior garden that was a typical feature of Roman houses. The setting reminds one of the garden within the heart, the lyric moment of recovery that is about to follow in the search for spiritual paradise. The two are far removed from the noise of the street crowds and their long journey from Milan to Ostia; they rest in preparation for the sea voyage that will take them back to Africa. One senses immediately that Monica's repose is preparing her for a quite different voyage. Yet far from communing without words, mother and son use language as

12. Joseph A. Mazzeo, "St. Augustine's Rhetoric of Silence: Truth vs. Eloquence and Things vs. Signs," in *Renaissance and Seventeenth-Century Studies* (New York, 1968), 9, 11, 17, 22.

a means of reaching understanding, for after their contemplation they return "to vocal expressions of our mouth, where the word spoken has beginning and end." This experience of beginning and end leads to a perception of the Word of God, "who endureth in Himself without becoming old, and maketh all things new." Thus the "mother of silences" is not herself silent. The poet asks her both to speak and listen:

> Speak, that we may hear;
> Listen, while we confess
> That we conceal our fear;
> Regard us, while the eye
> Discerns by sight or guess
> Whether, as sheep foregather
> Upon their crooked knees,
> We have begun to die.

She is his confessor, the person who both listens and advises and shepherds the sinner into right actions. She herself is neither brooding nor silent, but a vigorous figure of motherly involvement in the fortunes of her sons. She is both the sibylline prophetess who points toward the future and the spokesman for a world greater than the bounds of the conscious self.

It is Augustine's description of their conversation, however, that gives the key to Tate's poem as a whole, for in this mystical moment of contemplation the notion of silence receives its definitive articulation:

> We were saying then: If to any the tumult of the flesh were hushed, hushed the images of earth, and waters, and air, hushed also the pole of heaven, yea the very soul be hushed to herself, and by not thinking on self surmount self, hushed all dreams and imaginary revelations, every tongue and every sign, and whatsoever exists only in transition, since if any could hear, all these say, We made not ourselves, but He made us that abideth for ever—If then having uttered this, they too should be hushed, having roused only our ears to Him who made them, and He alone speak, not by them, but by Himself, that we may hear His Word, not through any tongue of flesh, nor Angel's voice, nor sound of thunder, nor in the dark riddle of a similitude, but

> might hear Whom in these things we love . . . were not this, Enter into thy Master's joy? [13]

This silence is a putting behind of "the images of earth, and waters, and air," the elements that form the physical motifs of the first three parts of Tate's poem. The poet wishes to hear from the lady he addresses "Whether your kindness, mother,/ Is mother of silences." The complex figure of the old woman and mother who can save her sons as they descend into "the burning cave" is a reminder that her guardianship in enduring love is extended to every stage of the journey. The confession at the end of "Seasons of the Soul" is an admission of helplessness and dependence. It is the first movement toward conversion. Louis Dupré has noted the necessity of finding this new perspective through silence that allows one to see himself for the first time: "To know oneself is to remember onself, and to remember onself entirely is to remember one's origin. At this point immanence turns into transcendence, and autobiography into confession." [14]

The meaning of confession in "Seasons of the Soul" is tied closely to the ability to remember and to speak. In poems like "Sonnets at Christmas" and "Autumn," Tate has explored the deep-seated experience of guilt that seems to be central to a discovery of the true self. In guilt and fear, man paradoxically comes to a realization of his dependence on another, and in that realization he opens the way to his acceptance of that part of himself which transcends the natural world. History, confession, alienation, fear, and love are all brought together in the last lines of "Seasons of the Soul" through the centrifugal force of the Augustinian perspective. But the moment of silence introduces a further theme: the rediscovery of the self through the soul's powers of memory, understanding, and will. They are the guardians of man's psychic integrity, opposed to an unsubmissive rationality driven by a narrow egoism. Echoing Blake, Tate calls this egoism "seeing *with* rather than *through* the eye." [15]

This loss of the ability to see things in their analogical relation to a

13. Saint Augustine, *The Confessions*, trans. Edward B. Pusey (New York, 1949), 187–88.

14. Louis Dupré, *Transcendent Selfhood* (New York, 1976), 74.

15. Allen Tate, "The New Provincialism," in *Essays*, 546. The phrase echoes a sentence of Blake in his "A Descriptive Catalogue."

significance beyond them is the subject of a poem Tate published after "Seasons of the Soul" and before his conversion to Catholicism. "The Eye" is a negative confession, a last purging from the modern soul of its blindness. The poem is a parody of a mystical experience; in a succession of perceptions, it leads from the child's to the mature man's vision of emptiness. In place of silence, modern man's "ascent" has taken him to a vision of nothingness. What he has lost is the tradition, emanating from St. Augustine, of dealing with the world as a text. In speaking of the exegetical techniques of the Middle Ages, Beryl Smalley has compared the ability to see *through* the letter with the "pierced technique" in medieval art, where we are "invited to focus our eyes not on the physical surface of the object, but on infinity as seen through the lattice." This, she says, "is also an exact description of exegesis as understood by Claudius, if we substitute 'text' for the 'physical surface' of the artists' material and 'truth' for infinite space. We are invited to look not at the text, but through it."[16]

Like "The Meaning of Death," Tate's "The Eye" offers a direct picture of what happens to the soul when letter is preferred to spirit, the City of Man to the City of God, the "beam in the mind's eye" of "Jubilo" to the moat of our imperfect existence. "The Eye" offers a succinct history of contemporary man's death wish as an alternative to despair over the loss of transcendence. The child roves "under the clean sheets" in order to hide from evil, but sanitation alone cannot provide a sufficient order to oppose the dangers lurking beyond his crib. As an older man, he sees nothing through the lattice of the sky except "a black hole." (Tate's poem is too early to be an allusion to the now familiar astronomical phenomenon.) His sky, become abstract, infinitely tall, and "sphereless" (like the sky in "Summer"), is the only cover that the "natural man" can pull over him for protection, but that sky leaves him more exposed than ever. Nor can nature offer any relief, for modern man sees the natural world as his enemy and the seasons as his destiny in death.

"The Eye" depicts a world that has misused memory. It has equated illness with the childlike, evil with love, happiness with maturity, elegance with abstraction. The past is lost and history dissolved in the "carbolic" dissipation of the "nuclear eye." The destructive technology

16. Beryl Smalley, *The Study of the Bible in the Middle Ages* (Oxford, 1952), 2.

that Western man evolved during the Second World War has turned a decadent civilization into an infernal one. Man has descended to the very pit of hell,

> Down, down until down is up
> And there is nothing in the eye.

Robert Fitzgerald has seen in these lines an allusion to the last stages of Dante's journey through Hell. Having reached the bottom, Dante moves again toward the light even though he has not changed direction.[17] If Fitzgerald is correct in this identification, then "The Eye" has a certain ambivalence in its conclusion. Perhaps Tate is suggesting that modern man will end by exhausting himself. The black crows of death, which Davidson accurately identified as referring to the world of the medieval English ballad,[18] are summoned by the dying to finish them off. The eye has become the "shut shutter" of a mere mechanism, the "mineral man/ Who takes the fatherless dark to bed." He has become an object among objects; he no longer exercises the vision or perspective that enables one to see the whole of things. His memories are partial; they cannot give him an imaginative view of the totality of existence. His is the "linear sight" which, as Tate predicted early in his poem "Homily," will lead to self-destruction.

"The Eye" is a bitter summation of themes that go back to Tate's early work, to "Idiot" and "Light" among those poems in which he explores the exclusive domination of the space-imposing eye. Yet it is different from them in one significant concept. Modern man, like Dante in the pit of Hell, can go no further in the direction of damnation. The destruction of the eye and its contents can mean the utter loss of all humanity, or it can point to a new beginning in a genuine psychic coherence. Once the eye is emptied, it loses its domination, and the soul can be reordered. That reordering can take place only when soul and memory are restored to their feminine character as bearers of meaning and released from the masculine dominion of the one-dimensional letter that kills.

Sight is associated by Augustine with space, but hearing is associated with time. Tate uses the eye as a symbol for the rational ego, that

17. Robert Fitzgerald, "The Poetic Responsibility," *New Republic*, CXVIII, 33.
18. Donald Davidson to Allen Tate, January 1, 1963, in *Correspondence*, 388.

sense with the highest powers of abstraction and analysis. The plunge through the mirror in "Last Days of Alice" is a phenomenon that takes place in space under the guidance of the visual imagination and through the rigid exclusion of the other senses. In "The Trout Map" the eye dominates through the "egoed belly's dry cartograph." In order for the soul to achieve wholeness, one must balance this overemphasis on sight and rational ego with sound and the childlike playfulness of the imagination. When the eye learns to sing through poetry, it learns to bring two levels of reality into consciousness and engage these two complementary senses in a broader unity of perspective.

Tate makes an awkward but amusing attempt at achieving this radical breakthrough in a pair of satirical lyrics published after "The Eye." Though some critics find them to be almost embarrassingly silly, they are important evidence of the sudden emergence in Tate's poetry of a new discovery. Here for the first time he allows the real depth of a self unbounded by the narrow limits of the letter to be disclosed. The childish extravagance of "Two Conceits for the Eye to Sing, If Possible" is the bursting forth of a suppressed part of the self, and it is the kind of undignified manifesto that is part of the confessional risk.

The first of the conceits is based on "Sing a song of sixpence." It includes references to Shakespeare's "Phoenix and the Turtle," to Freudian psychological theory, and to "Comin' Through the Rye." There is a hint of Louis XIV's "l'état, c'est moi" conjoined with the public fireworks of the modern state. An allusion to "Two billion Messieurs Gide" is another way of speaking about this odd publicizing of the private and the private appropriation of the public, for the French writer has promoted a message of egoism all over the globe: "Loving's in the I" rather than in the eye of the beholder. His counterparts are the "Two billion Turtle-doves/ Mourning in a sty." Venus' bird of love has become a pig wallowing in mud or an infection in the eye. The phoenix and the turtle devour each other instead of uniting.

The first part of the poem is concerned with the theme of love; the second, consisting of two stanzas, is about the city: "London/ Paris and Berlin/ Washington and Moscow/ Where the Ids are in." The first part is about the ego, the second about the id. Their opposition and separation have led to the perversion of another city and another love, Bethlehem and the incarnation, into vague symbols of well-being:

Star of all the Idmen
Everybody's Jesus
Now if never then.

As Tate says earlier in "Retroduction to American History," "every son-of-a-bitch is Christ, at least Rousseau." The modern city is the domain of self-serving but mechanical messiahs, all "Defunctive in the sense." The turtledove, now degraded into an uncontrolled libido, has become a devourer of "King Jesus." The attempt to extend the state into the stratosphere with the long-range rocket is a parallel assertion. The soul is indulged in both its severed dimensions of ego and id and unified only in the "mutual flame" of blind and ignorant passion.

The second conceit takes its point of departure from the nursery rhyme "Hey, Rub-a-Dub," playing on a slightly bawdy hint of illicit pregnancy. All has been turned inside-out. "Small" has become "a little Great" and the "Apple" is now "round the pig." The sky looks down with its "voluminous eye," suggesting that, like the three men in a tub lost on the ocean, the ego awaits a rebirth. But all is a joke, for the heavens are now the "belly-sky" and something surprising is about to occur:

So the dubbed conceit
Played nursery of cheat
To clear the I of sleet;
Wiped Eye dripping conceit
And tipped by tubby fear
Slipped into the ear
All the I's old gear,
Semicircled a tear
With blind sound.

The spinning tub and the odd transformations serve the purpose of disorienting the eye, which can now sing in "blind sound." Though the poet has not yet arrived at a level of comfortable psychic unity, he can see ahead of him the image of the Virgin, dancing "light as a green fairy." The color of hope, the dance, the fairy figure of a small girl, the tear, and the pun on "I" all point forward to a rewriting of this sketch into three more serious poems, each of which traces the movement from alienation to a refound wholeness.

The component themes of Tate's last poems are memory, light, and love. They correspond well to the tripartite division of the soul described by Augustine in his *The Trinity*: memory, understanding, and will. In Book Nine, Augustine anticipates this triad with a simpler one: "the mind itself, its love and its knowledge are a kind of trinity; these three are one, and when they are perfect they are equal."[19] Later, during a long analysis of the mind in Book Ten, in the course of asking how the mind may seek and find itself, he develops this more complex psychic trinity. The point of his analysis is that, according to doctrine, man is made in the image of God. If that is so, then it must be the soul rather than the body that is the bearer of this image. In examining the structure of the mind, Augustine seeks to find that within it which reflects the transcendent image of God as Trinity. Yet at the end of Book Fifteen, he recognizes the limitations of these analogies, for he is as careful to point out the flaws in his comparisons as he was to make them sound convincing. Despite his impressive pages of often exhaustive analysis, Augustine is wary of an over literal application of his psychology to his theology.

This caution is unnecessary for the poet, who works in the realm of fiction and image, where everything he creates must be recognized as a figure of something else. Tate's access to the Augustinian analysis of the soul does not seem to have been through a reading of the philosophic passages in *The Trinity* but through an assimilation of Dante's presentation of it in his poetry. It is not surprising to find this Augustinian psychology at the heart of *The Divine Comedy*, for Dante's poem is triadic to its very core, and Augustine's tripartite division of the soul was still operative in the language of the seventeenth-century Spanish mystics some three centuries after him. What is of particular note, however, is that Dante, like Augustine and Tate, chooses to represent the soul and its faculties through images of the feminine.

Augustine sometimes refers to his three divisions of the soul as memory, vision, and love; and it is in this form that the Dantesque parallel is most clearly seen. Fortunately, Tate himself was familiar with a book in which the union of the trinitarian with the feminine image of the soul is explored, and a brief survey of its main points helps to high-

19. Saint Augustine, *The Trinity*, trans. Stephen McKenna (Washington, D.C., 1970), 274.

light the features of Tate's own Augustinian and Dantesque imagery. In speaking of the "proposition: God is light," Tate adds that this idea is perhaps, "under Neo-Platonic influence, the prime Christian symbol, as Professor Fletcher and others have shown in reducing to their sources the powers of the Three Blessed Ladies of *The Divine Comedy*."[20] The book to which Tate refers, J. B. Fletcher's *Symbolism of the Divine Comedy*, places a great deal of emphasis on this idea in his central chapter, "The 'Three Blessed Ladies' of the Divine Comedy."

In Fletcher's interpretation, there is a poetic relationship between the "masculine" Trinity of Father, Son, and Holy Spirit and the feminine trinity of Mary, St. Lucy, and Beatrice. He interprets each member of this feminine trinity, drawing parallels between Mary and God the Father, Lucy and God the Son, and Beatrice and God the Holy Spirit. If his reading of Dante is combined with Augustine's analogy between the human mind and the Trinity, a psychological relationship emerges that makes the action of *The Divine Comedy* an articulation of the three powers of the soul.

In the chain of command from Mary to Beatrice that awakens Dante from his spiritual torpor, it is obvious that the Virgin, who instigates the intervention, is love or will and that Dante's remembered earthly love, Beatrice, is *memoria*. This leaves St. Lucy, who is the intermediary between them and represents vision or understanding. But St. Lucy is, in all probability, a symbolic figure within Dante's poem, despite his belief in her historic reality as a person who once lived in Syracuse. As Fletcher notes,

> Dante's dependence on the actual St. Lucia is more doubtful. He may have invoked her to cure his poor eyesight. At least, such healing power was accredited to her. He may have invoked her aid in more spiritual issues. But the suspicion arises that her personal prominence in the story of his redemption is due rather to the derivation of her name from *luce*, light, and the neat way this signification fitted in with her healing-power, especially if this power were conceived to extend to spiritual vision as well as to physical. For light is the natural aid to vision. . . . The actual

20. Allen Tate, "Tension in Poetry," in *Essays*, 62.

> light-giver to the dim of sight becomes the symbol of Light itself, physical and spiritual.[21]

Tate may not have recalled this argument when, fresh from an acquaintance with the work of Charles Williams and Francis Fergusson on Dante, he set out to fashion a modern poem in the style of the *Comedy*; but Fletcher's analysis sheds some light of its own on Tate's choice of St. Lucy as his guide and guardian. He could not invoke the name of Mary because she is no longer a living reality for the modern world, as Henry Adams noted in his celebrated discussion of "The Virgin and the Dynamo." Beatrice as guide would seem the merest affectation, for she is too closely tied to Dante's biography to apply to a modern writer. Thus Tate deliberately chose a symbolic figure, the only kind acceptable to a modern reader, as representative of the kind of illumination he was seeking. His terza rima poems are not devotional, then, but symbolist in the modern sense, using certain imaginative figures to stand for otherwise impalpable presences or realities.

Fletcher comes close to recognizing the Augustinian matrix behind Dante's feminine trinity when he interprets it as an embodiment of will and understanding; and since *The Divine Comedy* itself is a long exercise of *memoria*, it is a simple matter to extend his reading without doing violence to it. The important point that he makes concerning the feminine trio is that all three figures form a unity that "illumines the mind as well as kindles the will."[22] Though Mary is the true originating source, the sun, and Lucy and Beatrice are light and heat respectively, any one lady may stand for the influence of the others. As Augustine sees each power of the soul flowing from the other, so Dante's feminine trinity, symbol of the feminine anima, acts as one. Tate's choice of St. Lucy to stand for all three, like his choice of Monica to stand for Venus, Sibyl, and the Virgin Mary, is a matter of emphasis and practical poetic necessity.

Augustine outlines the stages of the mind's quest to find itself in Book Ten, Chapter 8 of *The Trinity*: "When it is, therefore, commanded to know itself, it should not seek itself as though it were to be withdrawn from itself, but it should rather withdraw what it has added to itself. For it is more deeply within, not only than those sensible

21. Jefferson B. Fletcher, *Symbolism of the Divine Comedy* (New York, 1921), 125–26.
22. *Ibid.*, 156.

things which are evidently without, but even than their images which are in a certain part of the soul." The mind knows itself immediately, for as Augustine argues in Chapter 10, "who would doubt that he lives, remembers, understands, wills, thinks, knows, and judges?" Finally, in Chapters 11 and 12, Augustine closes this part of his discussion by showing that the mind has an essential unity that makes it impossible to distinguish the action of understanding from that of memory or will or that of will from understanding and memory. Nevertheless, "these things can be more plainly explained even to those who are slower of comprehension when we discuss those subjects that the mind learns in time, and which happen to it in time, since it remembers what it did not remember previously, sees what it did not see previously, and loves what it did not love previously."[23]

Thus the search for self-understanding may be reasonably presented in a narrative form as an imagined sequence from experiencing to understanding to willing, provided that the spiritual action be portrayed analogically in terms of the world one comes to know as a temporal being. Dante's three ladies in their chain of command go from Mary's love for and will to save him, through Lucy's illuminative understanding, to Beatrice's remembrance. In his journey toward transcendence, Dante encounters them in reverse narrative order. These two "processions" in opposite directions symbolize the necessity of presenting in imagined stages the soul's grasping of its inner reality, but their circularity also stands for the simultaneity of the mind's grasp of itself. Fletcher's interpretation of the three ladies comes close to this insight: "The distinction, therefore, between Lucia and Beatrice is not absolute, but analogous to that between the Son and the Holy Spirit. The procession of the Son, or the Word, is by the mode of the intellect, which is Wisdom; that of the Holy Spirit by the mode of the Will, which is Love."[24] Although there is a discrepancy between Fletcher's implied model of the soul and the Augustinian trinity of the mind, the identification of St. Lucy, understanding, with the Word, second person of the Trinity, suggests that Tate chose her as his muse because she stands more obviously for the end of the poetic process in understanding. The poet begins in memory, of which he is the archeologist, and

23. Augustine, *The Trinity*, 305, 313.
24. Fletcher, *Symbolism of the Divine Comedy*, 177.

moves to vision. He must stop short of will, however, for that lies outside his limits. In choosing St. Lucy to inspire him, Tate is saying that poetry and the imagination can bring man understanding and knowledge but reach their limits on that level of the mind. It is the "romantic will" that would seek to make of poetry a form of love that it cannot sustain by its very nature.

The form of Tate's terza rima poems has an importance beyond its Dantesque allusiveness. By adopting the formal versification of *The Divine Comedy*, Tate has returned to the conflict of cyclical and progressive movement in history that he explored in "Winter Mask" and "Seasons of the Soul." The tercets invite progression within repetition, combine the thrust of narration with the contemplative stillness of the lyric. They also suggest a return to something that has already occurred or has always been present. The center of the confessional mode is the rediscovery in the memory of a presence that has existed from the beginning, but it is not a simple return. The elevation of memory to understanding provides a new perspective on the past that can redeem it in time and make what was fragmented whole. The city of memory, reconstituted by the poet, returns to the present as a place understood. Tate's tercets lead back through all the themes of his poetry and forward to the vision of an inner paradise which, like Dante's Garden of Eden presided over by Matilda, is guarded by the feminine understanding.

Tate's unfinished sequence, consisting of "The Maimed Man," "The Swimmers," and "The Buried Lake," offers special difficulties of interpretation. Though the poems possess sufficient unity to be treated together as a complete entity, large interpretive gaps remain despite the valiant attempts of several critics to elucidate their complexities. Indeed, uncertainties over the identity of specific figures in the poems are evident in the opening lines of "The Maimed Man":

> Didactic Laurel, loose your reasoning leaf
>   Into my trembling hand; assert your blade
>   Against the Morning Star, enlightening Thief
>
> Of that first Mother who returned the Maid.

In these opening lines of invocation, Tate introduces a new style, which he is willing to call "didactic," into his poetry. Henceforth, he intends to oppose its "blade" to the morning star, which represents an enlightenment that is also a theft. These complex symbols unite pagan and Christian figures in an original but coherent fashion. Venus is usually understood to be both the morning and evening star, but as early as the sixteenth century, the morning star was called "Lucifer," and the words "enlightening Thief" fit it perfectly (cf. Satan in *Paradise Lost*, IV, 192: "So clomb this first grand thief into God's fold"). If the laurel is identified with Phoebus Apollo (and therefore with the sun), then the light of dawn that dims the planet Venus is the beginning of a new day for the speaker. The poem begins with a new enlightenment that will overcome the old, an assertion of the light of understanding against the Luciferian and Venereal temptations of evil and the senses. The basic opposition is between laurel and myrtle, Apollonian understanding of self and the "sleek senses" of Venus.

If this reading is at least consistent with what is in the poem, it may be extended further, even at the risk of appearing less persuasive as it gains in complexity. Both laurel and myrtle are evergreens used to crown poets, and often no distinction is made between them. One recalls the beginning of Milton's "Lycidas":

> Yet once more, O ye laurels, and once more
> Ye myrtles brown, with ivy never sere,
> I come to pluck your berries harsh and crude,
> And with forced fingers rude,
> Shatter your leaves before the mellowing year.

Entertaining for a moment the not unlikely possibility that Tate is alluding to Milton, one notices that the older Tate does not pluck the leaves with violence, as the young Milton must. Instead, he asks the laurel to "loose" its leaf into his "trembling hand," suggesting a reticence in approaching so exalted a theme. Perhaps the "didactic laurel" may be understood as a reference to heroic poetry of the kind written by Virgil, addressed to a whole society as a means of sustaining its ideals. Myrtle might then refer to love poetry, the other side of the epic coin. Both are united in Dante; can it be that Tate is here asserting his intention to follow the path of those poets who explore the theme of self-understanding rather than those who devote themselves to erotic love? If so, he has defined his theme from the start, but he does not intend to seek Dante's great synthesis of the two loves. He has put aside the temptations of the "sleek senses" as subject for his verse.

The Apollonian self-understanding is a discipline that will allow the poet to see the true light for what it is:

> Return, Laurel! Dying sense has cast
> Shadow on shadow of a metal tear
>
> Around my rim of being. Teach me to fast
> And pray, that I may know the motes that tease
> Skittering sunbeams are dead shells at last.

The language is certainly consonant with the traditional Christian ascetic vocabulary, and the speaker knows that he must make a descent into a kind of twilight if he is to separate the light of life from the empty bodies that encumber it, the self from that which is extraneous to it. At the same time, he must also confront his own past hell in the person of a strange figure called "the maimed man." Is this journey to the underworld in search of that transcendent part of the self lost to consciousness like Orpheus' quest for Eurydice? The phrase "metal tear," an extremely curious image, may be an allusion to another Miltonic poem, "Il Penseroso":

> But, O sad virgin, that thy power
> Might raise Musaeus from his bower,
> Or bid the soul of Orpheus sing
> Such notes as, warbled to the string,
> Drew iron tears down Pluto's cheek,
> And made Hell grant what Love did seek.

The suggestion is attractive because the melancholy mood of Milton's poem seems to fit the serious tone of contemplation that suffuses "The Maimed Man." Again, when the speaker rejects the enticements of Venus and the senses—"Beguiling myrtle, shake no more my ear/ With your green leaf: because I am afraid/ Of him who says I have no need to fear"—one recalls the god who touched the "trembling ears" of the poet in "Lycidas" and Satan's deception of Eve in *Paradise Lost*, IX, 702: "Your fear itself of death removes the fear."

Whatever one makes of these possible references, appropriate enough in their contexts, it is clear that the speaker is following a typical confessional scheme in rejecting the temptations of the world and the senses and entering into a long meditative examination of his own past. The fifth tercet, beginning, "Then, timeless Muse," implies a shift from the discipline of the didactic laurel to something deeper. The muse is asked to

> reverse my time; unfreeze
> All that I was in your congenial heat;
> Tune me in recollection to appease
>
> The hour when, as I sauntered down our street,
> I saw a young man there.

The "timeless Muse" seems to be different from the "didactic Laurel" invoked at the beginning of the poem; subsequent lines suggest that she is the same Lady of Light who is the muse of "The Buried Lake." If so, her light is of a different sort from Apollonian reason, and the speaker must begin by confronting himself and his past before he can expect to go forward under her tutelage. He must first be led to a clearer perception of the natural world and his place in it before he can attempt to move beyond it.

This second invocation is continued after an interlude in which the encounter with the maimed man is described:

> Thence, flow! conceit and motion to rehearse
> Pastoral terrors of youth still in the man,
> Torsions of sleep, in emblematic verse
>
> Rattling like dice unless the verse shall scan
> All chance away; and let me touch the hem
> Of him who spread his triptych like a fan.

The muse transcends the claims of the visual sense; she can "tune" the poet "in recollection" by unblocking his memories and allowing the suppressed depths of the self to flow to the surface. Venus would draw all attention to things outside the soul; the Virgin Muse will not allow the frozen past to be neglected and forces the poet to trace back the hidden dimensions of his theme—"Torsions of sleep, in emblematic verse"—as expressed in his difficult early poetry. Tate's description of his youthful verse, "rattling like dice," suggests Mallarmé's "Un Coup de Dés," that strange work in which the French symbolist speaks of the throw of dice that can never abolish chance unless the poet provides order through his verse. But Tate has left behind this stage of modernist inspiration for the example of an earlier poet, Dante, the "hem" of whose poetic garment he is not worthy to touch. Tate hesitantly speaks of the mantle of a great poet that he cannot hope to wear and suggests that his adoption of terza rima is a homage to, rather than an imitation of, the author of *The Divine Comedy*.

A third appeal to the muse appears in the last lines of the poem. Having rehearsed his own past through memory, the poet can look forward to a kind of rebirth under the guidance of the Virgin Muse. What the muse has allowed him to see once more is a strange scene, a nightmarish vision of himself as a maimed young man lacking head and feet. In the central episode of the poem, the speaker encounters a strange, scarecrow-like man whose feet are hidden and whose head is gone, replaced by the "rusty play" of twilight. Recognizing the "grains of sand" under his eyelids that foretell sleep, the speaker concludes that he need not fear, since what he sees, "the charm and secret double of night in wakeful day," is no more than a dream. The grotesque figure is only a monster from a nightmare, not a reality that must be confronted. The poet's reaction is "stupor" and astonishment coupled with curiosity. Unable to tell whether the man is "live or dead," he retreats "to a ragged clump/ Of buckberry bushes in the vacant lot," a hiding place that contrasts with the laurel and myrtle that vied for his attention in the opening verses. The heart is still intact in the body of the headless man, but his feet are rooted "blue grass."

It is difficult to assign any single meaning to this unusual figure, but two features of this image are familiar. The maimed man, rooted in a place but also merely vegetating there, is akin to the person of Pier delle Vigne, alluded to at the end of "Winter." His blue-grass feet signal an attachment to the land of Kentucky. He must stand for the modern southerner, mindlessly attached to a place without attempting to understand the meaning of that attachment. He has lost his ability to understand and resides near an empty tract of land like the headless guardian of a vacant present. He is the remnant of a whole way of life that has become as impotent and purposeless as the limp hand that dangles by the young man's feet. The poet knows that he must bury this part of his past if he is to proceed further in the progressive world represented by his "football coach."

"If you live here," I said to the unbending
   Citizen, "it will not seem to you
   Improper if I linger on, defending

Myself from what I hate but ought to do
   To put us in a fast ungreening grave
   Together, lest you turn out to be true

And I publicly lose face."

The maimed man is the symbol of the passive remnant of a once flourishing people. Traditional man now takes on the sad figure of a person who has lost the good of his intellect. Nevertheless, though it will cost him embarrassment, the poet must acknowledge the scarecrow and recognize him as one of his own, even if he feels awkward in the confrontation:

Our manners had no phrase to let me broach
   To friends the secret of a friend gone lame.
   How could I know this friend without reproach.

The speaker does not know how to draw the attention of the community to this scarecrow in their midst. Yet he cannot neglect his duty to search for some means of healing and renewal. The result is an "expense of spirit," echoing Shakespeare's Sonnet 129, as the poet continues "witching for water in a waste of shame."

The second encounter with the maimed man comes later. Having seen this figure of death-in-life at the heart of his own community, the speaker struggles to cope with these "pastoral terrors of youth still in the man." The "man all coat and stem" has not ceased to haunt him in his maturity, but the poet remains unaware of the scarecrow's identity until one day he realizes that the terrible image is simply a reflection of himself. The distorting mirror in which this image appears is "glass swirled/ By old blowers." The glass is, of course, the mirror that art holds up to nature, but it is not flat-planed like the products of a machine world. It is produced by craftsmen, and every distortion in its reflection reveals something deeper about the human image. In his first encounter, the poet had suggested that the best thing he could do for himself and the maimed man would be to recognize that both were dead and required a decent burial. But now, through the mirror of poetic form, the speaker realizes that he is the maimed man. The "secret of a friend gone lame" that the poet could not communicate is his secret and the father of this mirror image. When he looks deeply into himself, the poet sees a picture of his own imperfection.

The scarecrow is an image buried in the self; the "black trunk without bloom" has taken the soul for its "tomb." God's image, the *memoria dei* or *imago dei* in man that is the true sign of a transcendent dimension in human nature, has been repressed by the personal will, the ego that recognizes only its own immanence. Tate gives a brief definition of the ego that connects it with the analytic narrowness of the eye:

> (By *I* I mean iambics willed and neat;
> I mean by *I* God's image made uncouth;
> By eye I mean the busy, lurked, discrete
>
> Mandible world sharp as a broken tooth.)

It is the ego that has maimed the soul and disfigured the *imago dei*. The "iambics willed and neat" are the product of the modern aesthetic attitude, the Mallarméan form of art that imposes a man-made order—the only kind he can admit—on the seemingly chaotic natural world. The poet would like to give the maimed man a decent burial, but to do so would be to bury part of himself. He would reinforce the action of the eye, which conquers the world by dividing it into discrete, assimilable fragments that it can "devour" analytically. The eye of the ego creates a maimed world by dominating and excluding from its purview everything that does not fit its perceptions.

The "small half-hell" following the terrible revelation drives the speaker to look for succor in nature and the family, but there, too, he fails to discover a sustaining order. Having lost his innocence, the poet cannot recover it; but he can remember the experience of a world that possessed wholeness:

> Where the sleek senses of the simple child
> Came back to rack spirit that could not tell
>
> Natural time: the eyes, recauled, enisled
> In the dreamt cave by shadowy womb of beam,
> Had played swimmer of night—the moist and mild!

Having left their womblike ignorance of evil and death, the eyes can be "recauled" only by a false light, a "shadowy womb of beam." In their flight from a harsh, destructive reality, they sought the kind of night that is a comfort, a nihilism of "moist and mild" return to the "dreamt cave" of the womb. Though the spirit cannot be satisfied with the temporal existence that the world of nature offers, neither can it regress to a state of unborn ignorance. It must be led "up the deeper stream" to something larger. The return to a world of order and to a communal life cannot be accomplished alone, however, and only the "Virgin Muse" can lead the poet back to the light:

> As a lost bee returning to the hive,
> Cell after honeyed cell of sounding dream—
>
> Swimmer of noonday, lean for the perfect dive
> To the dead Mother's face, whose subtile down
> You had not seen take amber light alive.

The subtle transition that occurs in these concluding lines of the poem is difficult to interpret, even if its general action is clear. Light has changed into sound; the dream can be heard but not seen. The hive is an image of collective life that has a natural order, unlike the disordered alienation of the nightmare corridor in "Autumn." The eye cannot be the guide to this order; only a figure—in this case St. Lucy—who can see without eyes is capable of steering the soul out of the darkness. The laurel leaf has been taken in the hand, not grasped by the eye. The Luciferian brilliance of the morning star has yielded to the noonday sun. The poet is being led back to the "first Mother" by the "Maid" who is his muse. But who is the "dead Mother"? Is she Eve, the Virgin Mary, or the poet's biological mother? Or is she all three? What is the poet's destination? He is returning not to the womb but to the "dead Mother's face," the image of *memoria* that is the object of his "perfect dive" into the self. The noonday swimmer has found the waters, but they belong to the conscious mind of the laurel, and he must recover through a restored image of the soul that image of woman that all men both pursue and flee.

The death of the mother is her rebirth. Tate was not able to witness the last hours of his own mother's existence, as Augustine was able to witness and profit by Monica's death, but he does present her passing as both a sunset ("amber light") and sunrise (the "subtile down" is like the light covering of a newborn child). The dead mother represents the complete cycle of birth and death, but no living man can claim to have experienced it firsthand. Yet he can know it through memory and imagination. It is this point of contemplation that reverses the poet's time. The first mother and the maid who stand at the beginning of the poem return at its end. Lucifer's thievery consisted of stealing man away from God, but Christ, born of a virgin, repaired that theft with his own death. Love and death, light and darkness, innocence and guilt are so intertwined in human existence that the enlightenment of Lucifer, who taught man the knowledge of good and evil, can only be overcome by the "felix culpa" that made Mary into the Second Eve. The poem begins with the morning star and ends with the amber light of sunset after pointing to the expectation of noonday; Apollo and Christ, the resurrection of the sun, will triumph over the moist and mild womb of Venus, mother earth, and the narrow perspective of the senses. Memory has yielded to understanding.

Nine

Light

It is not altogether certain that Tate intended "The Maimed Man" to be followed immediately by "The Swimmers," but a transition at the end of the first poem seems to point directly to the second. The references to water, for instance, are amplified in "The Swimmers." In this poem, the actions of diving and "witching for water" are given specificity by a recalled incident from the poet's memory, and the movement of the poem as a whole has the same pattern of discovery, peripety, and recognition that characterize its predecessor. Again a young man is plunged into a terrifying experience. Once more there is a succession of dawns and twilights. Even the country setting of "The Swimmers" appears to be anticipated by the "Pastoral terrors of youth" described in "The Maimed Man." But the difference between the two poems is considerable. Both are about "maimed" men; but the first poem describes a dream experience, while the second takes its main scenes from an actual event in the life of the poet. Because it has a more readily discernible story to tell, "The Swimmers" has tended to attract the kind of reader who prefers straightforward, easily accessible narrative.

The poem is an evocation of the free-wheeling pleasures of boyhood. During the "dog-days" of Kentucky summer, the speaker and his childhood companions go out in search of water. Theirs is an "odyssey" where, if they cannot expect to meet a real Nausicaä, the natural world of mullein and grapevine is almost as enticing as a girl's hand. But before Odysseus was washed ashore on the coast of a fairyland Phaiakia, he underwent many trials; and the fun these boys experience is not altogether idyllic. The poet describes it as "sullen" and "savage as childhood's thin harmonious tear." Once again Tate seems to be alluding to "Lycidas" ("He must not float upon his watery bier . . . without the meed of some melodious tear"), reminding one that water is traditionally associated with death and sorrow as well as with birth and joy.

The innocence of the "sleek senses" must yield to the more discriminating power of the mature eye:

> O fountain, bosom source undying-dead
> Replenish me the spring of love and fear
>
> And give me back the eye that looked and fled
> When a thrush idling in the tulip tree
> Unwound the cold dream of the copperhead.

In "The Swimmers" the opposition between laurel and myrtle is altered to a complementarity. The thrush and the copperhead, love and fear, the "undying-dead" fountain with its systaltic rhythm, the carefree and the didactic are all at the "bosom source" of the heart, mortal and immortal. The plunge into the water is both an escape from the summer's blast and an acceptance of the drowning sea. Is the fountain to be understood as *memoria*, the "clear springs," or the "harmonious tear" or all of them? The feeling of alienation from community and from the depths of the self is not as important in this poem as it is in "The Maimed Man." "The Swimmers" is about the larger dimensions of guilt and alienation that a whole community discovers in itself. The poet's memory returns him to an incident he witnessed in which the City of Man and the City of God, like the other oppositions disclosed by Tate's poetic dialectic, intersect in a specific time and place.[1]

As the "shrill companions" appear now in the eye of memory (rather than in the eye of the ego), they take on symbolic overtones. The rich descriptive language that chronicles their walk along a creek road under a clear, hot sky moves from a visual to an auditory emphasis. There is a delight in the music of words that was absent from "The Maimed Man." The catalog of heroes, five boys whose real names are given, may have no intended significance, but it is interesting that two besides Tate are identified by more than their names. One is a doctor's son and the other is a flautist. Medicine and music are also complementary arts, one for healing the body and another for soothing the soul. They are also traditionally associated with Apollo, their patron. Tate, the lad who even then was "maimed" before his time "with water on the brain," is obsessed by the need for water (and redemption); he is al-

1. Allen Tate, "Speculations," *Southern Review*, n.s., XIV, 232.

ready the "dull critter of enormous head" from "Sonnets at Christmas" who looks at the sky in search of transcendence. It is amusing that he has these Apollonian figures in his entourage.

The increasing predominance of sounds over sights points to some impending revelation. As the boys follow the "bells and bickers" of the noisy waters, they hear another sound, which seems "at first a song" but turns out to be horses' hooves. Like the thrush who revealed the snake, these sounds are soon followed by a posse and sheriff, whose face is as worn as a tombstone. The mood shifts abruptly. Day suddenly seems night; the reality, a nightmare. The boys walk into a world on the edge of fear, "where sound shaded the sight." Seeing yields to hearing, but when sight returns, the boys discover the sheriff leaning over the dead body of a lynched Negro. The boy Tate never gets a chance to swim, but he is plunged immediately into a drowning fear:

> We stopped to breathe above the swimming hole;
> I gazed at its reticulated shade
>
> Recoiling in blue fear, and felt it roll
> Over my ears and eyes and lift my hair
> Like seaweed tossing on a sun atoll.

When he regains his bearings, the boy hears only two phrases: "That dead nigger there," and "We come too late." As he watches the men, the boy notes both the sheriff's casualness in the face of death and his reluctance to touch the body, his regret for what has happened and his scant respect for the dead man. The sheriff removes the rope from the hanged man's neck with his foot and attaches it to the feet. The body is drawn forward, like a Hector pulled around the walls of Troy; yet the ignominious treatment of the body seems to flow from embarrassment or even fear, rather than hatred. The dead man, brought to dust, is made to advertise his earthly destiny prominently as the body is dragged to town "boxed . . . in a cloudy hearse" and taking only "the sun for shroud." The event occurs in broad daylight, though the sun will soon begin to set. The eleven "Jesus-Christers" of the posse abandon the scene "unmembered and unmade" like the fearful apostles who abandoned Jesus; they fail to see the significance of the "dirty shame" that they have witnessed. Yet the "three figures in the dying sun" are an emblem that the poet in retrospect sees as a kind of new Calvary.

Tate's daring evocation of crucifixion imagery is made convincing by the incidental details, like the sheriff's unintended irony in uttering "Goddamn" or the "butting horse-fly" that pauses on the ear of the corpse. There are no accusations, no moral heroes, and no villains in the scene. Even the argument that led up to the lynching is ignored as irrelevant. The terrible scene has been witnessed by "all the town." Lynching is another form of the scapegoat ritual, as René Girard has shown,[2] a means of attempting to restore order by going beyond established order in the name of the sacred. Like original sin, the responsibility for what has happened must be shared equally by all in the community:

> Alone in the public clearing
> This private thing was owned by all the town,
> Though never claimed by us within my hearing.

The community has not given its sanction for the execution nor expressed publicly its regret for what has happened. The event lies rather on the borderline between universal guilt and universal responsibility that cannot be articulated without diminishing its impact.

In a remarkable simile, Tate describes the dead body when it is first pulled forward:

> I saw the Negro's body bend
> And straighten, as a fish-line cast transverse
> Yields to the current that it must subtend.

Though the Negro has been lynched, not drowned, the comparison is rich in implications, for it connects his death with the feeling of helplessness that overcomes the boy when he first sees the awesome sight. The behavior of the fishline, like the dead body, manifests both a yielding and a resistance that are like the desperate plight of the lynched man. The tug of the rope is a crucifixion of sorts, but it also seems to merge the body with some larger force beyond it. The body is now part of the greater current of an anonymous natural power that sweeps all things before it. The "faceless head" of the body makes the death appear both terribly impersonal and yet symbolically particularized. The boy who has never managed to go swimming and the dead man whose

2. René Girard, *Violence and the Sacred*, trans. Patrick Gregory (Baltimore, 1977).

body swims only in simile have merged. The faceless death's head that the boy encounters upon emerging from his plunge is a grim counterpart of the dead mother's face that was the object of his dive in "The Maimed Man." The maimed man that the poet discovered within himself in the first poem has now merged with the hanged god of Frazer. Memory has disclosed the identity of fear with love, guilt with transcendence. In recognizing that he is guilty, man acknowledges that he is imperfect and incomplete. That acknowledgment is the confessional act that opens the mind to an awareness of its need for some transcending power beyond it, a dimension that can restore wholeness to the self and deliver it from alienation and dissociation.

The concluding poem of the sequence as we now have it, "The Buried Lake," brings these themes to their climax. Indeed, it is the climactic poem of Tate's career, resolving the conflicts of his earlier poetry and summing up the implications of the Augustinian imagination for modern man. It cannot be a coincidence that the epigraph Tate has selected for this poem, from Ecclesiastes, begins with the words "Ego" and "mater." For the poem is about the coming together of self and transcendence in an act of understanding deeper than either laurel or myrtle can offer. This biblical mother of beauty, fear, knowledge, and hope seems to embody all the qualities of Tate's vision of reality.

The "Lady of Light" who is invoked at the beginning of the poem is St. Lucy, patroness of eyesight, and the virgin muse of "The Maimed Man." This identification seems warranted by a reference in the fifth tercet of "The Buried Lake," where the poet says, "You set my time to flow/ In childhood." Moreover, the opening lines allude once more to the intertwining—though not to the opposition—of myrtle and laurel. The theme of the first poem was didactic and its inspiration Apollonian. Dante had to be led by Virgil, or reason, through the dark realms of the soul before he was fit to encounter his lady Beatrice. But now reason and the senses can be reconciled, for in the healed soul they are integrated. Likewise, the eye can be restored to its proper place as king of the senses once the ego has abandoned its narrow domination over the whole self. Lucy as understanding and vision is more than reason; she is the poetic imagination, where the memory of things past can be united with the love of things tenuous ("Aeneas at Washington") in a moment that transcends the temporality it fulfills.

While St. Lucy, the third-century Syracusan martyr who lost her sight, is certainly a rich figure for Tate to have adopted, it is principally as a protagonist in Dante's poem that she figures in "The Buried Lake." Tate actually compresses into his poem the crucial transitional dream of "Purgatorio," Canto IX. Readers of Dante will recall that St. Lucy is mentioned in only two other places: once briefly in "Inferno," Canto II, and again in "Paradiso," Canto XXXII. In the traditional reading of *The Divine Comedy*, Lucy stands for "illuminative grace," and Tate takes this aspect of her activity—her "gracing light," as he calls it—as central to his narrative. In Dante's Purgatory she intervenes directly to help the protagonist over a difficult transition. Dante has struggled from the perilous sea below to reach the entrance gate at the mount of Purgatory. But the bodily frailty that is the lot of all "sons of Adam" overcomes him, and he is soon immobilized in sleep. In a dream that includes several mythological stories of escape, Dante is lifted up and transported beyond the gate. When he awakens on the other side, Virgil explains to him that St. Lucy herself has carried him across. Francis Fergusson's commentary on this episode underlines its importance for Tate's poem:

> The darkness paralyzes the will, and therefore one cannot climb upward, though one might descend as though by gravitation back down the Mountain, toward that dead center we passed at the botton of Hell . . . ; sleep, the sign of our bodily being . . . , is an image of death. But when this mortal weakness is obediently accepted, the sleeping spirit is in a sense freed for another mode of life.[3]

It is for this reason, then, that Tate asks the "Lady of Light" to take his dream in her hand and lead him from his "edge of darkness." Sleep is the symbol of man's weakness, but dream is the sign that there is something within him that leads to transcendence and wisdom. At the beginning of the sequence, he asked the didactic laurel to loose its leaf into his hand; he must ask the muse to take from him the dream that he is now willing to turn over to another. By deciding to "admit a dream" to her, the poet confesses his vision and admits his guilt with a trusting confidence in her custody.

Without this fostering of the muse, the dream is a dead thing of purely private interest. Only her illumination can bring the dream to

3. Francis Fergusson, *Dante's Drama of the Mind* (Princeton, 1953), 31.

life, "let it in a gentle stream/ Of living blood." The dream is the dive into the buried lake of the heart; it reveals an image deep within the memory that can be recovered through the imagination. The image seems to be connected with the mother's face and the Old Testament figure of divine wisdom to which the epigraph refers and whom Tate seems to associate with *memoria*, that "is like a woman," and all the feminine figures evoked in his mature poetry. It is important to note the rest of the passage in Ecclesiasticus (24:24–44) from which Tate cites the opening sentence, for the Vulgate version from which he is quoting contains a section not found in the later received text of the Bible.

> I am the mother of fair love, and of fear, and of knowledge, and of holy hope. In me is all grace of the way and of the truth: in me is all hope of life and of virtue. Come over to me, all ye that desire me: and be filled with my fruits. For my spirit is sweet above honey: and my inheritance above honey and the honeycomb. My memory is unto everlasting generations. They that eat me shall yet hunger: and they that drink me shall yet thirst. He that hearkeneth to me shall not be confounded: and they that work by me shall not sin. They that explain me shall have life everlasting. . . . I, wisdom, have poured out rivers. I, like a brook out of a river of a mighty water; I, like a channel of a river, and like an aqueduct, came out of paradise. I said: I will water my garden of plants, and I will water abundantly the fruits of my meadow. And, behold, my brook became a great river, and my river came near to a sea. For I make doctrine to shine forth to all as the morning light: and I will declare it afar off.[4]

The "gentle stream" and the garden flowers, the morning light and the enduring memory are only a few among the key images in this passage that Tate has recalled in the opening and closing of his last long poem. The mother's face is the visage of wisdom herself, whose "doom is dark and deeper than any sea-dingle," as W. H. Auden wrote, citing from a medieval English version of verse thirty-nine. It is to these depths that the poet must prepare himself to dive.

4. *The Holy Bible: Douay Version* (London, 1957). Tate's citation is ultimately from the Latin Vulgate text, but its immediate source is the "Little Office of the Blessed Virgin Mary," where these Old Testament passages are applied to Mary. See *Correspondence*, 371.

The poet will be guided by St. Lucy, but he will not receive her light in a totally passive manner. He must "remand" it, return the gift of illumination in another form. Because Lucy was blinded in the course of her martyrdom, this remand must be a sound, the "pulse upon [her] ear" that is the music of poetic language. The dream has been sent by Lucy's "command," just as Dante was given his dream of the eagle while she carried him beyond the gate of Purgatory. But Tate seems to require more of Lucy than did Dante, however, for she must sustain the poet throughout his crisis lest he slip back into the darkness. Sleep is a little death that can bring the "edge of darkness near" and blind one to his own hope. The "edging slough" that he must avoid is from the "dying sense" that "cast/ Shadow on shadow of a metal tear" around the poet's "rim of being" in "The Maimed Man." The shadow that lurks within the soul is confronted only at great risk; the "edge of fear" must be lit up by some powerful source to prevent the soul from being overcome by its own darkness. St. Lucy, who met darkness in both ways by being deprived of her eyes and of her life, is an appropriate model for this journey into the shadows of the self.

The key to understanding lies in the memory, and so Lucy must lead the poet on "the way back" before she can guide him in the way to redemption. Both ways are difficult, but they are not the same. In "The Symbolic Imagination" Tate uses similar imagery: "If the way up to now has been rough, we may expect it from now on to be even rougher." The way to Paradise is rougher than the way through memory. This "way back" is the "Illuminative Way," which Tate speaks of in the same essay as "the way to knowledge through the senses, by means of aided reason,"[5] and it is the way guided by St. Lucy. She will teach the protagonist to "fast/ And pray," so that he may recognize the "dead shells" that obscure the light and cast off the "slough" from his eyes. At the end, the goal is the unitive way,

Where Myrtle twines with Laurel—single glow
Of leaf, your own imponderable stuff

Of light in which you set my time to flow
In childhood, when I tried to catch each flake
And hold it to deny the world of snow.

5. Allen Tate, "The Symbolic Imagination," in *Essays*, 441, 433.

Light and love have been available to the poet since the beginning, but his denial of them has also been exercised since childhood. In his youth he attempted to control nature and deprive the world of snow by not allowing its flakes to fall to the earth. The passage can also be interpreted as meaning that the speaker's action was an attempt to deny that "the world of snow" is real. In either sense, the implication is the same. Snow is an emblem of time and the death-oblivion that will cover all. Yet it is also a frozen form of water that can be set to flow once given warmth. The snow, like the motes in the sunbeam, must not be feared but accepted for what it is.

The hidden dimension that the speaker has "kept opaque" is the "sullen spectrum of a buried lake," a gloomily lit part of his soul that no one, including himself, has been aware of. It is the "congenial heat" of the muse that can unfreeze this "sullen" or sluggish body of water and allow it to flow to the surface. Lucy's way, the illuminative that leads to the intuitive and eventually to the unitive, is through analogy, which Tate describes in terms of mirror symbolism in "The Symbolic Imagination." She is the initiator of the poetic action, however, not the achiever of it. She is to "mirror" the poet's mind, which is already "styled/ To spring its waters to [his] memory." The heat her light provides will unfreeze what has been congealed, and her grace will "tune" him "in recollection," as Tate puts it in "The Maimed Man." Because Lucy was blinded, she could not be tempted by the domineering eye; because she was a martyr, she could not be imprisoned by her own ego. The poet who discovered the maimed image within himself by means of a mirror ("The Maimed Man") and his oneness with all maimed men in the human community through sound and music ("The Swimmers") will now combine mirror and music through Lucy's light of memory.

The journey through memory takes one back in time but forward in understanding. That is the way of Augustine in *The Confessions* and of Dante in *The Divine Comedy*. But Tate's feminine memory, as he says, possesses her own will independent of his desire; self-revelation is fluid, like a stream with its own movement. To immerse onself in it is to become a swimmer with the choice of going with or fighting the current.

> I fumbled all night long, an ageing child
>   Fled like a squirrel to a hollow bole
>   To play toy soldier, Tiny Tim, or the mild

Babes-in-the-Woods: sunk in their leafy hole,
The terror of their sleep I could not tell
Until your gracing light reduced the toll.[6]

The protagonist has made and will continue to make false starts. He first looks for the way in a "pinched hotel" by "a lakeshore." His stumbling on the shore recalls Dante's efforts to climb the mount of Purgatory beyond the sea; as Dante moves "up the dark stream," he emerges, with face stained and darkened, in the presence of Cato. Virgil is commanded to cleanse him; and after his face is washed, they move "to the deserted shore/ whose waters had never been sailed/ by anyone who afterward was able to return."[7] But Dante already knows that he is "moving over better waters," as he says in the opening lines of "Purgatory" and asks the muses to give him music for his song as he leaves the "dead air" of Hell. The way to the gate of Purgatory is "rough and hard" (*aspra e forte*), as Virgil points out in Canto II, but it is a road uphill that leads somewhere.

Tate's version of the movement from Hell to Purgatory is not a replica of Dante's, despite occasional echoes of word and image. Rather than plunge into the depths of the lake, he attempts to take up a narrow residence inside the "pinched hotel" of his "small half-hell" ("The Maimed Man") and recover his lost soul with music, as though he were Orpheus rescuing Eurydice:

But then exulting in my secret plan,

I laid my top hat to one side; my chin
Was ready, I unsnapped the lyric case;
I had come there to play my violin.

From the beginning there is something inadequate about this music forced into a box by a bow "erect and sinuous as Valence lace/ Old ladies wore." His music is all bravura and frill; it is stiff with age and rigid with self-consciousness. A "dreaming face" emerges that belongs not to the "dead Mother" but to a "small dancing girl who gave the

6. In his recorded reading of the poem, Tate gives a different version of the third and fourth lines of this passage: "To play toy soldier, Tiny Tim, and mild/ In death, the babes with autumn leaves for stole." *Allen Tate Reads from His Own Works* (Decca DL9130; Carillon Records YP300, 1960).

7. Dante Alighieri, *The Divine Comedy*, trans. H. R. Huse (New York, 1954), 175.

smell of dill." Unlike his music, she has some flavor; and she quickly shuts him up "in a soft surd." This scene perhaps refers to Tate's disappointment as a musician, but the event has been transformed from the literal to the symbolic by the dream. The piece he is playing, Tartini's difficult "Devil's Trill," suggests a demonic music. The music is an assertion of his will; his virtuosity as a satanic violinist is a display of his own ego. Having lost his Beatrice along with his youthful hopes, he turns to elegiac silence: "I mourned the death of youth without a word."

Fallen from the pinnacle of his personal ambitions, the poet is weighed in the scales by his "friend Jack Locke," whom Tate identified as fellow poet John Hall Wheelock,[8] and found wanting as a craftsman:

> And could I go where air was not dead air?
>   My friend Jack Locke, scholar and gentleman,
>   Gazed down upon me with a friendly glare.
>
> Flicking his nose as if about to scan
>   My verse; he plucked from his moustache one hair
>   Letting it fall like gravel in a pan,
>
> And went as mist upon the browning air
>   Away from the durable lake, the blind hotel,
>   Leaving me guilted on a moving stair
>
> Upwards, down which I regularly fell
>   Tail backwards. . . .

Like Yeats, in "The Circus Animals' Desertion," Tate now sees the inadequacies of his early verse. His mature mind, "styled" through the discipline of Augustine and Dante to "spring its waters" to his memory, is now capable of seeing what has been wrong not only with himself but also with his poetry. This confession runs throughout the sequence. In "The Maimed Man" Tate accuses himself of writing "iambics willed and neat" (with a pun on "I-am-bics") because his own ego demanded a too simple satirical posture. In "The Swimmers" he points to an early tendency to overintellectualize through a head grown too large ("Tate with water on the brain"). Finally, in "The Buried Lake," he depicts his

8. As reported by Alan Williamson, "Allen Tate and the Personal Epic," *Southern Review*, n.s., XII, 729.

early poetry, under the guise of violin playing, as "pelts of mordents" on the Devil's Trill, with a pun on the demonic energy of his mordant youthful verse. It cost him his sense of love, feminine grace, and youthful idealism. It also cost him an audience, as the small dancing girl demonstrates in her gesture of refusal. In the depiction of his friend Jack Locke's comic reaction to his "emblematic verse/ Rattling like dice," he makes fun of his affectation of modernity. Jack Locke disappears, in a Dantesque phrase ("browning air" is an echo of Dante's "*aer bruno*" in "Inferno," II, 1), and the poet is left alone once more with no one to hear him. His effort to escape from his prison through poetry is Sisyphean. Like the Jack and Jill of the nursery rhyme alluded to in "Spring," he falls from the heights where he has gone to fetch "water."

Having lost his audience, the poet is determined to continue his music: "If I am now alone I may resume/ The grey sonata"; but his instrument has also vanished. Instead, he sees the air clear to reveal a picture (one of the few visual images in the poem) of "a stately woman who in sorrow shone." The woman is ghostly, despite the clarity of her painterly image; the encounter that follows is difficult and mysterious but crucial to the poet's release from his captivity.

> I rose; she moved, she glided towards the hall;
> I took her hand but then would set her free.
> "My love," I said.—"I'm back to give you all,"
>
> She said, "my love." (Under the dogwood tree
> In bloom, where I had held her first beneath
> The coiled black hair, she turned and smiled at me.)
>
> I hid the blade within the melic sheath
> And tossed her head—but it was not her head:
> Another's searching skull whose drying teeth
>
> Crumbled me all night long and I was dead.

These lines are among the most intricate in all of Tate's poetry. Who is the woman with the "coiled black hair"? Is she a phantom of the poet's dead mother, as the setting, so like the ghostly scene in "Autumn," might suggest? Is she some lost early love? Or, less literally, is she tradition, the South, the historical imagination? Somehow she seems to draw all these motifs together in a single figure. She is a luminous vision that turns out to be something else. Her "coiled black hair" is ominous, suggesting a snakelike energy. It is as though Eurydice had been transformed into Medusa, whose gaze paralyzes. In this spectral apparition there is an apparent offering of love, but the poet is wary of her smile. If this is the dead mother's face that he has sought, then the speaker must both acknowledge and destroy her power. Perhaps the Perseus myth may serve as a useful analogy. The hero must destroy the "terrible mother" represented by Medusa in order to free his own "blessed mother," Danaë. But he cannot look directly at the head with the snakelike hair. He must observe her in a mirror, provided him by Athena, goddess of wisdom and understanding, and cut off Medusa's head with a magic sword. After Perseus has managed to accomplish this feat, the winged horse Pegasus, a symbol of imagination, springs from the severed neck.

The poet's weapon is the "blade" of his "didactic Laurel," hidden in the "melic sheath" of his verse. He guides his sword toward Medusa's head by means of the mirror of analogy, avoiding the paralysis of the will that a direct approach—the "angelic imagination," as it were—would bring about. Having lost the violin "box," the poet attacks the specter with the blade of his wit rather than with the bow. The ghostly love, like the small girl who emerges after he has "unsnapped the lyric case," presents the false hope of the "dogwood tree/ In bloom." She is the beguiling myrtle that must be held back until the poet can unite laurel and myrtle in a single imaginative complex. Yet the encounter is deadly. Instead of love, the poet finds hatred. He is attacked by a death's head that gnaws on him as Ugolino crumbled the skull of Archbishop Ruggieri. But the kind of love the mother-fury offers (one recalls "Sonnets of the Blood" and "Mother and Son") bears a spectral light that strikes like a snake at the sick heart of a man seeking release from his prison. It is this "shade of pompous youth" who "clutched shades forbearing in a family well" that Tate is leaving behind in his last poems. For the memory can be dangerous, just as it can be redemptive. Louis Dupré warns: "the person who is neurotically obsessed by the past does not really *remember* the past, but rather attempts to *repeat* it and, in reliving the painful events of his past, to attain a new ending different from the one he cannot accept."[9]

Having discovered the inadequacy of eros, of familial ties, of un-

9. Louis Dupré, *Transcendent Selfhood* (New York, 1976), 71.

aided tradition, and of the historical imagination, the speaker learns that he must both sacrifice his memories and be overcome by them if he is to discover true love. He must acknowledge what is wrong in himself, but he must balance his confession with a recognition that within him is the means of discovering a deeper level of existence. William F. Lynch speaks of this distrust of nature in ourselves as a fear of dependence: "It is the secret fear of most people that they cannot have both dependence and independence, just as it is their secret hope that they can. . . . We are often forced by our culture to deny dependence, passivity, the wish and ability to receive."[10] What must die is the "spirit that could not tell/ Natural time" ("The Maimed Man"). The plunge into water, mentioned in all three poems, is a confession of dependence. Only after the "shuttling eye" is drowned in the "green reviving spray" of nature and the "whispered" dream listened to, can the self begin to find its freedom:

> Down, down below the wave that turned me round,
>
> . . . .
>
> . . . while sight within me, caved . . .
>
> . . . .
>
> Till come to midmost May I bent my knees,
> Santa Lucia! at noon—the prudent shore,
> The lake flashing green fins through amber trees—
> And knew I had not read your eye before
> You played it in the flowing scale of glance.

Like Lucy, the protagonist has been deprived of sight as he hears the whine of the bees, bearers of a sting who are also makers of honey. Even the lost music of the poet's youth is recovered through Lucy; the auditory character of the Augustinian imagination is restored through the "light choir," at the end of the poem, whose song is no burden on his shoulder. Sound and sight have become one. The speaker has become a bee who returns to "cell after honeyed cell of sounding dream." He is no longer the mordant satirist of the "discrete/ Mandible world," busy without harmony, "lurked" but not revealed, a "gaol without a cell." He

10. William F. Lynch, *Images of Hope: Imagination as Healer of the Hopeless* (Baltimore, 1965), 202.

is no longer the captive of his own isolation; he has entered "cell upon cell" of an interdependent community signaled by the beehive murmur.

The waters of divine wisdom in Ecclesiasticus are linked with these echoes of the old theme of death and regeneration through baptismal waters, Dante's "bitter" and "cruel" sea of Hell that he escapes on the shores of Purgatory, and the deeper stream of time and memory that the protagonist has begun to enter. He has learned to taste life in death at the very moment he thought to have tasted death in love. The eye, now "caved" by being deprived of direct light, takes on its proper role, pouring "stinging dark on cold delight"; the dark night of the soul has overcome the beguiling myrtle. The soul has returned to Plato's cave to study its shadows and reemerge with the swarm of bees, an emblem of the City of God presented as a natural image and akin to the great flower in Dante's Paradise (Canto XXXI, 7–12). The "unfaced" shore has now become "prudent," a place of entry into purgatorial cleansing. Like Christ, whose "Head" descended into Hell (Tate's phrase is a pun on "Godhead"), the poet attends a resurrection of the captive past from its infernal dwelling and raises it to the present. He has learned to read Lucy's eye, as Dante learned to withstand the brilliant gaze of Beatrice, through indirection. For her glance is not the paralyzing angel's stare, the "brute curiosity" of some gorgonic Medusa, but a "flowing scale." The bitter, frozen sea has yielded to the freely moving waters.

What the poet has gained are the virtues, present in Purgatory but absent in Hell, which he had lacked before: fair love and holy hope. His skeptical attitude toward himself was a refusal to admit his capacity to know transcendence:

> I had not thought that I could read the score,
>
> And yet how vexed, bitter, and hard the trance
> Of light—how I resented Lucy's play!
> Better stay dead, better not try the lance
>
> In the living bowl: living we have one way
> For all time in the twin darks where light dies
> To live: forget that you too lost the day
>
> Yet finding it refound it Lucy-guise
> As I, refinding where two shadows meet,
> Took from the burning umbrage mirroring eyes

Like Tellico blue upon a golden sheet
Spread out for all our stupor.

Santa Lucia is more than a literary symbol, the figure of understanding and the character who intervened to send a dream to Dante and lift him across the entry into Purgatory. She is a model, like St. Augustine, of one who "lost the day" and refound it. The usual picture of Lucy, carrying her blue eyes on a golden tray, is combined with the flow of a river (the Tellico) to symbolize release of the self from its narrow confines in the ego. One can "read the score" of Lucy's music without his eyes. Though the quest is difficult—like the grail quest of Perceval, it requires facing the waste land before finding the sacred relics, the "lance/ In the living bowl" of Christ's blood—the "twin darks" of Lucy's "mirroring eyes" light up the place where "two shadows meet" at the edge of "blinding slough" and the edge of fear.

Lucy, then, is a feminine image of eternity, of that permanence which will never leave:

Lady coming,
Lady not going, come Lady come: I greet

You in the double of our eyes—humming
Miles of lightning where, in a pastoral scene,
The fretting pipe is lucent and becoming.

The "fretting pipe" of the protagonist's poetry now plays a new theme that combines the visual and the auditory, the quiet ("humming") and the brilliant ("miles of lightning"), space and time in a single act. ("Becoming" seems to be a pun meaning both "fitting" and "changing.") The Lady of Light, unlike the small dancing girl and the woman in sorrow, will stay, for she is an image of that deepest aspect of the self, eternal and unchanging, which is the *memoria dei*. Like Dante and Donne, who saw their own reflections in their ladies' eyes, the poet sees in Lucy the triumph over blindness that he had sought from the beginning of his career.

Having glimpsed the *imago dei* within the self, one has a natural desire to perpetuate it in some way:

I thought of ways to keep this image green
(Until the leaf unfold the formal cherry)
In an off season when the eye is lean

With an inward gaze upon the wild strawberry,
  Cape jasmine, wild azalea, eglantine—
  All the sad eclogue that will soon be merry.

The image can be kept green in the memory until nature revives it in due season, but the experience need not be sustained in its highest intensity; for the poet has learned to entwine in the memory two evergreens, laurel and myrtle. He is their constant reviver, the archeologist who rediscovers memory again and again in a reconstituting act. All the fragrant blooms that the poet lists are associated in traditional lore with spring, poetry, delight, intoxication, and love. They are part of natural time. It is the "inward gaze" that is given by the mirror of art and the laurel—symbol of inspiration, fame, success, prophecy and vision, victory and hope and the light of the sun, the first plant to be used in wreaths for a Christmas decoration and associated with Christ's victory over sin and death—that complements the symbol of love and the senses in the myrtle. Nature can be kept literally green for a while—cherry twigs will keep green, even in December, if immersed in water until they blossom a few weeks later—but nature cannot transform anything. The poet now knows

        that nature could not more refine
  What it had given in a looking-glass
  And held there, after the living body's line

Has moved wherever it must move—wild grass
  Inching the earth; and the quicksilver art
  Throws back the invisible but lightning mass

To inhabit the room; for I have seen it part
  The palpable air, the air close up above
  And under you, light Lucy, light of heart—

Light choir upon my shoulder, speaking Dove
  The dream is over and the dark expired.

The image of his maimed self that the protagonist glimpsed in the mirror cannot be changed by the natural order. Lucy has not brought the poet into the presence of the true light by driving him to the sun (as in "The Eagle" or "More Sonnets at Christmas") or by merging him with his image (as in "Last Days of Alice"). She has taken him across the threshold of alienation into an inward world where sufferings are meaningful. The dream has transformed the poet from a gloomy twilight traveler into a man "light of heart" who can face future suffering as a lighter burden. The last line of the poem—"I knew that I had known enduring love"—is a recognition that love is not only possible but has actually been known, if only for a short while, in human experience as something eternal. The concluding verse brings together the three aspects of the Augustinian model of the soul—memory, understanding, and love—in a single phrase. The poet has moved from recollection to vision to the unified will and sensibility.

It is not clear why Tate failed to go on with his terza rima sequence, but one may hazard the guess that he had, literally and figuratively, nothing more to say. The last line of "The Buried Lake" is the goal toward which all his work moves, the meaning and crown of his entire imaginative experience. One misses, of course, other details and events that would fill in the narrative action; but on its own terms, Tate's terza rima sequence is as complete as it need be. It is no less coherent, really, than many a modern poem of comparable scope. Unless further fragments of his work are published in the future, there is no reason not to treat the three pieces as a completed triad about the quest for and achievement of some knowledge of transcendence in the depths of the self. For the trio of poems suggests something that the quartet of "Seasons of the Soul" does not. A sequence of four units implies a cycle. A series of three suggests a dynamic unity of the one in the many. I suspect that the terza rima series is meant to be incomplete, because there is no definitive conclusion to the kind of life for which it stands.

For Allen Tate is not a religious poet, certainly not in the sense of a St. John of the Cross or even a Hopkins. He does not write about religious experiences but the desire for some dimension beyond the narrow limits of immanence. At the same time that he was writing his terza rima poems and his superb essay "The Symbolic Imagination," he was reflecting on the limits of poetry and the imagination and concluding that

> what we are confronted with in a work of literature, and I suppose also in the other arts, is human *action* translated into *being*—morals moving towards metaphysics. And that is why we get into trouble when we try to get our ethics from works of the

> imagination. Even if all men could agree on the moral soundness and depth of a given poem, it would still be dangerous to appeal to it as a sufficient guide to conduct. Action as it appears in a poem has been given another kind of reality which is no longer in motion, though it may *seem* to move: it has arrived at the reality of being, the end for which the poem exists. If we imitate its action, we are imitating an imitation, as some persons have been said to do when, after reading *The Divine Comedy* a few months, they decide to enter the Roman Catholic Church.[11]

Tate has insisted throughout his career that poetry cannot save men. At best it can offer images of transcendence. Though periods of great religious fervor and cultural unity may or may not ease the difficulty of redeeming oneself, they are of distinct benefit to poets, who can find in such times more interesting topics than alienation, fragmentation, or emptiness. The great temptation for a sincere poet, aware of the disorder of his own times, is not to attempt saving the world through art but to remain silent.

Despite the fitting climax to his career reached in "The Buried Lake," Tate did not remain totally silent as a poet. Though he published only two new original poems after the fifties, he did not neglect the necessary step of beginning anew. His last short poems are a mixture of images of hope and amazement; they show forth a fresh wonder at the ability of the world and the self to be renewed. The first, a sonnet tucked inconspicuously in a middle section of the 1970 edition of Tate's poems, is in the complex style typical of his poetry, but it has less of the dense allusiveness of his earlier work. It is addressed to his wife and first son, and it explores a paradoxical situation unlike those he had known before. While the poet had difficulty speaking out in his early poetry, here he fears that he cannot live out the love that his words promise. The poem reverses the situation of Shakespeare's Sonnet 73, "That time of year." Love can never be repaid and time can never be reversed. No "interior" lie of youth can halt the irresistible force of time, but a lifetime would not be enough to explore the mystery of an older man's happiness. The biblical handwriting on the wall and the shadows of Plato's cave, "the glyph/ That the mind's eye strikes on my

11. Allen Tate, "The Self-Made Angel," *New Republic*, CXXIX, 21.

shadowy wall," are the terms of man's judgment of his own achievement; but man's "chronic" sentence, his own temporality, is never overcome with such "timely" lies that his will would impose. The purpose of God is mysterious. Why has he favored man, who understands Him and himself so little? The final couplet is addressed to his wife and child:

> Who let me love you two? Have I been wrong
> To love you well who cannot love me long?

The sonnet is a brighter, happier version of Shakespeare's famous melancholy meditation. For in Sonnet 73, it is the young man who must learn to appreciate the older, who must "leave ere long." But in Tate's poem, the older man wonders if his love in old age can ever be repayment for the great showering of grace he has come to know. He worries that his very happiness in love may be unjust to those he loves.

The last poem—which is actually three poems grouped as one—appears in the *Collected Poems* of 1977. In it Tate leaves behind the intricate syntax of his "Sonnet" for a total simplicity of statement. Titled "Farewell Rehearsed," it extends the theme of the poem published seven years earlier. Here the plain style appropriately manifests the full power of joyful resignation. These three touching little epigrams have a kind of neoclassical ring of delicately allusive sophistication in their poise. The first stanza, "To My Son Benjamin," is almost Jonsonian in its light tetrameter couplets. It is perhaps meant to remind the reader overtly of Jonson's poem on his son Benjamin, deceased at an early age, in which the poet laments, "My sin was too much loving thee, dear boy." But in Tate's version, the situation is reversed, for the father knows that his son will surely outlive him. The elderly father knows that his remaining days are few; his son is the exemplar of innocence that the parent must become. The boy is the "leaven" that will cause his soul to rise toward its goal. The playful game they play together is a prelude to the oneness of all through love, but it is the son who teaches the father to bear the slight discomforts of the game for the joy it gives. Ben is a teacher of love and a *memento mori*, a guide to the existence on another plane where all will be transformed.

The second stanza ("To My Son John") carries forward this idea that there is a unity of presence after death. The younger son is the leaven of the father's spirit; the older will affect him in a different fashion. It is the dead father who will preserve the image of the living, for the poet's memory of persons outlives him through language. Death is the realm of memory, the place where all things and persons eventually reside. It is the son's "happy little face" that the father will bear in his memory "to the fount of grace." In memory the terror of death becomes transformed into the joy of a happy life, where young and old, living and dead are reconciled. The son may retain the image of his father as he reaches maturity, but the father will immortalize the most joyous moments of his son in an eternal gaze.

The final stanza, "To My Wife Helen," is the most complex. It alludes with graceful wit to Campion's "When Thou Must Home to Shades of Underground." Once more, Tate turns his model around. It is the speaker who will "reach the shady underground" first, and not the person spoken to. Campion's fanciful image of pagan afterlife, where the "newe admired guest" will arrive and be surrounded by "The beauteous spirits . . . White Iope, blith Hellen, and the rest," is transposed into Dante's journey:

> When I have reached the shady underground
> With but sad hope of coming up again,
> I shall implore your ghost to hover round
> And guide me to a land of lucky men,
> Even luckier than the land that I had left.

The wife who helped nurse her husband through illness cannot accompany him to the underworld. Dante, alive, found in the dead Beatrice his leaven, image of joy, and guide to Paradise. The poet hopes to persuade her spirit to conduct him as well, even if she, as a living person, can do so only through prayer. He would hope to have her company, even in the afterlife, for she is the beautiful Helen who has saved him for happiness and allowed him to find a land "even luckier" than the one he will be leaving. Tate cannot imagine an afterlife without the image of the beloved, and he knows that his "empty spirit" requires the presence of the beloved in some fashion even after death. She is the Beatrice who will not abandon him.

Even in his final published poem, Tate creates a fable of feminine guidance and fulfillment in remembrance that presumes the necessary existence of a human community. What the understanding brings together is a people, united, as Augustine says every society must be, by a common love. As epigraphs to his last volume, the *Collected Poems*, Tate cites two Latin passages:

> Sunt lacrimae rerum et mentem mortalia tangunt.
>
> Ne avertas faciem tuam a puero tuo quoniam tribulor velociter exaudi me.

The first is, of course, the familiar passage from Virgil's *Aeneid* (I, 462). In a brilliant analysis of this passage, Adam Parry has provided the larger context for Tate's Virgilian reference; he speaks of Virgil's "public voice of triumph" and his "private voice of regret," his recognition of "the capacity of the human being to suffer."

> For Aeneas . . . is man himself; not man as the brilliant free agent of Homer's world, but man of a later stage in civilization, man in a metropolitan and imperial world, man in a world where the State is supreme. He cannot resist the forces of history, or even deny them; but he can be capable of human suffering, and this is where the personal voice asserts itself. . . .
>
> The sufferings of the Trojans, as Aeneas sees them in Carthage, have become fixed in art, literally: they are paintings. And it is here first, Virgil tells us, that Aeneas began to hope for a kind of salvation. Here he can look back on his own losses, and see them as made beautiful and given universal meaning because human art has transfigured them. "Look here!" he cries. "There is Priam; there are tears for suffering, and the limitations of life can touch the heart."[12]

The second citation is from the Vulgate version of Psalm 68 (69 in the Authorized Version), which begins "Save me, O God: for the waters are come in even unto my soul." The verse Tate cites repeats a familiar phrase that occurs several times in the Psalms: "And turn not away thy face from thy servant: for I am in trouble. Hear me speedily" (v. 18). In these two quotations, Tate sums up the achieved theme of his final verse. It is interesting to compare them with his first epigraph, from Blake's "London," which appeared initially in *Mr. Pope and Other Poems* and was used in later collections:

12. Adam Parry, "The Two Voices of Virgil's *Aeneid*," *Arion*, II, 79–80.

For oft in midnight streets I hear
How the youthful harlot's curse
Blasts the newborn infant's ear
And blights with plagues the marriage hearse.

This is the City of Man, where birth is a kind of death. It is interesting to note that Tate's misquotation ("ear" for "tear") has an appropriateness, in light of his emphasis on sound, all its own, but Tate has spoken elsewhere of the tears into which man is born. In a short prose meditation written for his seventy-fifth birthday, Tate ruminates on death by commenting on a selection of texts, among which is Tennyson's "Tears, Idle Tears":

> One must say, with this lyric as his authority, that we begin at birth to die. Whatever one's age, one's degree of consciousness shifts up and down. One saw trees yesterday morning, but this morning only a glimmer. If one here is dying, what is one doing in the last stanza? "Dear as remembered kisses after death."
>
> After one's death one remembers in that next life the moment of love? Is one dead but still conscious of the deepest frustration that man can suffer? That is, hopeless love. I am stretching the meaning. But isn't it equally grim to face dead love in this life? "O, Death in Life!" We are still alive but at every moment something with us dies, until there is nothing left to die, and we are dead.[13]

But the final answer is not so grim, for Tate's commentary is an exploration of what the poets have said about us and a testing of the truth of their claims. He suggests that what Landor, Whitman, and Sandburg have had to say about nature is no longer true, if it ever was. The lady that is nature has changed from a "Thou" to an "It" in the modern world; we have all but destroyed her. But the Lady of Light who stands to guide us on the other side of darkness is eternal: "Love is not mere love, whatever mere love may be; it is love gathering from the flying dark."[14]

13. Allen Tate, "A Sequence of Stanzas," in *Memoirs*, 213.
14. *Ibid.*, 215.

Index

I. BOOKS AND ESSAYS BY TATE

III. NAMES AND TERMS